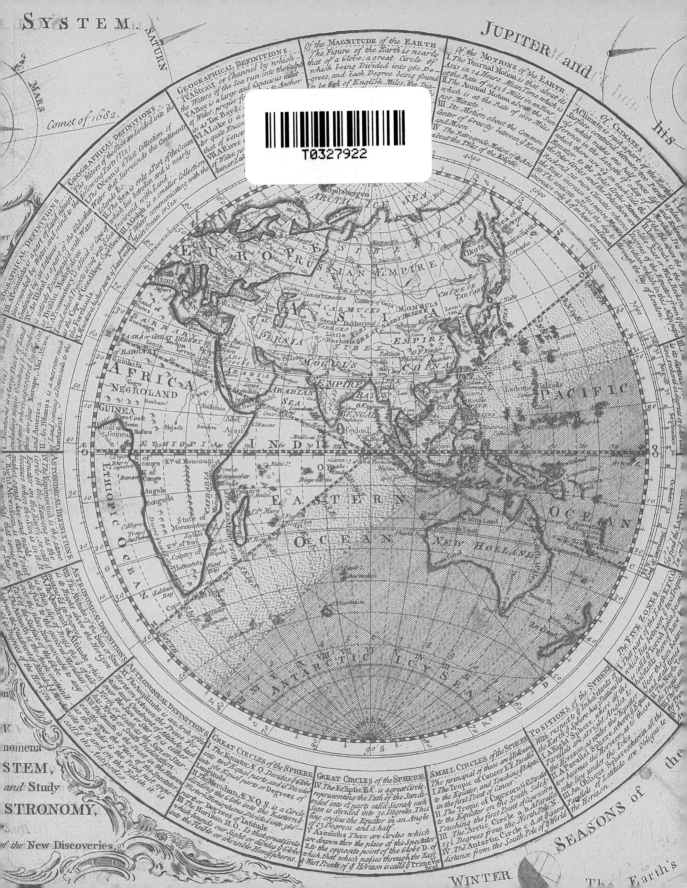

THE
ATLAS
OF
ATLASES

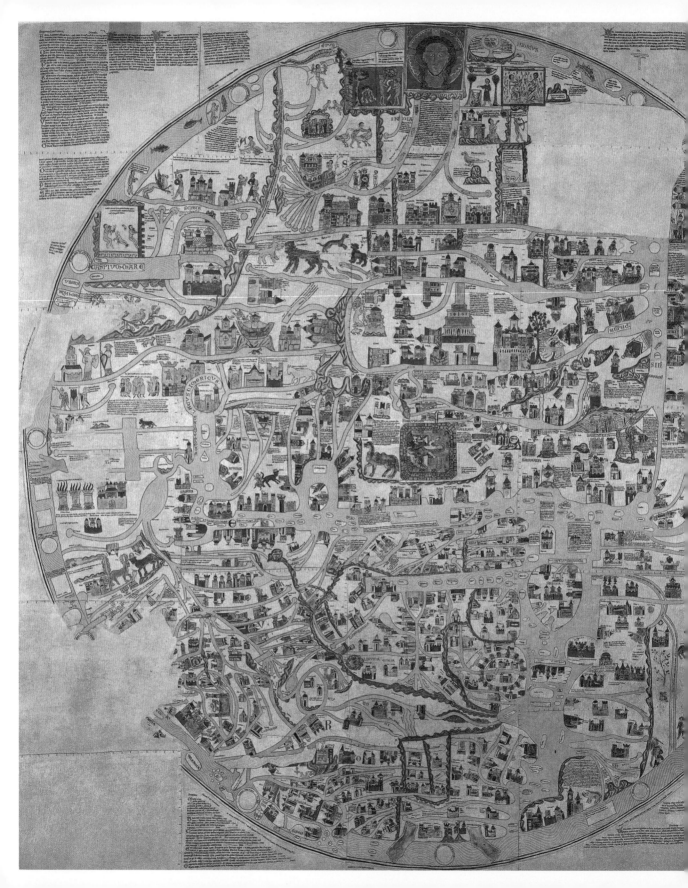

THE
ATLAS
OF
ATLASES

PHILIP PARKER

IVY PRESS

First published in 2022 by Ivy Press,
an imprint of The Quarto Group.
The Old Brewery, 6 Blundell Street
London, N7 9BH,
United Kingdom
T (0)20 7700 6700
www.Quarto.com

A catalogue record for this book is available from the British Library.

ISBN 978-0-7112-6805-0
Ebook ISBN 978-0-7112-6749-7

10 9 8 7 6 5 4 3 2 1

Text by Philip Parker
Design by Kevin Knight

Printed in Singapore

MIX
Paper from
responsible sources
FSC™ C007207
FSC
www.fsc.org

CONTENTS

INTRODUCTION

BELOW

Statue representing Atlas holding up the world, Kolkata, India

OPPOSITE

Frontispiece, *Atlas sive Cosmographicae*, Gerardus Mercator, 1595 edition

The first work explicitly to describe itself as an atlas.

For a brief (and presumably agonizing) few hours, the Greek hero Heracles held the whole weight of the World on his shoulders. In exchange for relieving Atlas, the titan whose fate it was to support this intolerable burden, Heracles received the stolen golden apples of the Hesperides, which the hero needed to fulfil the 11th of his 12 labours. It is from this ancient myth that we derive the title of the genre of books which are designed to carry the whole weight of our knowledge of the world within their pages (and which we hope will deliver their own bounty of golden nuggets of information to us).

The Atlas of Atlases considers the origin and development of the atlas, from its distant beginnings in mankind's first attempts to map the world in the ancient Near East in the fifth millennium BC (thus long predating the Heracles story), to the digital mapping systems of today which can create a bespoke map of a region in seconds, a task that once would have taken a trained cartographer months to complete.

Maps have always carried an ideological freight. The very earliest were attempts to understand and organize the world in terms that made sense to the viewers. For example, the Babylonian Map of the World created around 600 BC (p.13), is not an exact description of terrain, nor a means to navigate – aims to which far later maps aspired. It is instead a bold statement of the position of its creator's hometown at the centre of the

world, a sentiment which was still being echoed in the nineteenth century when British cartographers used bold red shading to highlight the vast extent of their empire. Maps could be statements of belief, of power, of agency, long before they were viewed as an attempt to mirror reality on the ground.

Trade and travel have long been two of the primary drivers of mapping. As time went on, information gathered by merchants, pilgrims and adventurers added texture to maps (though medieval cartographers were not above adding fantastical elements such as dog-headed beings, dragons and giants to their maps, despite the fact that no one could plausibly have encountered them). Collections of maps in the forms of itineraries, views and plans of cities, and single maps of countries or of the world (enhanced by the European voyages of discovery from the fifteenth century) approached but did not quite reach the bar of encompassing the whole world within a book.

That was a development that had to wait for the mid-sixteenth century, by which time the demands of navigators for a convenient form of detailed mapping which they could hold in their hands (rather than have to unroll), advances in printing, and the appetites of a growing class of literate city-dwellers with money to spare led to the issuing of the first atlases. The *Theatrum Orbis Terrarum* ('Theatre of the Globe of the World', p.114) by the Dutch cartographer Abraham Ortelius, published in 1570, was the first modern atlas, consisting of a series of regional maps, which reconciled recent advances in knowledge with the time-hallowed system of the ancient Roman geographer Ptolemy, all bound within a single cover. Before long it was joined by a European atlas published by Gerardus Mercator (p.110) (whose devising of a projection to display the curved surface of the Earth on the flat surface of a map has made him perhaps the most famous cartographer of all), which was the first publication to bear the world 'atlas' in its title.

The Ortelius and Mercator atlases ushered in a golden age for the atlas, as cartographers from the Netherlands and Italy produced an ever-wider variety, from grand world atlases such as Ortelius's, to practical navigation guides (known as rutters and wagoneers), and the first atlases which concentrated on a particular theme, most often with maps illustrating bible history or that of classical antiquity. The Dutch and Italian pioneers were soon joined by German, French and British cartographers, while the heirs of other ancient mapping traditions, such as the Ottoman Turks, Mughals and Ming and Qing Chinese began to produce their own versions. While many were practical, others were works of art, or expressions of power – perhaps none more striking than the *Klencke Atlas* (p.143), presented by a Dutch merchant to Charles II on the occasion of his restoration to the British throne in 1660, which is an unwieldy 1.75 x 2.3m ($5^3/_4$ x $7^1/_2$ft) when opened and takes six people to move.

More practical considerations, however, drove the move to a more modern form of mapping, generated by scientific surveys which, from the seventeenth century, laid down networks of base-lines and triangles across states, beginning with France, to produce national maps of a precision which their predecessors only a century before could not have dreamed of. These national surveys and their products, such as those of the British Ordnance Survey, are increasingly represented in the later chapters of this book, as are the diverse uses to which mapping came to be put (and then placed within atlases). These first thematic atlases were historical or biblical, but as printing technology and that of transport advanced, they encompassed everything from atlases of railway networks to those showing disease (and, by the twentieth century, almost any subject that lent itself to graphic presentation).

Atlases faced the greatest challenge to their long dominance of the cartographic sphere from what at first seemed an unlikely direction. The very first computer maps, in the 1960s, were primitive, clunky affairs, and the technology seemed more suited to storing information in databases than presenting it to the public. The advent of the internet in the 1990s and the appearance of smart-phones of ever-increasing sophistication in the early twenty-first century changed all that. Before long consumers could consult maps of almost any city or region with a few clicks, threatening to render the printed atlas redundant.

Yet in one way, the new form of atlas has solved a problem posed by the Argentine writer Jorge Luis Borges, when he mused in one of his short stories on an empire in which cartography had become so sophisticated and detailed that a map of it was on a scale of nearly 1 to 1 and so massive that it covered up a whole province. Borges's dream is now possible. We can comprehend the whole world without, as Atlas or Heracles did, having to carry its weight, or creating the impossible map of which Borges conceived. Now we can carry the whole world in our pockets. Though questions remain as to who owns the data and how technology companies choose to present or redact it, this in some ways is no different to the ideological choices made by an ancient Babylonian map-maker or the efforts of the sixteenth-century Spanish Crown to keep sensitive information about its new empire in the Americas from falling into the hands of foreign cartographers. It is a controversy which is unlikely to die down while there are still maps and anyone left to read them.

Far from dying, the atlas has now become ubiquitous.

1

THE PREHISTORY OF THE ATLAS

(TO *c.* 1200)

Before humans made atlases, they created maps. The urge to understand or control the world by reducing it to representational or symbolic form on stone, clay, papyrus or paper long preceded the assembly and compilation of these maps into something resembling an atlas. Although there are markings and scratches on stone dating from the Upper Palaeolithic around 11,000 BC which it is claimed could represent the birth of mapping, the first really plausible candidate for the earliest map comes from the Neolithic settlement of Çatal Höyük, near Konya in Turkey. Its inhabitants, who earned a living around 6200 BC from an early form of agriculture and trading in obsidian (a volcanic glass valued for the sharp blades into which it could be worked), lived in a close-knit huddle of rectangular mud-brick houses, stacked on top of each other like ancient shipping containers.

Amid leopard frescoes and the plastered skulls of bulls with which they adorned the walls, the people of Çatal Höyük painted the world's first picture of a volcanic eruption, the triangular cone of Hasan Dağ (which provided them in good times with the bounty of obsidian) spewing out angry red wisps of fire and lava. In the foreground, a network of rectangles with black dots inside unmistakably represents the layout of the town itself. Even before writing – which would not be invented for a further 3,000 years – the long prehistory of the atlas had begun in the shape of this unlikely town plan.

The wedge-shaped cuneiform script of Mesopotamia and the enigmatic pictographs of Egyptian hieroglyphic writing emerged at around the same time, about 3200 BC. In both locations, this innovation served a double purpose, the practical one of recording commercial transactions, and the more political one of glorifying the deeds of rulers. We are somewhat hampered by the bias in what survives, as many of the more day-to-day

documents have doubtless been lost, despite the preservative qualities of Egypt's dry, desert conditions, leaving us with the carefully curated (and often boastful) inscriptions in stone that relate the victories of its pharaohs and the spells to guarantee survival in the afterlife painted on the dark walls of their tombs.

Tantalizingly, though, one map does survive. A fragile document originally a little over 2m (7ft) in length, the Turin Papyrus was discovered by agents acting for the avid Italian antiquities collector Bernardino Drovetti (1776–1852). Serving as French consul in Egypt between 1821 and 1829 (and in an earlier stint for Napoleon's regime from 1806 to 1815), he amassed an enormous array of sculpture, papyrus scrolls and other artefacts. His sometimes questionable acquisition techniques mean we cannot be entirely sure where and from whom he obtained this papyrus, though it was probably at Deir el-Medina, the ancient workmen's village close to the Valley of the Kings at Thebes. Created by the scribe Ammennakhte, son of Ipuy, the manuscript formed part of Drovetti's personal collection, which was not sent back to Paris, as the 'official' portion was. It was instead bought in 1824 by the Kingdom of Sardinia, finally ending up in the Museo Egizio in Turin. The map depicts the Wadi Hammamat, a bone-dry river course in Egypt's Eastern Desert, which acted as a conduit to the pharaonic kingdom's principal gold and stone-quarrying regions. Probably compiled for an expedition during the reign of Ramesses IV (1151–1144 BC) which went in search of *bekhen*, or greywacke, a green-tinted sandstone which was particularly prized by the Egyptians for royal statuary, it is also the world's earliest geological map. As well as the wadi itself, a strong bold streak in the lower part of the map, a subsidiary wadi leading off to the east in the direction of a gold-mine at Bir Umm Fawakhir, and a speckle of dots representing rocks, there are colour-coded conical shapes which indicate hills, with black perhaps representing schist, and pink for granite. Inscriptions on the map in the flowing hieratic script that scribes used for day-to-day and administrative documents in place of the rather cumbersome hieroglyphs indicate 'mountains of gold', a well, a cistern, which may have been employed in the mining process to winnow out gold from crushed quartz, and a temple of the creator god Amun.

In Mesopotamia, Amennakht's Sumerian counterparts exhibited a similar thirst for geographical knowledge, compiling lists of rivers, mountains and placenames as far afield as Syria and Anatolia. By 2300 BC, the first maps appear in the region, one of them, from Yorghan Tepe, near Kirkuk, includes a wavy line that may represent a river and shows the dividing lines between plots of land, one of whose owners, Azala, is named on the map. By 1500 BC, plans were being drawn of the region's cities (which had been the world's earliest), including one of Nippur which shows the Euphrates River (whose plentiful waters gave birth to and sustained Mesopotamian civilisation), the Temple of Enlil and seven named gates punctuating the city walls. By the mid-seventh century BC, the heirs to a cartographic tradition almost two thousand years old turned their hands to a very different type of mapping. What has become known as the Babylonian Map of the World, a small clay tablet, just 12.2cm long and 8.2cm wide (5 x 3¼in), incised in bold cuneiform wedges, and with a series of circles and rectangles deployed around a central point in the tablet's lower portion, is very much a map composed in the service of an ideology, or at the very least a world-view.

Babylon was by then an ancient city. Its first heyday had been in the eighteenth-century BC under Hammurabi. It was he who decreed one of the world's earliest law-codes, with its eye-for-an-eye, tooth-for-a-tooth penalties; this discouraged medical malpractice by laying down that a doctor who contributed to the death of a noble patient would have his hands amputated. Now the city was enjoying a political renaissance under the rulers of the neo-Babylonian empire, most notably Nebuchadnezzar II (*r.* 605–562 BC), during which it was once again one of the Near East's main political powers.

The map shows the world as a disk surrounded by a boundary ocean, which was a common device in ancient world views where the water represented the division between the form of the created land and the shapeless chaos beyond it. Beyond the ocean ring are triangles that denote mythical lands either bathed in sunshine which made them 'brighter than stars' or plunged into permanent darkness. In the centre of the main circle stands a rectangle, which represents Babylon itself. Around it are arrayed eight smaller circles, each standing for other regions in the Babylonian orbit, with Assyria, the kingdom of Urartu and the Elamite capital Susa to the right, and two vertical lines running the length of the circle probably standing for the Euphrates. Never a map intended to provide directions (as the Turin Papyrus, to some extent, was) or even to show a topographically accurate representation of the landscape, it was very much a symbolic map, presenting the Babylonians' view of the world, in which their city sat firmly at the centre.

The ancient view of geography was very much a dual one, caught between a desire to show what could be seen and an urge to explain how the world was organized and what its relationship was with the heavenly realm of the gods. Representations of belief systems yielded the haunting images of the souls' journey into the afterlife portrayed in the *Egyptian Book of the Dead*, painted on numerous high-status tombs, their protective spells reinforced by papyrus scrolls containing incantations. These included handy tips on how to pass the 'weighing of the heart' ceremony, which if failed, indicated the soul was sinful and would result in the deceased's spirit being consumed by the demoness Ammut and perishing permanently. The incantations also prompted the composition of cosmological maps, such as those on the coffins found at Deir el-Bersha, dating from around 2000 BC, during Egypt's Middle Kingdom. Adorned with a version of *The Book of Two Ways*, another magical text, they provide a visual guide for the soul in the afterlife, showing it the way past such supernatural obstacles as the Lake of Fire, and the Lake of the Knife Wielders, past a variety of supernatural guardians, such as 'He whose face is hot', and the disturbingly named 'He who eats his fathers, he who eats his mothers', pausing at the Field of Offerings and finally reaching an audience with Osiris and, if the two ways have been navigated correctly, eternal bliss.

Another type of cosmological map – and to modern sensibilities a somewhat more comprehensible one – appears not on coffins, but on the roofs of Egyptian tombs. Such star maps reflect a ubiquitous belief in the ancient world that heavenly bodies such as stars, the planets and comets were associated with deities and that their movements and relationship to each other had a corresponding effect on the Earth below. Understanding their position, therefore, was crucial. Among the finest examples is the star diagram found in the tomb of Senenmut, a royal steward and chief architect to the Eighteenth Dynasty queen Hatshepsut (*r.* 1479–1458 BC). As the mastermind behind her lavish mortuary temple at Deir el-Bahri, Senenmut secured himself a portal to the afterlife in the precinct of the royal tomb he himself had designed. The ceiling of his burial chamber is truly astonishing, not for the array of colours which enliven the decoration of many other Egyptian tombs – his is delineated in sombre blacks and greys, with the occasional touch of red – but for its intricate diagram of the stars, divided into 24 sections on northern and southern panels. Crowded with circles to denote the stars and miniature portraits of Egyptian deities, it is hard to associate the constellations shown with the ones we are familiar with today, for the Egyptians, in gazing at the heavens, made different pictures from the

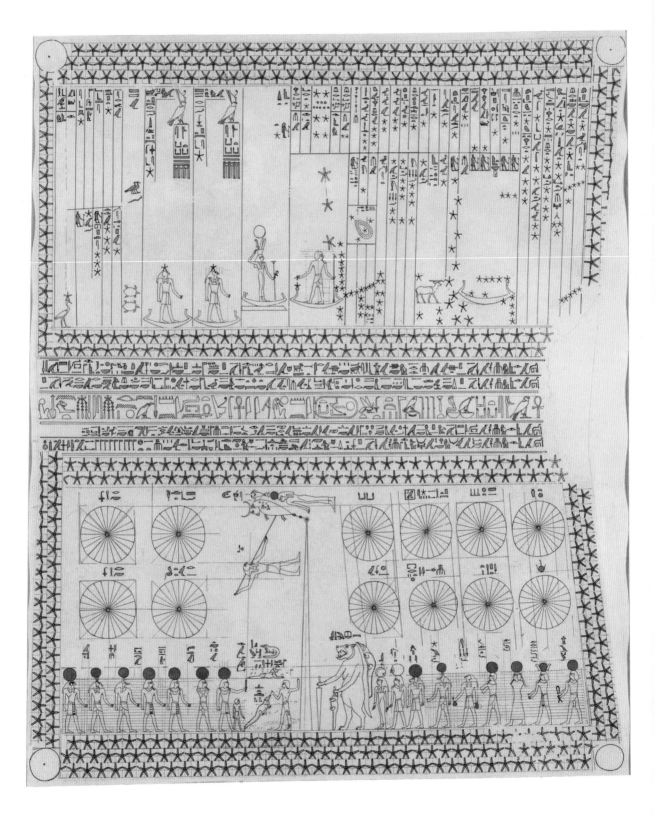

patterns they discerned there, such as the Cow, the Crocodile and the Two Tortoises. Yet, astonishingly, the pattern of stars on Senenmut's ceiling can be dated exactly, as it depicts a conjunction of planets around the longitude of Sirius in May 1534 BC.

Few other ancient maps can be dated so precisely, but a concern with measuring the heavens and linking them with divine personages continued to drive early astronomers right down to the dawn of the Classical Age. Then, in the early sixth century BC, in Ionia on the west coast of what is now Turkey, a new approach emerged. Rather than seeking to link the phenomena they observed to the capricious actions of the gods, thinkers such as Thales of Miletus (c. 620–540 BC) sought to explain them in more natural terms. Thales himself thought that the basic stuff of the Universe was water, which later differentiated into all the substances that make up the world, while his slightly younger contemporary Anaximander (610–546 BC) claimed, more inscrutably, that the basic component of matter was the *apeiron*, or boundlessness. Perhaps more importantly, he devised a cosmological system based on mathematical principles in which the Earth sat at the centre of the cosmos (where it was, as far as most scholars were concerned, to remain until the sixteenth century). He was also the first named person to produce a world map.

Nothing of Anaximander's map has survived but judging from later Greek versions for which it established the template, it probably showed the world as three large islands (Europe, Africa and Asia) with the Mediterranean and its coastlines – areas with which Anaximander and his imitators would have been most familiar – at its centre. Around 500 BC, Hecataeus, another Milesian, wrote the *Periodos ges* ('The World's Circuit'), the first known geographical treatise, which described the peoples inhabiting the lands bordering the Black Sea and the Mediterranean, going clockwise from Gibraltar and ending back up in Morocco. In his work he included another map, which again divided the world up into three roughly equally-sized continents.

OPPOSITE

Astronomical ceiling of tomb of Senenmut, *c.* 1479–1458 BC

BELOW

World map, Hecataeus, *c.* 500 BC (19th-century reconstruction)

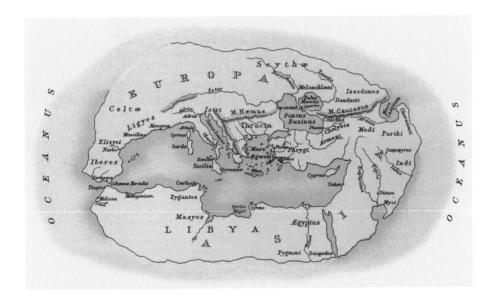

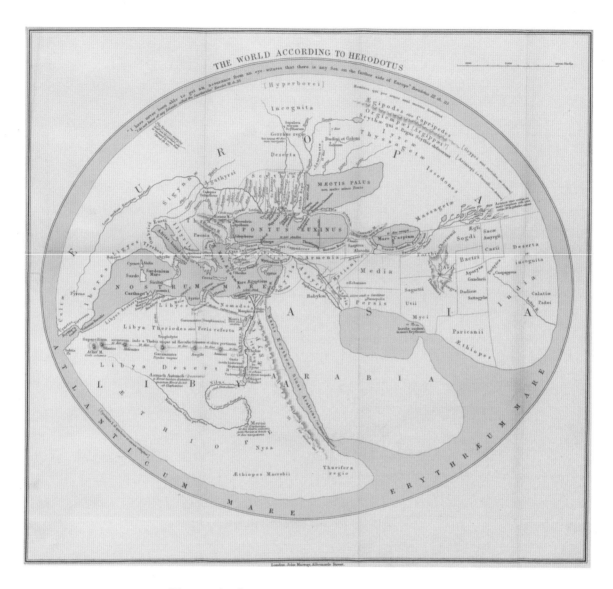

THE WORLD ACCORDING TO HERODOTUS

Hecataeus's other career as a statesman was blighted by his failure to dissuade his countrymen from becoming involved in the Ionian Revolt against Persian rule (499–493 BC), which led to decades of warfare between Greeks and Persians that, despite famous Greek victories against massive odds at Salamis and Marathon, still left Ionia under the thumb of the Persian Achaemenid King of Kings. Even so, his example was followed in other respects, including another (again lost) world map composed around 320 BC by Dicaearchus of Messana (in Sicily), a pupil of Aristotle. Among his numerous works, which included one on the heights of mountains (which he was the first to attempt to determine by triangulation, taking measurements from known points and using geometry to calculate the distance to the unknown one, in this case the height of the peak), he wrote another world geography, again entitled *Periodos ges*, which also incorporated his world map. This one contained reference lines across it, one running from Rhodes in the east to the traditional gateway from the Mediterranean to the Atlantic known as the Pillars of Hercules (one of which is Gibraltar; the other, known in ancient times as Mons Abila, is most likely the much less prominent Monte Hacho, a hill overlooking the Spanish enclave of Ceuta). The other runs north-south through Rhodes, and between them they represent the first sense that the division of a map using such lines (the distant ancestors of latitude and longitude lines) might help both cartographers in their assembly of the maps and their readers in understanding them. His map, too, seems to have been an advance on Hecataeus's in that he calculated that the known world was more a rectangle of relative dimensions 3:2 than a square, allowing him to massage the shape of the continents somewhat and portray Europe correctly as rather less extensive than Asia.

By then, the Greeks were able to include information on lands about which Hecataeus, and even Herodotus (484–425 BC), the 'father of history', could only speculate. He borrowed lavishly from his competitor but criticized him, mockingly saying, 'I cannot help but laugh, at the absurdity of all the map-makers . . . who show Ocean running like a river around a perfectly circular Earth, with Asia and Europe of the same size.' The traveller Pytheas of Massalia (now Marseilles) explored the Atlantic coastlines of Europe from Iberia to France around 300 BC, and left us the first description of the British Isles, in which he observed tin being traded by the native peoples at a place called Ictis (which may have been St Michael's Mount). He went even further north, reaching the Orcades (the Orkney Islands), commenting along the way on the surfeit of rain and absence of sunshine in Britain, a sentiment with which modern travellers might concur, and while at this extreme point of his journey, he heard an account of an even more far-flung land named Thule which was so cold that the ocean froze around it and where, in the winter, it was permanently dark. It was precisely details such as this, which seem far-fetched but are correct, that led others to doubt his tales, yet they confirm that he had either seen these places or heard an account from someone with first-hand knowledge of them.

Alongside this more practical enlargement of their knowledge of the world – which was given a great boost by the campaigns of Alexander the Great (356–323 BC), who brought a group of scholars along on his world-conquering progress to study the flora, fauna and geography of his new acquisitions – the Greeks continued to theorize. As well as the traditional three continents, they began to divide the world into *klimata*, or zones, beginning with the philosopher Parmenides of Elea in the mid-sixth century BC. He considered that there were five of these zones, one hot, two cold and two temperate, or mild. It was a notion that was to have a very long lifespan and was refined by Aristotle (384–322 BC), whose quicksilver mind touched on almost every field of endeavour known to the classical Greeks, from cosmology to civic virtue and the classification of species. For him, the Equator, which formed the hottest *klima* formed an impenetrable barrier, beyond which must lie a temperate and a cold zone to balance those observable in the north, but which it would never be possible to access. He also deduced, from the way in which eclipses of the Moon proceed in curved sections and from observations of the way the visual horizon shifts as a traveller moves, that the Earth must be spherical.

World map based on Herodotus's writings, Herodotus vol. 2 (trs. Canon Rawlinson), 1897

Although Herodotus did not – as far as we know – compose maps, the wealth of geographical information in his *Histories* has allowed reconstructions of the world he knew.

As well as organizing and categorizing the regions of the Earth, the Greeks turned to the heavens. Here, too, the traditional explanations of the behaviour of heavenly bodies in divine terms was becoming insufficient. Instead, thinkers devised a more mechanistic model, beginning with Eudoxus of Cnidus (*c.* 395–340 BC), who proposed a system of celestial spheres, arranged concentrically, which rotated around a central axis formed by the Earth. He also made the first known estimate of the circumference of the Earth, coming up with a figure of 400,000 stades, although quite how accurate this was is tricky to determine, as the size of the Greek stade varied between a modest 177m (*c.* 580ft) for the Attic stade (used in much of mainland Greece) and a rather more substantial 209m (*c.* 685ft) for the Ionic stade preferred by the Phoenicians and Egyptians.

A more refined calculation was made around a century later by Eratosthenes (*c.* 276–*c.*194 BC), born in Greek North Africa, who served from about 240 BC as head of the Ptolemaic royal library at Alexandria, history's most renowned library and a powerhouse of intellectual achievement through its Mouseion, a kind of advanced study centre where scholars from all over the Greek world could study the library's collection (which amounted to an estimated half a million works). He came up with the bright idea of using the shadow cast by a gnomon (the central rod of a sun dial) at midday on the summer solstice in two different places (in his case Alexandria on Egypt's north coast, and Syene (now Aswan) deep in its southern desert). He noticed that there was no shadow at

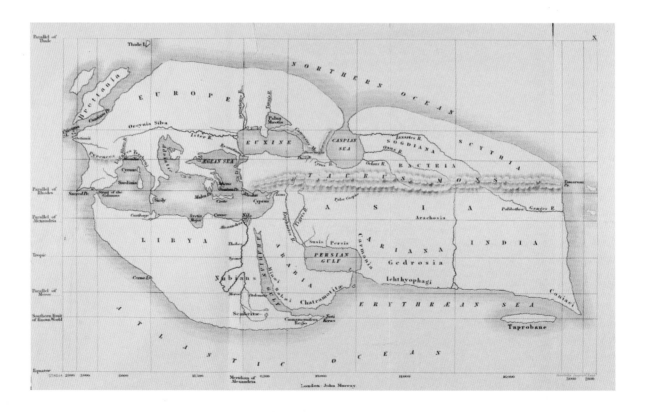

Syene (as the sun was directly overhead), but that at Alexandria the gnomon's shadow fell at an angle of 7.2 degrees (or one fiftieth of a circle). He took this to mean that the distance between the two locations represented a fiftieth of the circumference of the earth, and since he had already estimated that they lay 5,000 stades apart, he calculated the size of the earth to be 252,000 stades. This comes out at between 44,000 and 52,000km (27,340 and 32,311 miles), depending on the stade used, which is not too far out from the real figure of 40,075km (24,901 miles), measured at the equator.

Almost inevitably, Eratosthenes drew his own world map, showing it as a rectangle with truncated ends and employing Dicaearchus's device of parallel lines running from west to east (running roughly through Gibraltar as far as India) and north-south from the mysterious Thule in the north to Ethiopia, with the two sets of lines meeting at Rhodes. He calculated this known world, the *oikumene*, as 78,000 stades wide and tried to divide it further into *sphragides*, rhombus-shaped sections which are the first real attempt to solve the problem of mapping a spherical object (the Earth) onto a flat surface (the map).

The demise of the independent Greek city states after their conquest by Alexander the Great brought something of a renaissance in geographical speculation (not to mention some of the finest work by Greek mathematicians such as Euclid and Archimedes). Some of it remained theoretical, such as the terrestrial globe said to have been constructed around 150 BC by the philosopher Crates of Mallos, whose eclectic interests included the epics of Homer (on which he wrote a commentary) and sewage. The latter led to an unfortunate accident when he visited Rome and tried to inspect the main drain, the *Cloaca Maxima*; he fell in and broke his leg, which at least meant he had to prolong his stay in the city and earn a living by lecturing there, sparking a revival in Roman interest in grammar. His globe showed four symmetrical continents, with the *oikumene* known to contemporaries to the north, but a balancing *antipodes* to the south, a first mention of the term by which the elusive southern continent came later to be known.

Others took a more practical approach, compiling *periploi* ('sailings around'), manuals for travellers, principally navigators, describing the ports along the main trading routes, complete with details of the local peoples, their customs and the trade goods they might offer to merchants. The tradition began with Scylax of Caryanda (*fl.* sixth century BC), whom Herodotus tells us scouted out the coastline of India preparatory to an invasion by Darius I of Persia in the late sixth century BC, was continued by Pytheas of Massilia, and was in full bloom in the first centuries AD when the most famous *periplus* of all, the *Periplus of the Erythrean Sea*, written by an anonymous Greek-speaking merchant, possibly an Egyptian. Beginning at the great port of Berenice on the Red Sea, he describes the peoples a merchant might encounter along the coast (quaintly differentiated into 'fish-eaters', 'wild flesh eaters' and 'calf eaters'), down to the emporium at Adulis, where elephant and rhinoceros ivory can be obtained from the interior (and more locally gathered tortoise shell), and then across the Red Sea, fringing south-east Arabia (where precious gums such as frankincense make a handy addition to the cargo) and finally to India, the people of whose first major port, Barygaza, are said to have a penchant for Italian wine. In many ways, the *periplus* may seem a picturesque curiosity, but it represents an itinerary-based approach which would remain one of the principal approaches to mapping in the Roman era (and beyond into the Middle Ages, with a contemporary reflorescence in the era of Google Maps).

Another side of this was the compilation of geographical encyclopaedias, a kind of global *periplus* manual, of which the most all-encompassing was the 17-volume *Geographica* of Strabo (b. *c.* 64 BC), published around AD 21. Perhaps because of its comprehensive nature, this survived almost intact despite the disappearance of so many classical manuscripts in the disorders which accompanied the collapse of the Western Roman Empire in the fifth century and became one of the principal means by which ancient geographical knowledge was preserved through the Middle Ages. A Greek speaker from Amaseia (now Amasya in Turkey) on the southern shores of the Black Sea, he travelled to Rome and then became attached to the staff of Aelius Gallus, the Roman prefect of Egypt in the 20s BC, and includes in his work an account of his patron's misadventures during the attempted Roman invasion of Yemen in 25 BC, when the expedition became lost in the desert, led astray by their guide Syllaeus (who as the chief minister of the Nabatean state of Petra had clear motives for wanting the Roman presence astride the frankincense trade route that brought huge wealth to his city to be as brief as possible). Strabo's own travels and first-hand accounts from informants such as Aelius gave him a unique breadth of perspective. His brand of geographical details, historical accounts of the regions he describes, and what verges on current affairs, is very far from the fantastic tales of some of his predecessors. His description of the security situation at the head of the Arabian peninsula is typically matter of fact:

'And then, towards the parts inhabited promiscuously by Arabians and Ituraeans, are mountains hard to pass, in which there are deep-mouthed caves, one of which can admit as many as four thousand people in times of incursions, such as are made against the Damasceni from many places. For the most part, indeed, the barbarians have been robbing the merchants from

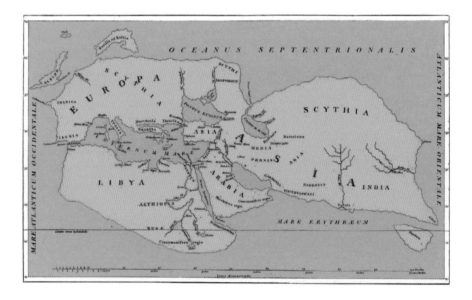

Arabia Felix, but this is less the case now that the band of robbers under Zenodorus has been broken up through the good government established by the Romans and through the security established by the Roman soldiers that are kept in Syria.' [1]

Strabo, too, tried his hand at determining the size of the *oikumene*, calculating it to be somewhat smaller than previous writers at around 70,000 stades wide and 30,000 stades north-to-south, an extent that was, not coincidentally, close to the size of the Roman Empire. He is not known to have produced his own map of the work, instead arguing (correctly, as it turns out) that the world could only be entirely accurately portrayed on a globe, which should be 'like that of Crates'.

The climax of the classical geographical (and astronomical) tradition came with a man of whom frustratingly little is known, but whose influence persisted for a millennium and a half and cast a long shadow over attempts to understand the working of the Solar System. Claudius Ptolemy (AD 100–c. 170) was a Greek-speaker and, though he is universally known as Ptolemy of Alexandria, there is no certain evidence that that is where he was born, although he did work from the Mouseion of the library at Alexandria. A polymath with an intimidating variety of interests, he wrote on astrology, music, optics and history (compiling a list of Assyrian, Persian and Roman rulers), but his main studies, and those for which he became best known, focused on astronomy and cartography.

Ptolemy's main astronomical work, the *Almagest* (a later Arabic corruption of the original Greek nickname for the book which means 'the greatest'), was probably written around AD 150, and was based on years of observations, and his desire to explain the irregularities in the orbits of the Moon and planets which ran contrary to the ancient expectation that these should be perfectly uniform. He devised a system by which the Sun, Moon and the five planets (he wrote over 1,600 years before the discovery of Uranus in 1781) all orbited around the Earth along a series of celestial spheres. Although this was not a new notion – Eudoxus of Cnidus's original scheme had 27 spheres, the mathematician Calippus of Cyzicus increased the number to 34 spheres, augmented by Aristotle to reach a tally of 47 – Ptolemy refined it, by adding epicycles, the main pathways or spheres along which the planets rotate, along with deferents, other points around which the epicycles themselves rotate, so helping to explain those troublesome irregularities, including the phenomenon of retrograde motion by which planets appear to 'overtake' each other periodically.

Ptolemy's geocentric system survived as the main theoretical basis for the description of the Solar System. Although incorrect, on the whole it worked, though complications in it, such as the equant (the point about which the epicycle rotated, which was slightly offset from the Earth's centre), and niggling inconsistencies which his mathematics still could not explain, greatly troubled later astronomers. It was only in the sixteenth century that the temptation to tinker with a system that was fundamentally broken was finally shown to be folly, and the Polish astronomer Nicolaus Copernicus (1473–1543) swept the whole Ptolemaic structure away, epicycles and all, when his *De Revolutionibus orbium coelestium* ('On the Revolutions of the Celestial Spheres'), published in 1543, came up with the revolutionary notion that it was the Earth (and the other planets) that orbited the Sun, and not the other way around.

Ironically, Europeans were throwing off the shackles of Ptolemy's mapping of the heavens not long after they had rediscovered his geographical works, which led them to try to shoehorn his view of the world into their knowledge about their own, just as this was expanding with the great discoveries of the fifteenth and sixteenth centuries that made the task equally in vain. Ptolemy's *Geography* is a curious work for one that inspired so many maps, as it does not – at least in surviving copies – include one that is indisputably the work of Ptolemy himself. Already in the *Almagest* he had given a clue to the way in which he would go about his work, remarking that, 'What is still missing in the preliminaries is to determine the positions of the noteworthy cities in each province in longitude and latitude . . . But since the setting out of this information is pertinent to a separate, cartographical project, we will present it by itself following the researches of those who have most fully worked out this subject, recording the number of degrees that each city is distant from the equator, along the meridian described through it.'[2]

Ptolemy took this up in his second major work, the *Geography*, an encyclopaedic eight-volume description of the known world. He used a huge range of sources, including many, such as the works of Marinus of Tyre (AD 70–130), which would otherwise have been completely lost to us. Crucially, he included in six of the volumes tables of geographical co-ordinates, giving the latitude and longitude of around 8,000 towns, other inhabited places and geographical features. His broad sweep begins in the west with Ireland (where, as a consequence, we have some of the earliest recorded place-names) and then moved eastwards, ending up in India. In the final book, Ptolemy divides the *oikumene* he had described into 26 segments and gives instructions about how to construct maps of them.

Whether he actually took the next step and drew those maps, or had someone else do so, is unknown. Had he done so, he would have produced something like the first world atlas, but his co-ordinates still had an enduring life, adjusted and added to by subsequent geographers, such as Pappus, who worked in Alexandria two centuries later, during the reign of Emperor Diocletian (*r.* AD 284–305). Then, after the collapse of the Roman Empire, all knowledge of his work seems to have disappeared in western Europe, although not in the Greek-speaking East (or the Islamic world, which absorbed many of the eastern Roman provinces in the seventh and eighth centuries). Ptolemy's *Geography* only re-emerged in Europe in the fourteenth century, when it had a huge impact on cartographical development there.

Ptolemy also bequeathed to subsequent geographers a handy definition of the subject, terming it as 'a representation in picture of the whole known world together with the phenomena which are represented within', so making it clear that as far as he was concerned map-making (or at least map description) lay at the core of the discipline. He differentiated it from chorography, which he defines as the study and detailed description of individual regions of the world (and so rather closer to what we might think of today as geography). As a mathematician, he was also very clear that mapping depends fundamentally on mathematics: he calculated his longitude co-ordinates with reference to the distance moved by the Sun in an hour and then provided one of the earliest sets of instructions for

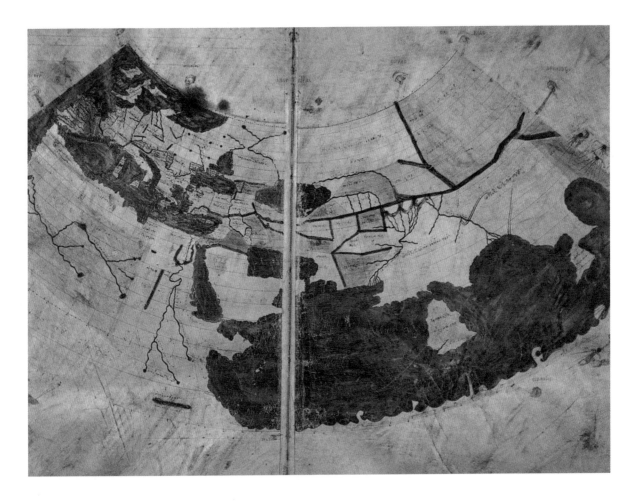

ABOVE

World map based on Ptolemy's first projection, *Geography*, *c.* AD 150 (*Codex Urbinas Graecus 82*, 13th-century)

a means of projecting the spherical Earth onto a flat surface. It wasn't the first, for around AD 100, Marinus of Tyre (whom Ptolemy roundly criticizes for his perceived errors) had produced a projection with straight meridian lines that yielded a more-or-less true area for the area on his prime meridian running through Rhodes, but distorted it elsewhere. Ptolemy was aware of this problem, and so he came up with a projection in which the meridians of the map were not quite parallel, but converged on the North Pole, making the regions to the south of the map larger than they should have been, and creating an overall conical effect, but with their ratio being fairly accurate in the Mediterranean. Still not satisfied, Ptolemy then created a second projection in which the meridians and the parallels that crossed them were actually curved, largely resolving the distortions to the north and south that his first attempt had created.

That Ptolemy was a practical, rather than a purely theoretical, cartographer is clear from the two instruments he describes for use in surveying. The first was a kind of brass astrolabe, with gradations marked on it for each of the 360 degrees of a circle. A movable

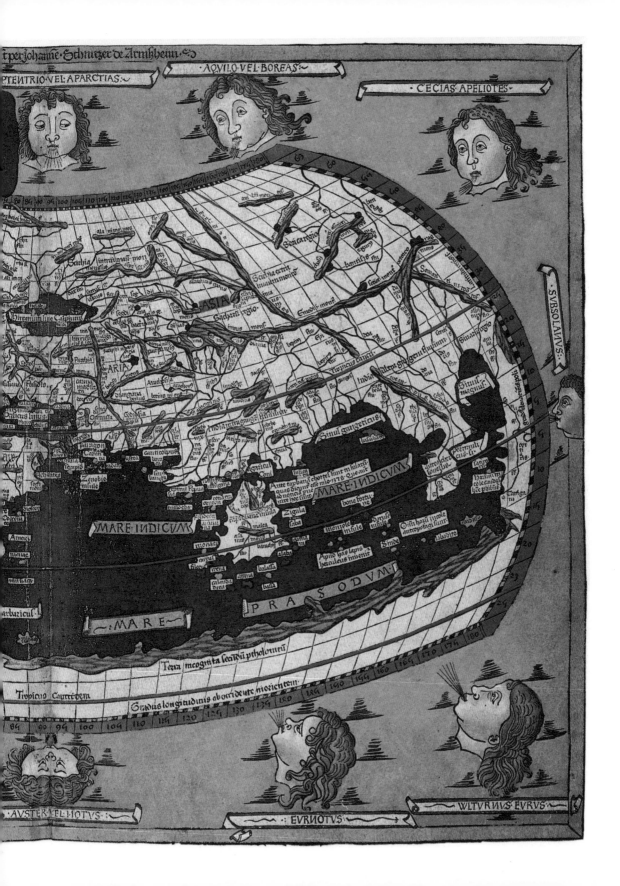

RIGHT

World map, Pomponius Mela, c. AD 43 (1898 copy)

Reconstruction based on the geographical descriptions of one of the earliest Roman geographers, Spanish-born Mela, in his geographical treatise *De Chorographia*.

OPPOSITE

Modern statue of a Roman legionary using a *groma*

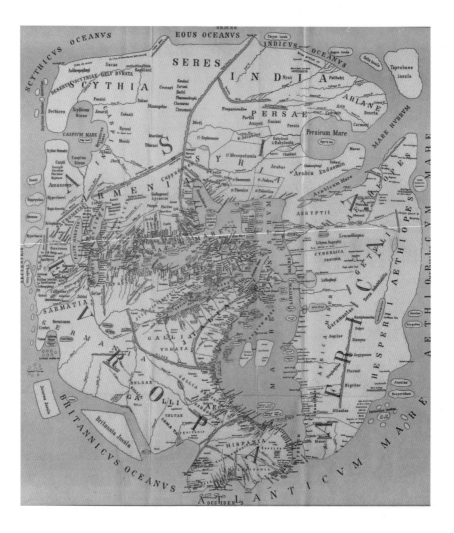

vane with a prism was then attached and plumb lines dropped from it to line up with the horizon and take measurements of the arc between that and the Sun. The second was a quadrant, a sun-dial-like block with markings for 90 degrees, further subdivided into 180 30-second sections, with a rod that could be set in an east-west direction and then plumb lines used to measure the angle of the Sun.

Ptolemy did make errors: his estimate of the circumference of the Earth was too small, foreshortening the overall north-south distances and so setting the equator some 650km (just over 400 miles) too far to the north (with confusing results once the Portuguese started to penetrate down the coast of West Africa, a region to which Ptolemy had no access). He also thought that Scandinavia was made up of two islands and that Ireland lay wholly to the north of Wales, but these mistakes had little effect. Of more influence was his location of the source of the River Nile in the towering Mountains of the Moon (or *Montes Lunae*), in the vain search for whose entirely imaginary slopes nineteenth-century European explorers expended a great deal of time and effort.

Just because a cartographer of the status of Ptolemy may not have produced a map did not mean that no maps were produced in the Hellenistic or Roman world. The rulers of an empire the size that Rome became needed some means of visualizing its vast extent; 3,500km (2,175 miles) separated its northern tip on the Antonine Wall in Scotland and the desert stronghold of Thamugadi in Algeria, and its east-to-west span from Portugal to Anbar province in modern Iraq was roughly 4,500km (2,800 miles). Julius Caesar (100–44 BC) is said to have begun a project to survey the entire Roman world – the *Cosmographia Iulii Caesaris* – and four Greek surveyors were appointed: Nicodemus for the East, Didymus for the West, Theodotus to survey the north, and Polyclitus to make measurements in the South. Their work took decades, with Polyclitus said to have spent a heroic 32 years on his task and, sadly, nothing of it survives, although the four are at least depicted on the corners of a medieval world map.

Caesar's grand-nephew and adoptive son Octavian, who became Augustus, the first Emperor, in 27 BC, carried on in his adopted father's footsteps. He commissioned his chief lieutenant Marcus Agrippa to oversee the compilation of a new world map that, despite the interruptions caused by Agrippa's death in 12 BC, was erected on Porticus Vipsania, not far from the Pantheon in the centre of Rome. Sadly, again nothing of it survives, save references by others. The naturalist Pliny the Elder accuses Agrippa rather acidly of getting the length of the Roman province of Baetica in southern Spain wrong. The map sets it at 475 Roman miles, rather than 280, and Pliny remarked, 'Agrippa was a very painstaking man, and also a very careful geographer; who therefore could believe that when intending to set before the eyes of Rome a survey of the world he made a mistake, and with him the late lamented Augustus?'[3]

Ever a practical people, the Romans seem to have devoted most of their cartographic energy to smaller-scale surveys, in particular the cadastration, or boundary-surveying, which was necessary to lay out the grid pattern along which new Roman towns – including the *coloniae* established for legionary veterans such as Timgad or Colchester in southern England – were built. The individual blocks of *centuriae* (from which the process is also called centuriation) were carefully measured out by *agrimensores*, who employed a specialist surveying device known as the *groma*, a cross-staff with an x-shaped swivelling metal attachment to which were appended plumb-lines used for sighting.

Official maps of the cadastral surveys and boundaries were kept in the Tabularium, a building in Rome's main Forum, which must as a result, have housed the largest collection of maps in the ancient world. Apart from a few sketches inserted in the *Corpus Agrimensorum*, a kind of ancient handbook for surveyors, all of these have perished. What does survive is a handful of Roman town maps and building plans inscribed on stone, in particular the *Forma Urbis Romae* (Severan Marble Plan), a large-scale map of Rome which was compiled between AD 203 and 208 during the reign of Septimius Severus (it includes an ornamental gate known as the Septizonium, which was only erected in 203). The original was

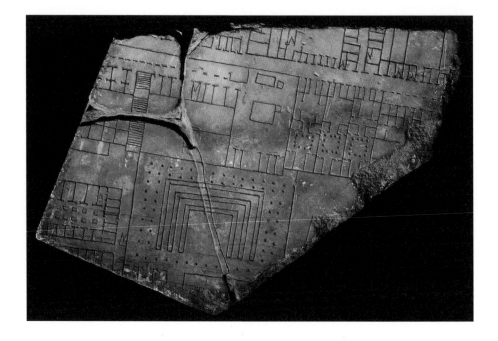

massive, some 18.1 x 13m (60 x 43ft). Although what we now have represents only fragments of the original (complete with the holes used to affix it to a wall on an annex of the Temple of Peace), and the scale wavers somewhat between 1:189 and 1:413, the *Forma* brings to life buildings such as a temple of the Egyptian god Serapis, close to the modern Via delle Botteghe Oscure, and the Diribitorium, where votes were counted in the elections for Roman magistracies.

If the map of Agrippa and the *Forma Urbis Romae* represent the public display of imperial might and administrative prowess, the Romans also met more humdrum needs through maps. In an exercise somewhat akin to the maritime *periploi* compiled in Hellenistic times, they developed a land-based version of these itineraries, comprised of lists of staging points on journeys (mainly along the vast network of roads that they constructed to link key cities in the empire), with the number of miles between stops listed. A few survive in rather eccentric mediums; the Vicarello goblets, a set of silver cups found in northern Italy, give the distances and intermediate stops on a journey from Gades (Cadiz) to Rome. A rather more traditional example is the Antonine Itinerary, which is named for its compilation during the era of the Antonine emperors, beginning with with Antoninus Pius in AD 138 and ending with the murder of Commodus who was strangled in his bath in 192 in an assassination organised by his own bodyguards. It sets out a series of journeys, some of them with branching alternatives. There are 225 in total, 15 in Britain alone, and the longest is that from Rome all the way to Egypt, a distance of 3,500km (2,175 miles), which would have taken many weeks.

None of these, though, were maps (although they could have been used to construct them). The closest thing that we have to a Roman itinerary map is something of a

conundrum. Named for the German scholar Konrad Peutinger (1465–1547),
who was bequeathed it by his friend the humanist Konrad Meissner
(who had in turn found it in 1494, probably in a monastic library),
the *Tabula Peuteringiana* ('Peutinger Table') was originally a single
long, narrow piece of parchment around 6.75m long and 0.34m
wide (22 x 1ft). Along its constricted canvas, a rather squashed
version of the empire was presented in the form of a large series
of itineraries with the roads snaking between major towns which
are painted in with a variety of symbols. These are sometimes
quite lavish, with Rome ornamented with a personification of
the city itself, crowned and seated on a throne, bearing an orb in
her right hand and a spear in her left, while Constantinople has a
similar portrait of its city-goddess, this time without an orb, but
sporting a helmet.

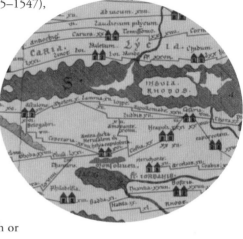

ABOVE AND OVERLEAF

Jerusalem and surrounding
region (above); Pannonia
(Hungary), top strip, Italy,
middle strip, North Africa,
lower strip (overleaf), *Tabula
Peuteringiana*, 4th century AD
(1888 copy, based on 12th-
13th-century version)

The map, though, is clearly a medieval copy made in the twelfth or
thirteenth century of some form of original dating from the fourth century AD.
This might itself have been based on an even earlier version, as it includes Pompeii and
Herculaneum, destroyed by the eruption of Vesuvius in AD 79, which were presumably
on the original archetype map then simply copied and amended without deleting
places long-since destroyed. It may have been a civilian document associated with the
cursus publicus, the Roman postal system of roads and staging posts along which official
visitors (and particularly emperors) were permitted to travel, as it shows no military
installations such as forts, but instead portrays 555 towns, 429 of which are depicted
with towers, which might indicate they had city walls. A number show local landmarks
such as temples and the Pharos lighthouse in Alexandria.

Even though it is not an original, and in the case of Britain only part of the south
coast survives, the *Peutinger Table* gives a hint of what the Romans were capable of in
mapping terms. By the time it reached its final form, however, the Roman world was
changing. The official toleration of Christianity which came when the Emperor
Constantine issued the Edict of Milan in AD 313, and the gradual decline in adherence
to paganism among the traditional elite, which culminated in the effective banning of the
old rites by the Emperor Theodosius in 391–92, created a new landscape of churches
and holy places, and a novel set of itineraries, as pilgrims trudged the long road to
the Holy Land. These pilgrims included the Empress Helena, Constantine's mother,
who went there in 326 and ordered the building of the Church of the Nativity in
Bethlehem and the Church of the Ascension on the Mount of Olives outside
Jerusalem as well as, reputedly, discovering the True Cross on which Christ himself
had been crucified.

A new world-view was emerging, too. Rome was no longer the sovereign of the
known world. Its empire in the west crumbled in the face of barbarian incursions
which overran the provinces one-by-one until in 476, the last emperor, Romulus,
nicknamed 'Augustulus' (the little Augustus) in a mocking reference to his illustrious
predecessor, was deposed by his Germanic army commander Odovacer. There was no
more *cursus publicus*, no more legions, no more shows of imperial might, and though

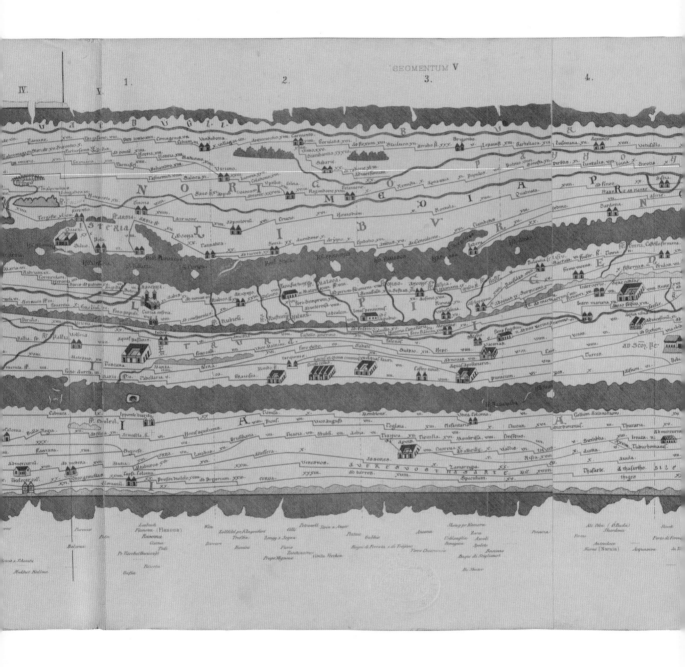

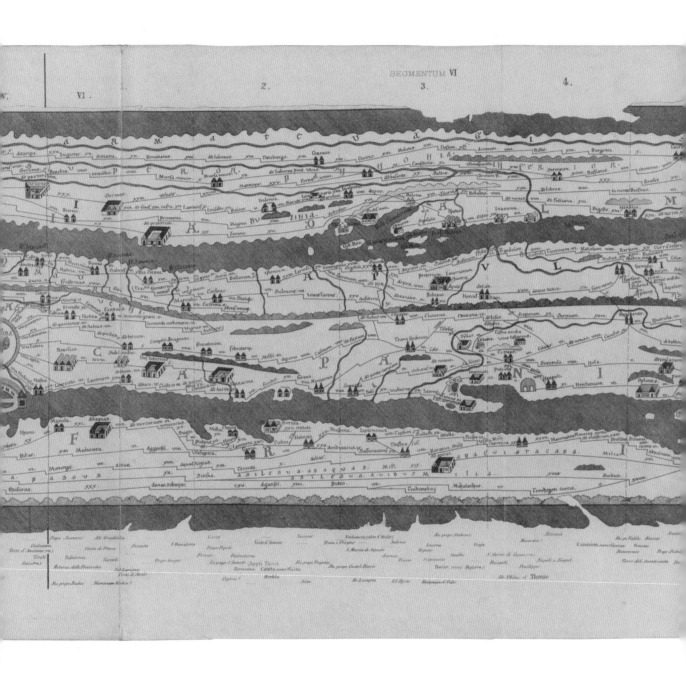

COMES. LIMITIS. AEGIPTI.

elements of the old administration were adopted by the gallery of Visigoths, Ostrogoths, Franks, Burgundians and Vandals who divided up Rome's territory between them, it was bishops, not consuls or centurions, who ran the show and decided what, from the great panorama of classical learning, was acceptable enough to Christian sensibilities to be copied and preserved, and what was quietly forgotten.

Mapping, at first, was not at the forefront of their concerns. In the east, the Roman Empire managed to cling on, despite constant crises such as the ravages of Alaric, the Gothic warlord, in the AD 380s and 390s and a tide of Slavic invaders who pressed down from the Danube and reached as far as Athens and the Peloponnese in the seventh century. This Eastern Roman Empire (which became known to later historians as Byzantine) underwent a revival in the sixth century under Emperor Justinian, whose armies reconquered North Africa, and in an ultimately ruinous series of campaigns between AD 535 and 554 retook the broken shell of an Italy destroyed by war. In 538, they even seized back Rome, but it was by then a hollow consolation prize, whose once-proud monuments served as little more than a convenient repository from which the Byzantine emperors could loot statuary to beautify their new eastern capital at Constantinople.

A mapping tradition survived in the East; there the emperors saw themselves as the rightful heirs to the Roman Empire, rather than the upstart barbarian monarchs such as the Frankish ruler Charlemagne, whose coronation of himself as emperor in 800 caused outrage in Constantinople. A shadow of it can be discerned in the *Ravenna Cosmography*, a list of 5,000 locations drawn up around AD 700 by an anonymous cleric in the capital of Byzantine Italy. The choice is rather haphazard, and many placenames are in the wrong order. Its utility as a practical document is also rather undermined by the omission of distances between the places itemized: as the cosmographer notes, 'We could, with the help of Christ, have written up the harbours and promontories of the whole world and mileages between individual towns.'[4] Although clearly not an official document, it hints that late Roman maps and itineraries were still available for consultation, even as Roman power in Italy was slipping away once more.

Imperial authority remained strong in the eastern Mediterranean until that, too, was swept away by the advent of Islam and the Muslim armies which overwhelmed it in the seventh century. The Byzantine church of St George in Madaba (now in Jordan) bears witness to this time of transition between the classical and Christian worlds in the form of an astonishingly beautiful mosaic map of the Bible lands. Its depiction of the towns and cities of the region looks almost as though it could have been lifted from the *Peutinger Table*, though its focus is clearly on sites of Christian interest. Discovered in 1884, having been covered over for centuries, the mosaic map probably originally extended to an area of 24 x 6m (*c.* 80 x 20ft), depicting the area from Thebes in Egypt to Damascus. Only about half of this now remains, but it is enough to gain a sense both of the workmanship involved in the placement of the two million or so mosaic tesserae that fill the floor with a panorama of greens, reds, blues and more subtle shades in between. The attention given to showing the Holy Places, and in particular Jerusalem, whose size is grossly exaggerated to allow the portrayal of landmarks such as the Church of the Holy Sepulchre and the Church of the Theotokos (or Virgin Mary) is evident. As the latter was only consecrated in AD 542, it gives an earliest date for the mosaic, which was most likely completed before the end of the reign of Justinian in 565.

We have a Christian successor to the old Roman itineraries from about the same time. Cosmas Indicopleustes, who lived in the mid-sixth century AD, was a merchant from Alexandria (his name means 'sailor to India', which suggests he was involved in long distance trade). As well as a series of works, now lost, on geography and astronomy, he composed a 12-volume *Christian Topography*. His extensive travels – he had been converted to Christianity by a cleric in Persia – gave him first-hand knowledge of India's Malabar coast, where he mentions local Syriac Christians for the first time, and took him to the Christian state of Aksum in modern Ethiopia, where he describes the gold trade and speculates that the precious metal comes from 'regions that contained the sources of the Nile'. His manuscript also includes a number of small-scale maps, including one showing four Ethiopians trudging the road from the Red Sea port of Adulis to the capital, passing on their way one of the famous *stelae*, or memorial

BELOW

Jerusalem, Madaba mosaic map, 6th century AD

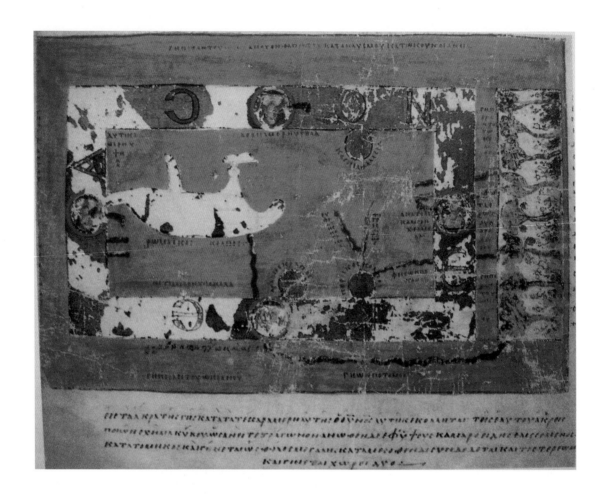

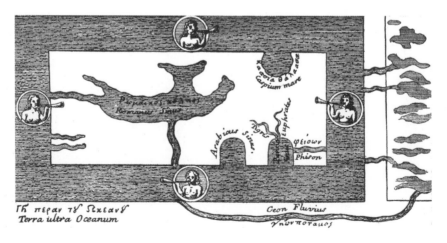

obelisks, of Aksum. The imposing remains of these can still be seen in the town and one of the largest, at 24m (nearly 80ft) tall and weighing in at 160 tons, so impressed the Italian dictator Mussolini that he had it carted back to Rome when he invaded Ethiopia in 1936. He had it erected the following year near the Circus Maximus, where it remained, despite an agreement to repatriate it in 1947. The Ethiopians finally got it back in 2005 (despite a last-minute hitch when it was found the runway at Aksum was too short).

Despite his worldly experience, Cosmas was something of an arch-conservative in geographical terms. He took it as his personal mission to disprove the assertion that the Earth was spherical, reserving particular scorn for Ptolemy. He even used an illustration of four giants standing on top of a small sphere to portray how absurd the notion was. Instead, he argued that the world was shaped like the Ark of the Covenant, a kind of vaulted box with a curved lid, with the realm of God and the divine contained in the curved section and the box part representing the human world. Rather than the elongated cylinder of the *oikumene* of Eratosthenes and his successors, Cosmas's world is rectangular with four seas draining into the Ocean (the Caspian, Arabian, Persian Gulf and Mediterranean), with Paradise situated just beyond the eastern edge of the Earth, from which flows the four great rivers of the world (the Nile, Tigris, Euphrates and 'Pheison', which may be the Indus or Ganges). Somewhere beyond the ocean that bounds the earth (rather as it did in the Babylonian map of the world a thousand years before) lies 'the earth beyond the ocean'. It was not, though, a sign that Cosmas had a premonition about the discovery of the Americas, but a marker suggesting humankind's homeland before the Flood.

Cosmas's scheme, a curious mixture of the classical and the Biblical, is a sign that the rationale for mapping had shifted once more (and in some ways back to a more ancient conception). His purpose is not really to show the world as it is (although he might have argued that his depiction was more accurate than those of 'sphere-earthers' such as Ptolemy). Instead it is a much more symbolic one, organizing the world to show how it reflected the truth of the Christian Gospel. For him, speculations on the *antipodes* are fruitless since, not being mentioned in the Bible, they are irrelevant to the way in which God's message is embodied in the Earth. Cosmas's final rhetorical flourish was to assert that it was clearly impossible that the world could be a sphere, since the water in the lakes and seas on the other side of the world would pour out and mankind could not trample on snakes and scorpions (as God clearly wishes) if we were walking upside down.

The mixture of hair-splitting logic based on dubious Biblical precedent and a potpourri of selective classical sources is typical of much medieval scholarship, but within this a definite cartographic tradition emerged. The principal focus was on maps of the world or *mappae mundi* (the name originally deriving from the Latin *mappa*, meaning 'napkin' or 'cloth'). In the later Middle Ages, these became quite elaborate, but in their first development they were simple affairs, many oval in shape, following the lead of classical world maps since Eratosthenes, but the bulk circular or rectangular (in a nod to Biblical references to 'He that sitteth upon the circle of the Earth'[5]). Their purpose was two-fold: principally to translate an image of God's

OPPOSITE

World map,
Christian Topography,
Cosmas Indicopleustes,
c. AD 540 (top); 19th-century
engraving (below)

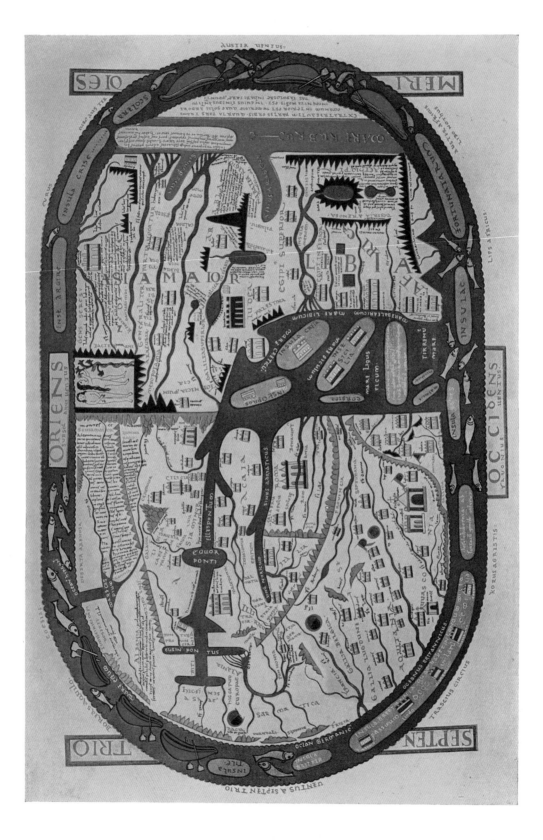

earthly creation into a neat visual form, but also to provide some geographical image, in some cases to allow reflection on stories found in the Bible, but in others as an aid for planning pilgrimages.

Those that linked most obviously to the waning classical tradition were the 'zonal' maps, also called Macrobian, from their origins in the ideas expressed by the late Roman author Macrobius (AD 370–430) in his commentary on Cicero's *Dream of Scipio* (in which the general Scipio Aemilianus has a vision in which he sees the world (and the solar system) from a point high above Carthage, Rome's arch-nemesis, which he will finally conquer and destroy in 146 BC). Macrobius follows Crates of Mallos (p.21) in dividing the world into a series of climatic zones, which are shown in the Macrobian maps as five strips (six if the ocean running between the northern and southern continents is included). The two zones close to the Poles are labelled as *'frigida'* and unsuitable for habitation (a not-unrealistic description) and that close to the equator as *'perusta'* or uncrossable, leaving the two temperate zones, the one in the north familiar to Macrobius and his imitators, and the unknown southern one. The Macrobian maps were popularized by the fifth-century author Martianus Capella. His *Marriage of Philology and Mercury*, with its attractive presentation of the seven liberal arts – grammar, dialectic and rhetoric making up the basic 'trivium'; and geometry, arithmetic, astronomy and music constituting the 'quadrivium' that together formed the basis of a cultivated medieval education – was frequently copied in the Middle Ages, ensuring that the zonal map tradition was still thriving as late as the twelfth century, when Lambert of St-Omer reproduced one in his *Liber Floridus* (*c.* 1120).

The simplest in form among the *mappae mundi* were the T–O maps, which take their name from their depiction of the world as a circle (or 'O') bounded by the ocean within which the great rivers which crossed the three (or sometimes four) continents formed a 'T' shape. Most are included as illustrative material in other manuscripts, sometimes only a few square centimetres in size. Among the earliest examples are those which accompanied the *Etymologiae* (or 'Etymologies') of Isidore, an early-seventh-century bishop of Seville. Steeped in the classical knowledge still available in Spain, his 20-volume work, created between AD 622 and 633, was a favourite of subsequent copyists, with its store of obscure and fascinating knowledge (such as that whoever drinks from the Lake of Clitorius in Italy will develop a distaste for wine). Though the original map that accompanied it has not survived, dozens of the copies do, with their neat and rather stark partitioning of the world into Asia (at the top), and Europe and Africa (at the bottom, or west), divided by the rivers Don and Nile and by the Mediterranean, with the *antipodes* sometimes tacked on to the right (or south) as something of an afterthought. A little more complex are the maps which supplement the *Commentaries on the Apocalypse* by Beatus of Liebana, another Spanish cleric, which were written around 776. Mainly rectangular in form, the Beatus maps show the growing influence of an Arabic tradition transmitted by the Islamic armies which overwhelmed the Visigothic kingdom of Spain in 711, with their colours brighter than the subdued monochrome of most of the Isidorian maps, and the fish swimming breezily in the margins of the world ocean.

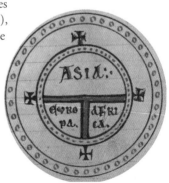

The centre of the early *mappae mundi* had always been
the point at which Europe and Asia meet, which formed
a kind of sacred crossroads as the location of Jerusalem,
even if the city itself is not always marked. The era of the
Crusades, which began with Pope Urban II's declaration
in 1095 of a sacred war to recover the Holy Land for
Christendom (and never mind the opinions of local
Orthodox Christians, let alone those of the Muslims who
by then had been in residence for over 450 years), brought
new practical knowledge of the East to Europe. The
renaissance in western European scholarship of the twelfth
century, which sparked a renewed interest in natural
science, was facilitated by new access to classical manuscripts
(such as Ptolemy's *Almagest* itself) which had been preserved
and translated in Islamic libraries and now began to be
translated back into Latin at the school which developed
in Toledo in Spain.

The thirteenth century brought a broader geographical
knowledge, too, as the growth in interest in empirical science exemplified by scholars
such as Roger Bacon (*c.* 1220–92) and William of Ockham (*c.* 1287–1349) was
complemented by the missionary and diplomatic journeys undertaken by their fellow
Franciscan friars. The travels of men such as John of Plano Carpini, dispatched by
Pope Innocent IV in 1245–47 to seek the aid of the Mongol Khan against the Muslims
(and, if at all possible, to convert him to Christianity), did not succeed in their overt
mission, but brought back invaluable first-hand intelligence about Central Asia, as did
the follow-up mission of another Franciscan, William of Rubruck in the 1250s.

The travel narrative of Marco Polo (1254–1324), dictated while he languished in a
Genoese prison after being on the losing end of a naval battle between Genoa and his
native Venice, is a stirring set of tales of the wonders of the Mongol empire, and about
whose veracity argument has raged ever since. Even in his own time he was nicknamed
'Marco Millioni' because of his perceived penchant for exaggeration. Yet the appetite
for what he had to say after his final arrival back in Venice in 1295 after a 15-year
odyssey through the East was typical of a society that increasingly wanted to know
what lay beyond the borders of its perception. It was an era in which the previously
quite simple *mappae mundi* grew ever more complex and lavish, helped by a burgeoning
interest in cartography and cosmography at the universities which had begun to spring
up as centres where learning might be acquired at a distance from the stifling embrace
of the Church. The Scot John of Sacrobosco (or Holywood) was typical of many.
Educated at Oxford, he taught at the University of Paris in the 1220s and wrote the
De sphaera mundi ('Of the Sphere of the World'), a textbook with a set of instructions
on cosmography, complete with world maps.

Among the more significant cartographic productions of the age is the Ebstorf map.
Discovered in the Benedictine Abbey at Ebstorf in Lower Saxony in 1830, it was probably
produced in the 1230s (a date of 1284 inscribed on the map was most likely appended

later), and was the largest *mappa mundi* known, at 3.58 x 3.56m (11¾ x 11½ft). Sadly, it was destroyed in 1943 during an Allied bombing raid on Hanover, where it had been kept in the Museum of the Historical Society. As a result we are dependent on a facsimile edition made in 1891. Its vast size encompasses both a presentation of t he world according to a Christian viewpoint, with labels carefully inscribed on the map for key events in the life of Christ and the birthplaces of the apostles Mark and Bartholomew. The author – who might possibly have been the Englishmen Gervase of Tilbury who was Abbot of Ebstorf until his death in *c.* 1235 – also clearly draws on a range of classical sources, from Pliny, Strabo and the Antonine Itinerary, to Isidore, Augustine and Jerome, referring as inspiration to both the much earlier world-mapping efforts of Julius Caesar and to the work of Orosius, whose *History Against the Pagans*, written around AD 420, contains much geographical information and spawned its own tradition of world maps in the early Middle Ages.

By then, England was already home to a deeply embedded cartographic tradition that had its roots in the Anglo-Saxon world before the Norman conquest. A manuscript known as the *Anglo-Saxon Scientific Miscellany*, which was probably compiled in the 1020s or 1030s (though a fire which ravaged the collection of the seventeenth-century bibliophile Robert Cotton in 1731 disordered the manuscripts and makes precise dating tricky), includes a map of the world in which the T–O form is flattened into a rectangle, oriented with east at the top, and a rather forlorn-looking Britain in the bottom left with the north of Scotland fragmented into a scattering of islands.

Perhaps the summit of the *mappae mundi* tradition (at least among those that have survived) is the beautifully coloured and gilded map held in the treasure of Hereford cathedral. At 1.59 x 1.34m (*c.* 5 x 4⅓ft), its size is surpassed only by the (now destroyed) Ebstorf map and, astonishingly, it was made from the skin of a single animal. It shows the world contained within a bounding circular ocean, divided into three continents – its compiler did not dabble in the matter of the *antipodes* – though the effect of the lavish gilding with which their names is picked out is rather marred by the monastic illuminator having got Europe and Africa the wrong way around. Its more than 1,100 inscriptions in Latin and the Anglo-Norman vernacular that had become established by the time of the map's compilation around 1300, together with the riot of pocket illustrations of towns, geographical features and fearsome beasts, create an almost anarchic effect over which Christ presides in majesty at the top and to which the Emperor Augustus sending out his surveyors for his own world map provides a secular counterbalance at the bottom.

It is uncertain who commissioned the Hereford map, though it may have been a certain Richard de Bello who was treasurer of Lincoln Cathedral in the 1270s. It is an appropriate memorial for a Christian cleric, in effect telling, as it does, a Christian history of the world, from the Creation in the earthly paradise, to the end times, interspersed with events such as the Flood, which is represented by Noah's Ark perched on Mount Ararat. At its margins, though, more esoteric references abound. In India, a manticore, with the body of a lion and a scorpion's sting-ended tail, menaces travellers, while in the unknown interior of Asia a griffin lurks. At the edge

Ebstorf map and details,
c. 1230s (1891 copy)

The massive size of the original,
made up of 30 sheepskins sewn
together, allowed the compiler
to include a wealth of religious
allusions. The head, arms and
feet of Christ are shown at the
cardinal directions of the map,
making it in a symbolic sense
the body of Christ. The map
is oriented with east at the top
and west at the bottom (with
Europe lower left) and in the
centre of the map Jerusalem
holds pride of place with
Christ's Resurrection depicted
as he steps out of the tomb.

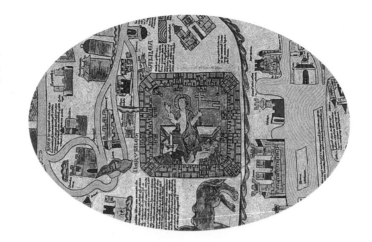

of the world, the compiler, overwhelmed by the exotic dangers, simply gives up and warns that 'Here are all kinds of horrors, more than can be imagined . . . Here are exceedingly savage people who eat human flesh and drink blood.'

These regions were of course not monster-infested blanks to those who lived there. In the vast Islamic caliphate, which stretched at its height in the eighth and early ninth centuries from northern Spain to the borders of Afghanistan and India, classical learning had, if anything, survived in more complete form than it did in northern Europe. A veritable industry sprang up centred on the Bayt al-Hikma (the 'House of Wisdom') in Baghdad, established by Caliph al-Mamun (*r.* 813–33), in which key works such as Ptolemy's *Geography* were translated into Arabic and where, around a century later, the works of Strabo became known. As part of this treasure-trove of classical learning, Arabic scholars inherited and built on the Greco-Roman tradition of cartography. This embraced both traditional mapping and celestial mapping, shown by the beautiful ceiling vaults in the eighth-century bath-house of the Qusayr 'Amra palace in the Syrian desert, with the northern constellations arrayed for those relaxing in the Roman-style *caldarium*.

The Islamic world had developed its own version of the Greek *periploi*, Roman itineraries and Christian missionary guides, with lists of routes for pilgrims travelling to holy places such as Jerusalem or Mecca. The *Kitab al-masalik wa-al-mamalik* ('Book of Routes and Provinces'), compiled around AD 846 by Ibn Khurradadhbih, who served as chief of the postal service in Baghdad, consists of routes throughout the Islamic world, with distances in between them, and extending even further, as far as China. Yet, even though it could have been used to create a *Peutinger Table*-style map, it does not contain one. A world map was created under al-Mamun, which was said, modestly, to have been better than anything that preceded it and seems to have been based on a Greek model such as Macrobius, including climatic zones (which Arabic scholars called *aqalim*).

More in the Ptolemaic tradition are the maps included in the *Kitab Surat al-Ard* ('The Book of the Image of the World') by the mathematician al-Khwarizmi (AD *c.* 780–*c.* 850) (who indirectly gave us the term 'algorithm' from the mangling of his name in Latin translation as Alghoarismus). In the style of his Alexandrian predecessor, the book, produced around 820, includes tables of over 2,400 placenames with their locations given in terms of longitude and latitude. The maps in the one surviving manuscript of the work (copied around 1037) include one of the Nile, which repeats Ptolemy's erroneous assertion that the Nile's source lies in the fabled 'Mountains of the Moon' (which in al-Khwarizmi's version seemed gripped by the claws of a double set of the river's tributaries).

The portrayal of the extent of the Islamic world and the routes by which it might be traversed formed the principal concern of the al-Balkhi school, the main Islamic cartographic tradition. It took its name from a Persian scholar, Abu Zayd Ahmad ibn Sahl al-Balkhi who worked in the early tenth century. Almost nothing is known about him and none of his maps survive, but his work was imitated on a sufficient scale for him to become regarded as the father of Islamic cartography.

OPPOSITE AND ABOVE

Hereford *mappa mundi*, *c.* 1280–90, (opposite) colour-enhanced, 2010; (above) 1956 copy

The detail of the Nile delta (above) includes some of the many fantastic and exotic beasts depicted on the map, including unicorns and a mandrake – a human-shaped root said to scream when uprooted, and capable of curing infertility or inducing madness.

These imitations include the intriguing maps produced by the geographer Abu Ishaq al-Istakhri for his *Kitab al-masalik wa-al mamalik* ('Book of Routes and Kingdoms') sometime around AD 930. Known only from later copies, they are unlike any map that had preceded them (and not much like anything that would follow for the best part of a millennium). Instead of carefully plotted locations, Istakhri's maps consist of a set of itineraries, with the stages included in squares or circles, colour-coded according to whether they were towns or geographical features, set apart from each other on the page at equal distance without any regard to the true scale on the ground. He concentrates on the Islamic world, with a map for each of its 20 provinces, and then a more conventional round world map to include the non-Muslim lands. Taken as a collection in the manuscripts in which they appear, we are finally approaching something like an atlas.

Before long, we even have sets of town plans, such as those which appear in the *Book of Curiosities of the Sciences and Marvels for the Eye*, an eleventh-century manuscript from the North African Fatimid caliphate. Its map of Mahdia, the spiritual headquarters of the

ABOVE

World map, *Kitab al-masalik wa-al-mamalik*, Al-Istakhri, mid-10th century

Fatimids, with its twin palaces of the imams, arch above the entrance to the harbour and twin gates punctuating the walls, show a real attempt to capture the reality of the urban space it portrays. The book's map of Sicily includes a zoomed-in view of Palermo, complete with towers, arsenal and the palace of the emir, built in AD 937, while the city's eight suburbs are neatly divided up by yellow border lines.

Sicily was at the time of the *Book of Curiosities'* production firmly a part of the Islamic world, but in the 1060s its Islamic era came to an end as a Norman army under Robert Guiscard surged over the Strait of Messina, delivered a series of stinging defeats to the ruling Zirids (another North African Islamic dynasty who had taken it over during a bout of Islamic infighting in 1053), and then took Palermo after a siege in 1071, following which all the Muslim strongholds fell one by one. Having emulated his Norman compatriot William the Conqueror, Guiscard was faced with a similar problem of how to reconcile two diverse cultures (whose differences far outweighed those between Anglo-Saxons and Normans in England).

Guiscard handed rule of the island over to his brother, Roger Bosso, who completed its conquest, and it was under Roger's son, Roger II (1105–54), first as count, and then as king, that the fusion of Norman and Arab influences, together with an element of the underlying Greek Byzantine culture that had preceded them, reached its height. In its lavish mosaics, gorgeous ivories, flowing interior lines and the pointed arches of its architecture, and thanks to the Christian, Muslim and Jewish scholars whom its rulers invited from all over the Mediterranean, Sicily became a rare example of cosmopolitan tolerance in a world where the violence of the crusades and the barbarity of anti-Jewish pogroms was rather more typical.

Among those whom Roger II attracted to his court was al-Sharif al-Idrisi, a descendant of the Idrisid dynasty which had ruled parts of Spain and Morocco from the ninth century and which by the time of al-Idrisi's birth in 1100 was just barely clinging on to a toehold in Ceuta. Around 1138, Roger invited him to come to Palermo, attracted by the geographer's reputation as an inveterate traveller (he had already visited Asia Minor, France and even England). Now in possession of a slice of North Africa (which the Norman rulers of Sicily held until 1160), Roger may have felt doubly in need of intelligence about the Islamic world. The principal result of their collaboration was the *Nuzhat al-mushtaq fi'khtiraq al-afaq* ('The Entertainment for He who Longs to Travel the World'), also known as the *Tabula Rogeriana* ('Book of Roger'), a geographical treatise accompanied with maps, drawn from existing treatises, al-Idrisi's own considerable personal knowledge and travellers' tales.

This had not, however, been the main purpose of al-Idrisi's labours, which were motivated by Roger's wish that 'he should accurately know the details of his land and master them with a definite knowledge and that he should know the boundaries and routes both by land and sea, and in what climate they were.'[6] After the initial gathering together of geographical information, a process which took 15 years, the material was collated on what al-Idrisi describes as a *lawh al-tarsim* (or drawing board) prior to its being engraved on perhaps the most extravagant world map of all time, a great silver disk described as '400 Roman *ratls* in weight, each *ratl* of 112 dirhams' upon which were inscribed 'a map of the seven climates and their lands and regions, their shorelines and hinterlands, gulfs and seas, watercourses and places of rivers, their inhabited and uninhabited parts, [and] what distances were between them.'[7] At around 2.97 grams per dirham, the whole thing amounted to 133kg (293lb) of pure silver (with the raw metal alone being worth around £75,000 at today's prices).

Unsurprisingly for such a precious object, which could be easily melted down for its bullion value, the silver map did not survive, leaving only the *Entertainment* and its accompanying maps as testament to the partnership between Christian king and Islamic scholar which ended with Roger's death in February 1154, just a month after the completion of the silver disk. A tantalizing glimpse of what it might have looked like is provided by the circular world map which accompanies many of the surviving copies of al-Idrisi's treatise. Together with the 70 other maps (al-Idrisi divided each of the traditional seven climes into 10, to create a map which covered 18 degrees, or one tenth of the known world at each particular latitude), it forms the most complete vision of the world available at the time. The climate for Muslims in Sicily began to darken under the rule of Roger's son, William I, who, though not opposed to his father's tolerant policies,

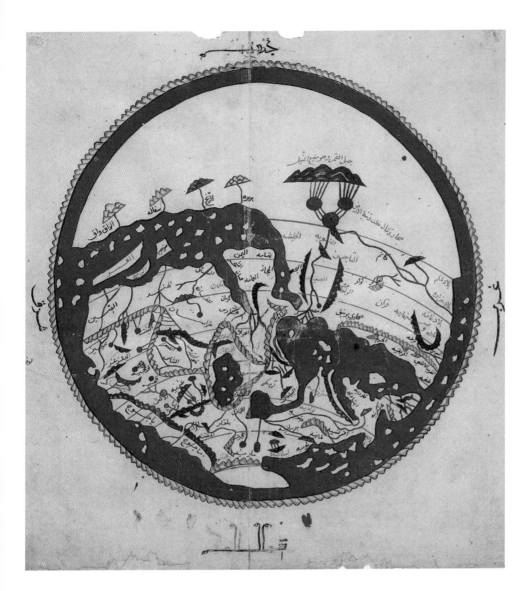

LEFT AND OVERLEAF

Introductory overview
map (left, 1456 copy);
Mediterranean Sea (overleaf,
1926 copy), *Tabula Rogeriana*,
al-Sharif al-Idrisi, *c.* 1154

was too young and inexperienced to manage the conflicting political and cultural currents
which cut across the island, earning him the unfortunate soubriquet of William the Bad.
With his work curtailed, al-Idrisi slipped away to his native Ceuta, where he died in
1165, while the Muslim community in Sicily suffered growing persecutions, interspersed
with revolts, and between the 1220s and 1240s were expelled to Lucera in southern Italy.

Through al-Idrisi, the ancient and medieval worlds had touched through the medium
of Islamic cartography. Though the moment was fleeting and its most spectacular product
vanished, it did at least, in the form of his 71 maps, produce something like the first atlas,
and the inkling of an ancient tradition which began to stir interest among travellers,
merchants and, crucially, navigators in Europe.

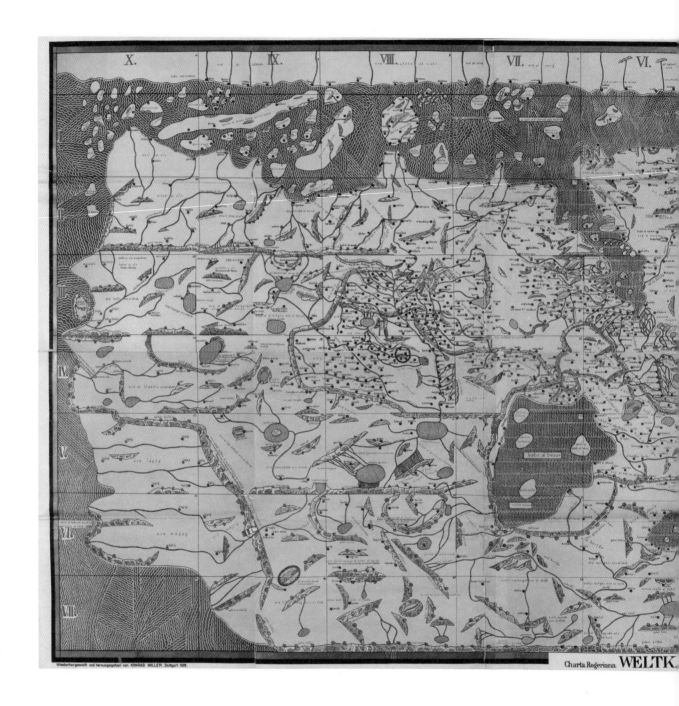

Wiederhergestellt und herausgegeben von KONRAD MILLER, Stuttgart 1926.

Charta Rogeriana WELTK

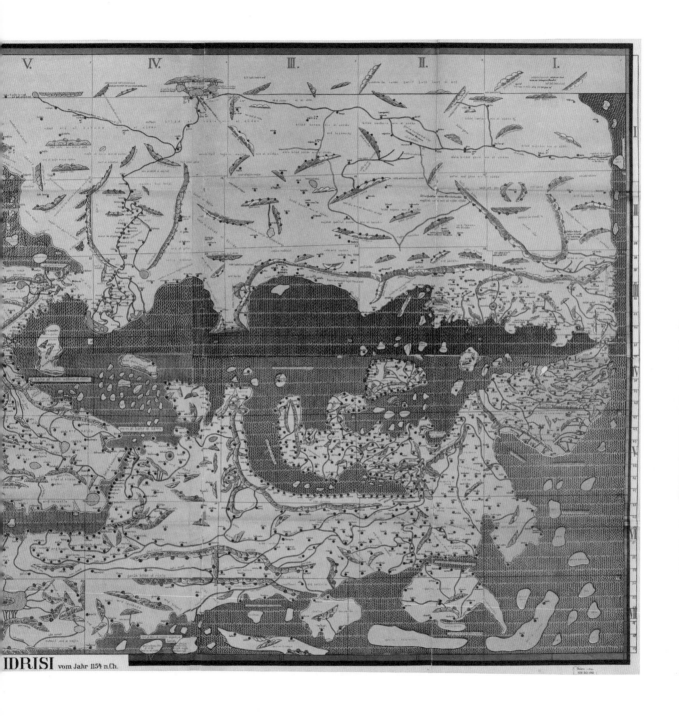

IDRISI vom Jahr 1154 n.Ch.

THE WORLD EXPANDS: THE EARLIEST ATLASES

(*c.* 1200–1492)

The three centuries from 1200 saw the beginning of processes that would eventually lead to profound change in the global political system. Far from being a period of stagnation and stifling conservatism, it was one in which innovation, sometimes tentative, in many fields laid the foundations for the greater strides of the Age of Discovery and the scientific revolutions that followed it. Although the horizons of Europeans had radically narrowed since the collapse of the Roman Empire and during the slow period of rebuilding that its Germanic successor states undertook in the early Middle Ages, by the thirteenth century centralized kingdoms were beginning to consolidate – most notably in England – while the vibrant commercial life of Italian city-states such as Pisa, Venice and Genoa were making (or renewing) connections with the eastern Mediterranean and beyond. Although the Byzantine Empire finally collapsed in 1453, with the Muslim Ottoman Empire that supplanted it occupying much of its former Balkan territory, and eastern Europe experiencing invasion (and in the case of Russia, occupation) during the period, these violent episodes showed a world within which – with the exception of the Americas – its component political systems were interacting more frequently.

Mansa Musa, the ruler of Mali, whose vast wealth – by some measures he is assessed to be the richest person who ever lived – elevated him to fabled status even in Europe, travelled right across North Africa on pilgrimage to Mecca in 1324–25, while the journeys of Moroccan explorer Ibn Battuta, whose three decades of travel from about the same time encompassed virtually the whole Muslim world (and beyond, to China), are emblematic of a world in which geographical knowledge and the thirst for intelligence about far-off lands was growing. In Europe, that process began to accelerate in the fourteenth century as the maritime states of the continent's Atlantic coast embarked on tentative probes into the unknown. The Portuguese discovered the Azores in the early fifteenth century, beginning a process that led to explorations down the west coast of Africa, reaching Cape Bojador in 1434, and culminating in Vasco da Gama's expedition to India in 1497–98, while the Spanish conquered the Canaries in 1478.

This extending of horizons required and produced maps, both in the old tradition of world maps, which with the rediscovery of Ptolemy's original works in Europe now became more sophisticated, and in an increase in the number of regional maps, as monarchs demanded visual displays of power and guides to their burgeoning realms. A more practical tradition emerged, too, as the growing web of trade routes spurred a rise in practical tools for navigation and the appearance of the first genuine maritime charts, for the coastal pilots who eased merchants' passage into local ports and for long-distance voyages.

Known as portolan maps, with their diamond patterns showing the fastest maritime route between two points, these charts mark the precursors to scientific cartography in Europe, but they were at first overshadowed by more traditional products. Typical of the older style is the European map produced by the Welsh clergyman Giraldus Cambrensis (Gerald of Wales, *c.* 1146–1223) around 1200 to accompany his *Topographia Hibernica*, a history and geography of Ireland, a work which drew from his experiences accompanying a military expedition dispatched to the island by Henry II in 1185. His text is replete with fantastic stories of bearded women, grumbles about the lack of fruit trees in Ireland and outbursts against the Irish, whom he accuses of living 'like beasts', but his map, at

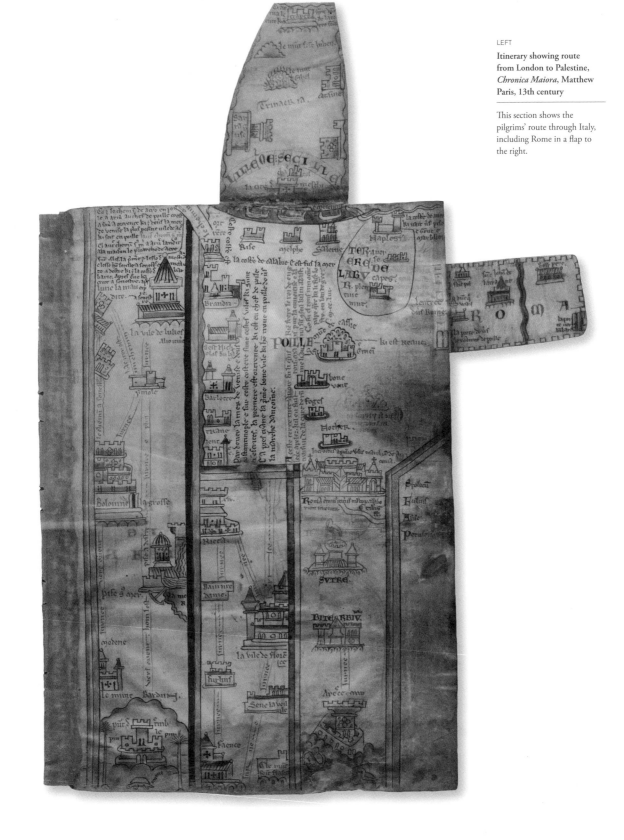

LEFT

**Itinerary showing route
from London to Palestine,**
Chronica Maiora, Matthew
Paris, 13th century

This section shows the
pilgrims' route through Italy,
including Rome in a flap to
the right.

least, is more refined. The squashed circles that represent Britain have few placenames: only four in England (including Lincoln and London) and four in Ireland (most notably Dublin), with none at all in his native Wales, but they do show it as part of a larger European system that is centred (as was fitting for a cleric's world-view) on Rome.

The text of the chronicle of the Benedictine monk Matthew Paris (1200–59) is perhaps a little more sophisticated, but his mapping is assuredly so. He spent most of his life cloistered at St Alban's Abbey, where he took it upon himself to complete the *St Alban's Chronicle* begun by his predecessor Roger of Wendover (who had died in 1236). The abbey had a well-endowed library and Matthew was well-connected, even meeting the king, Henry III, on several occasions when royal progresses brought the court into the area. His main work, the *Chronica Majora*, was accompanied by an itinerary map which took readers on an imagined pilgrimage all the way from London to Apulia (from where, one assumes, they would take a ship to the Holy Land, of which a separate map was also provided). The series of framed narrow strips in which the itinerary map is enclosed still finds space for miniature portraits of towns along the way, showing the pilgrims *le punt de lundres* (London Bridge) and the soaring spire of *seit pol* (St Paul's) in London at the beginning of their journey. They then travel via routes that bifurcate or even split into three alternative pathways, some of them constructed to take in Benedictine houses such as St Omer and Arras, which are shown on convenient flaps to overlay the main route, ending in the crowded profusion of central Italy and finally Apulia, each stage along the way marked with the number of *jurnees* (days) it is expected to take.

Paris also drew a series of four maps of Britain of different levels of complexity. On possibly the earliest, the Royal map (named for the manuscript of his itineraries on one of whose folios it is appended), the island seems grossly oversimplified, Scotland a series of indistinct curves and Wales (or Wallia) barely emerging from England. Yet the whole is boldly labelled 'Britannia' as though an assertion of the unity of England with the other still-independent parts of the islands. Although it contains more placenames than others such as the Cotton Claudius manuscript, particularly in Yorkshire (and shows a particular interest in the river systems of Scotland), the Royal map seems stark. It is a less lavish production than the polychrome Cotton Claudius with its more emphatic annotations filling much of the available space, though the latter's coastline seems more subtly drawn and Scotland in particular is better defined, with both Hadrian's Wall and the Antonine Wall dramatically scoring across the map to divide it from England to the south.

Paris drew overtly antiquarian maps too, which sprang from his interest in Britain's historical development. These include one of Anglo-Saxon England, drawn with the kingdoms of the Heptarchy (the traditional seven realms into which early England was seen to have been divided) presented as though petals of a flower, radiating out from the central figures of Alfred the Great (who ruled Wessex from AD 871 to 899), who represents both Wessex and the uniting of England under his successors. Around him are displayed roundels for East Anglia, Essex, Kent, Sussex, Mercia and Northumbria. As Paris explains in the accompanying text, 'By means of this circular diagram can be known the various kingdoms as they were formerly distinguished from one another by the English.' He then helpfully explains to any reader confused by his novel diagram that, 'Actually the form of England is oblong'. Together with his *Schema Britanniae*, a map of the four main roads of Roman

OPPOSITE

Britain, *Abbreuiatio chronicorum Angliae*, Matthew Paris, *c.* 1250

The most detailed of Paris's maps of Britain includes a wealth of towns, but the geography is sometimes uncertain, with Dover and Canterbury wrongly shown due south of London.

ABOVE AND RIGHT

Maps from the *Polychronicon*, Ranulf Higden, c. 1400

Both *mappae mundi* depict Jerusalem in the central position, but they show deeply contrasting styles. The sparse map (left) shows the T-O shape more clearly, and with relatively few towns, such as Carthage and Babylon shown. The more lavish map includes many additional adornments, including images of the 12 winds around the outer rim.

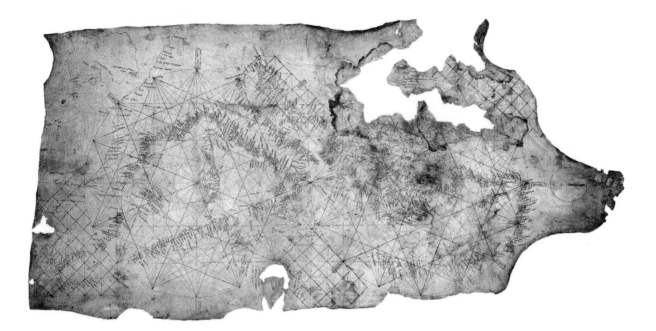

Britain (the Fosse Way, Watling Street, Ermine Street and, though in fact prehistoric rather than Roman, the Icknield Way), these constitute if not quite a historical atlas, then the birth of a tradition of presenting history through the medium of cartography.

Paris's learned, if rather conservative, approach was taken up by others, including Ranulf Higden (*c.* 1280–1364), another English Benedictine Monk, this time from the Abbey of St Werburgh in Chester, who composed a *Polychronicon*, or *Universal Chronicle* between 1327 and 1360. The first volume, covering the geography of the world – with the odd excursus into historical matters such as the foundation of Carthage and Roman divorce law – included in its second edition a map of the world in a developed form of the earlier T–O map, with the three known continents enclosed by a river representing the Ocean, while Adam and Eve are shown in the far east (or top) of the map, standing on either side of the snake that is about to provoke their expulsion from Paradise. This world map, by virtue of it being printed in translation by the pioneering printer William Caxton in a 1480 edition became the first printed map in English.

At about the same time as Higden's map, in the late 1360s or early 1370s, another advance in the cartography of Britain took place in the shape of the Gough Map. Named for the antiquarian Richard Gough, who acquired it in 1774, it is the first map to show a reasonably recognisable outline of Britain, particularly in the south (the coast of Scotland is still rather shaky, and its archipelago of islands rather blob-like). With its more than 600 place-names and the dense network of roads that it includes causing it to be labelled as 'Britain's first road map', it seems a world away in conception from the religious and didactic focus of many earlier medieval maps. If a king such as Edward III wished to regard his lands, with the Gough Map he could have come as close as any medieval monarch had the opportunity to do.

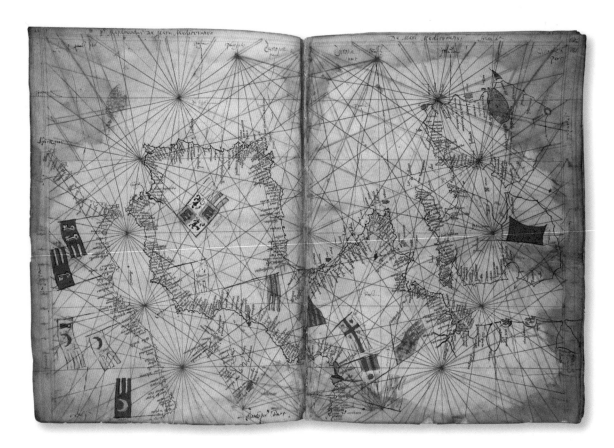

The Renaissance was a time of great intellectual ferment, which began in Italy in the early
fourteenth century with a growing interest in the recovery of the knowledge of the classical
era (whose ruins, after all, lay scattered about Italian cities for all to see). There were the first
reactions against the formulaic religious iconography of the Middle Ages by artists such as
Giotto di Bondone (*c.* 1266–1337) in his sublime frescoes in the Capella degli Scrovegni in
Padova, the elevation of the vernacular to the status of a literary language by Dante Alighieri
in his masterful *Divina Commedia* (completed in 1320), and the scouring of monastic and
ducal archives for Latin and Greek manuscripts which had lain there scarcely noticed for
centuries. The same impulse that drove these also manifested itself in cartography.

The change was brought about by three converging trends: the development of
the portolan charts from being of merely local use to representations of the wider
Mediterranean and Atlantic worlds and then to the world more generally; the merging
of this development with the more traditional *mappae mundi* of the earlier Middle
Ages; and the rediscovery in Europe of the works of the classical cartographer Ptolemy
in the late fourteenth century.

As medieval monks and early cartographers were projecting their varying images of the
world onto *mappae mundi*, a much more practical mapping tradition was emerging in

the maritime republics of the Mediterranean. Cities such as Amalfi, Pisa, Genoa and Venice, which had taken advantage of their access to the coast first to engage in local trade (and not a little piracy), had by the twelfth and thirteenth centuries elevated themselves to the status of maritime powers. Amalfi on the south coast of Italy was the early leader. As it declined into impotence and Pisa ceded its position after a bruising naval encounter with the Genoese at Meloria in the Ligurian Sea in 1284 (a defeat so total it lost almost all its 86-strong fleet of galleys), the struggle over the Mediterranean descended into a tussle between Genoa and Venice, with the Catalans' fleets in Majorca playing a secondary role in the West. The centuries-long struggle really revolved around trade and control of trade routes, or at least access to those under the domination of others (such as the Muslim powers which held Egypt and then, after 1291, the Holy Land, giving them control of the routes by which sugar, and most crucially, spices, reached Europe). Where there was trade, there needed to be maps, and maps of the world populated with fearsome beasts and entirely fictional islands would not do.

Cartographers in the maritime republics turned from the drafting of *mappae mundi* to the production of portolan charts with detailed outlines of the Mediterranean. The term was coined in the late-nineteenth century by analogy with *portolani*, which were medieval texts with sailing directions, although the portolan maps were not in fact associated with these in manuscripts. On them, the coastlines are studded with place-names, of towns, capes, promontories and headlands, while the inland areas, of little interest to merchants and mariners, are left comparatively bare. Around 180 portolans have survived – of the doubtless thousands that were originally made – often betraying, in the shape of their parchment, the outline of the animal skin from which the vellum used for their surface was made, with the neck protruding to one side.

The tradition seems to have sprung fully formed in the later thirteenth century, with the very first portolan appearing around 1275. This, the *Carte Pisane* (or 'Pisa Chart', from its probable origin in the city) is covered in a network of lines that form a mesh of triangles. These rhumb lines or loxodromes showed straight-line paths of equal navigational distance between two points. These all converge on 16 intersection points at equal distances from each other, a sequence which repeats across the larger maps, giving the rhumb-line network an almost hypnotic effect, but also signifying the four cardinal directions and four subdivisions of these (each of them often associated with a wind and illustrated with a 'wind rose'). The placenames are all written on the inland part of the map at right-angles to avoid obscuring the all-important coastline (even though that was often distorted to fit around the rhumb lines, giving peninsulas and headlands an unduly pointy feel), meaning that as the coastline shifts so does the angle of the text, and so it sometimes appears upside down to those used to more modern mapping conventions.

Although attempts have been made to link the portolans with a tradition that survived unbroken from the late Roman Empire or the Middle Ages (possibly via the *Ravenna Cosmography*, p.34), the *Carte Pisane* is the first datable portolan, and before it sailors may have been forced to rely on pilots

Der Permennter.

Ich kauff Schaffell/Böck/vñ die Geiß/
Die Fell leg ich denn in die beyß/
Darnach firm ich sie sauber rein/
Spann auff die Ram jeds Fell allein/
Schabs darnach/mach Permennt darauß/
Mit grosser arbeit in mein Hauß/
Auß ohrn vnd klauwen seud ich Leim/
Das alles verkauff ich daheim.

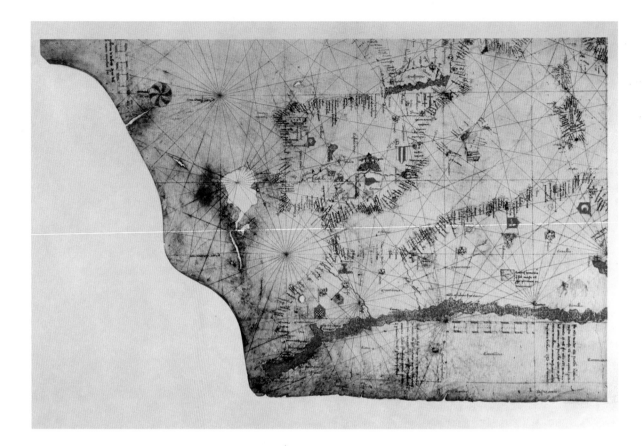

**Portolan of the known world,
Angellino de Dalorto,
c. 1325/30**

Sometimes considered to
be identical with Angelino
Dulcert, Dalorto was among
the pioneers of Catalan
cartography. This portolan
shows the breadth of detail
available to Catalan navigators
of the Mediterranean world,
including North Africa, but
barely a hint of the long
process of exploration of the
West African coastline.

with local, oral knowledge to guide them. It is hard to know what motivated its
(unfortunately anonymous) author to compile it or the sources that permitted him to
produce a good outline of the western Mediterranean and a reasonable one even of the
far-off Black Sea. His example, though, was soon followed by others, with the first named
cartographer being the Genoese Pietro Vesconte (*fl.* 1310–30). Vesconte produced a series
of portolans between 1311 and 1318, whose coastal outlines already show considerable
refinement from the *Carte Pisane*, particularly in the area of the Atlantic coast and the
English Channel ports to which Mediterranean merchants were making more frequent
voyages by the fourteenth century. Two of his portolans, produced in 1318, still have the
wooden boards to which they were pasted, presumably to stop the vellum shrinking when
it came, inevitably, into contact with salt-water aboard ship. Other portolans may simply
have been rolled up for easier storage.

Soon, the portolan tradition had spread to Catalonia, where a somewhat more
ostentatious style evolved, typified by Angelino Dulcert (*fl.* 1320–40), who may
originally have been a migrant from Italy, but who, once in Majorca, moved away
from the more austere chart-making tradition of his homeland to include some inland

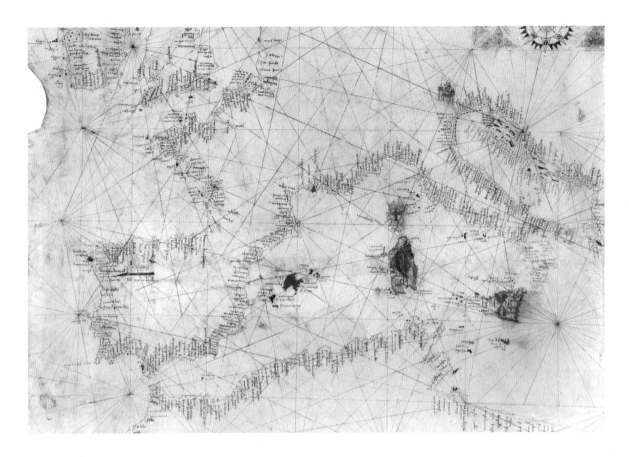

ABOVE

**Portolan of the
Mediterranean, Andrea
Bianca, 1436**

A Venetian galley officer,
Bianca produced a portolan
atlas in 1436, which includes
this map. Among the other
charts was a very early
one of Scandinavia, which
other southern European
cartographers rarely showed,
for lack of first-hand sources.

illustrations of towns in his 1330 portolan. By 1339, with his finest production, he was incorporating features such as a drawing of the Queen of Sheba in Arabia, and of a majestic enthroned king in Africa, all more redolent of a *mappa mundi* than a practical sailor's chart. Dulcert's 1339 portolan also includes details of the early Portuguese discoveries in Africa, extending further to the south than the traditional Mediterranean frame of such maps (and in the east reaching as far as the Caspian Sea).

Although we have the names of dozens of the cartographers who produced portolans between 1270 and 1500, we know relatively little of how they were drafted. It must have been a minor industry in its own right, with the need to source the animal skins and have them scraped away by a parchment-maker to produce a smooth surface. Examination of portolans has shown the pinpricks of a 'hidden circle' which must have been drawn first with a pair of dividers and a ruler, and which formed the basis of the network of rhumb lines that came next. Then, carefully, the cartographer would have inked in the coastline, adding the placenames and (if Catalan!) embellishing the map with appropriate flourishes, occasionally including flags of the nations portrayed fluttering over tiny tents.

Almost no Spanish portolan maps from before 1500 survive, even though in 1354 King Pedro IV of Aragon, an inveterate political schemer who spent most of his reign embroiled in wars with Castile and Catalonia, decreed that all Aragonese galleys must have two sea charts on board. There are also surprisingly few Portuguese survivals, particularly given the extensive exploration that occurred down the west coast of Africa: Gil Eannes (*fl.* 1421-36) in 1434 travelled beyond Cape Bojador, which his predecessors had feared marked the edge of the world, or at least the point at which the heat of the tropics became so fierce that further progress was simply impossible. Most extant portolan maps, therefore, are Catalan or Italian, and become progressively more sophisticated in their treatment as blanks at the edge of the map were filled in, but all retaining their overall look of single parchment sheets and rhumb lines.

Typical of the later portolans is one produced in 1470 by Grazioso Benincasa. Born in Ancona in southern Italy some time in the first decades of the fifteenth century, he was a prolific cartographer, and his portolans were the first to document in an extensive manner the Portuguese discoveries of the preceding decades, including the Cape Verde islands. In spite of his previous career as a ship's captain, he still credulously included in a 1463 atlas of portolan charts he compiled the entirely mythical island of 'Antilia'. European

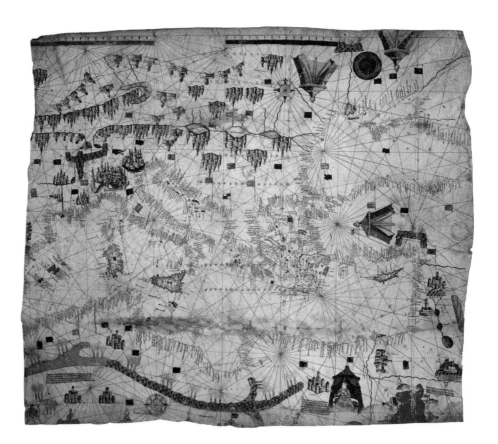

map-makers had started to site the island out in the Atlantic in the 1420s; perhaps its inclusion represented a sense that somewhere out there were lands yet to be discovered, which remained frustratingly just out of reach.

Portolans did not entirely displace the tradition of creating world maps, which continued into the later Middle Ages, although they began to evolve into a more elaborate, and to some extent more accurate, form. The work of Pietro Vesconte (p.64), pioneer of the portolan chart shows the beginnings of this change. He produced a series of maps for inclusion in the *Liber Secretorum Fidelium Crucis* ('Secrets of the Faithful of the Cross'), a work by the Venetian aristocrat Marino Sanudo (*c.* 1260–1343), who had taken it upon himself to promote a new crusade to the Holy Land. The final crusader stronghold there, including Acre, had fallen in 1291, just 15 years before Sanudo began his one-man, and

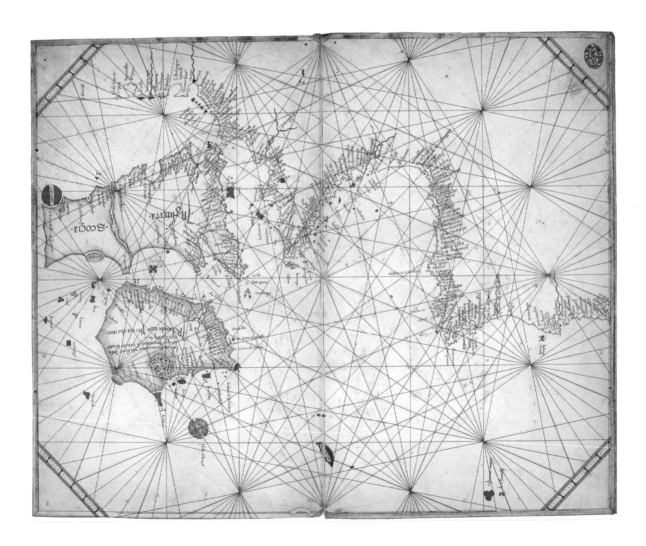

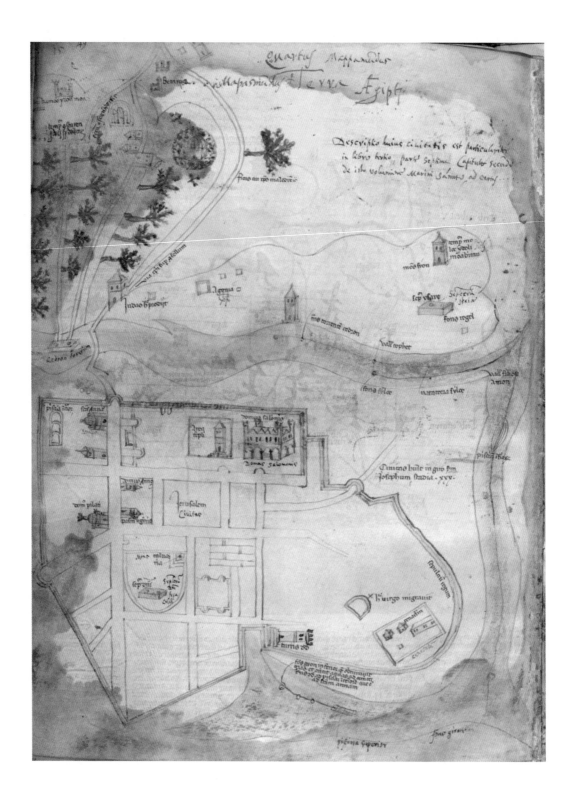

ultimately fruitless, attempts to interest European monarchs and the Pope in new expeditions to retake them. Vesconte's contribution to the work was more successful. Consisting of a circular *mappa mundi*, a more detailed map of the Holy Land, and city plans of Jerusalem and Acre (the latter of which, presumably, might have assisted any putative crusaders should Sanudo's master plan for the conquest of Egypt and then a thrust into Palestine have come to fruition), they are the work of a master cartographer who blends tradition and innovation. Although doubt was cast on his authorship for some time – and Sanudo, ungraciously, did not acknowledge the identity of his map-maker – the inclusion in the *Liber Secretorum* of a set of sea charts which are almost identical to those Vesconte assembled for his 1313 portolan atlas (and which he signed), make it highly unlikely another cartographer was involved.

For the map of the Holy Land, Vesconte applies some of the lessons he learnt in compiling his portolan maps, overlaying the terrain with a grid, with the sides of each square covering two miles, and including a sort of key on the side (so that Masada is indicated as being in 'row twelve, square 67' as the 'impregnable fortress which Herod built'). The Jerusalem map is freer than previous versions, not bound by the circular portrayal that convention dictated, and it includes a selection of sites for would-be crusaders (or pilgrims), such as the tomb of Isaiah and the Garden of Gethsemane, where Judas betrayed Christ, while scrupulously avoiding any mention of Muslim holy sites.

Vesconte's world map is a more complex fusion of the medieval *mappa mundi* and the portolan. It is oriented with east at the top and retains the traditional division into the three continents of Europe, Asia and Africa, with the bounding Ocean shaded in green. Around this, though, in a nod to the theory of celestial spheres, are bands of white and red to represent the spheres of air and fire that surround the world.

It is the mesh of rhumb lines that stretch across the map, extending from 16 points along its edge, that show the portolan heritage. The names of the winds, too, are included, such as *sirocus* (the south-east wind that blows in across the Mediterranean from the Sahara, known to the Arabs as the *khamsin*, or '50 days', from the length of the period in spring over which it casts its scorching pall). East and Asia continue to be at the top, in the tradition of medieval *mappae mundi*, but the continents and seas have a curved form like so many early sea charts and the Indian ocean is pocked with islands representing the sources of the spices, such as nutmeg, which were eagerly sought after in Europe, and which would in due course become the prime motivating force behind the voyages of the Age of Discovery. Amid useful indication of geographical locations such as Cathay (China) and the Caspian Sea, there are some errors, such as the addition of a fictitious 'Mare de Sara' between the Black Sea and the Caspian and, though Vesconte eschewed the *mappa mundi* custom of enlarging the Holy Land, he still felt the need to scatter his map with items from legends, such as the fabled giants Gog and Magog who are placed in the extreme north.

Perhaps the most famous of the transitional world maps, and without doubt one of the most lavish, is the Catalan Atlas, which was created in Majorca in the 1370s. Its six double panels, which were beautifully painted on vellum and then mounted on boards, allowing it to be folded up, produced an atlas that was a worthy gift for a king. It owes its survival to a request by Charles V of France for a world map which would show all the latest discoveries.

His Aragonese counterpart Pedro IV (*r.* 1336–87) obliged with an atlas produced in the Catalan workshop of Abraham Cresques (1325–87) and his son Jehuda (1350–1427).

The first two panels of the atlas are a conventional sea chart, with a thousand ports and coastal features marked in Europe, but with little in the way of pictorial adornment (save a few flags fluttering over cities such as Granada in Spain). Although the use of four rhumb lines intersecting to produce the first compass rose, indicating the four cardinal directions for the use of the map's readers, is an important innovation of the Catalan Atlas, it is from the final two sets of double panels, which cover Asia and Africa, that it earns its place as one of the most reproduced atlases of all time. The cartographers were clearly influenced by the accounts of the travels of Marco Polo (which were now nearly 80 years in the past), and the map is liberally sprinkled with beautiful miniature illustrations of tales, from both Polo and other travellers. Kublai Khan (or Holubeim, as he is labelled on the map) is shown east of the Caspian Mountains, and to their west a crowned Alexander the Great appears to be having a chat with a winged devil (who,

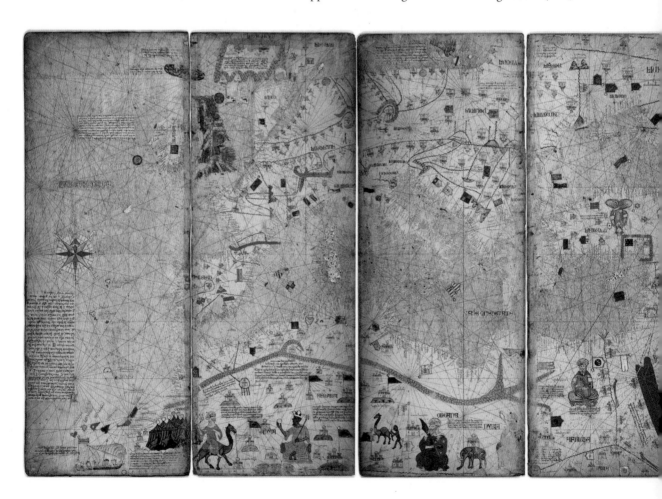

legend has it, is guarding the gates to the mountains against the Macedonian king's enemies). Polo's vagueness about Chinese geography – which led some at the time and subsequently to imply that he had never actually been there and that his whole *Travels* was a confabulation drawn from libraries and other travellers' tales – is reflected in the somewhat haphazard location of the 29 Chinese cities named on the Catalan Atlas and the repetition of his claim that there are 7,548 islands in the South China Sea. At its furthest reaches, the cartographer grasps for even more outlandish tales, with southeast Asia populated by mermaids, an island called Iana (possibly Java) which is said to be ruled by a queen, and a race of black giants who are said to have a particular taste for eating white intruders.

The portion of the map showing Africa is on even less secure ground, reliant on information that had trickled into Spain via the Arab trade caravans which bore salt, gold and slaves across the Sahara. It was still too early for the Portuguese expeditions that would later open up maritime routes around the continent, though one early pioneer is

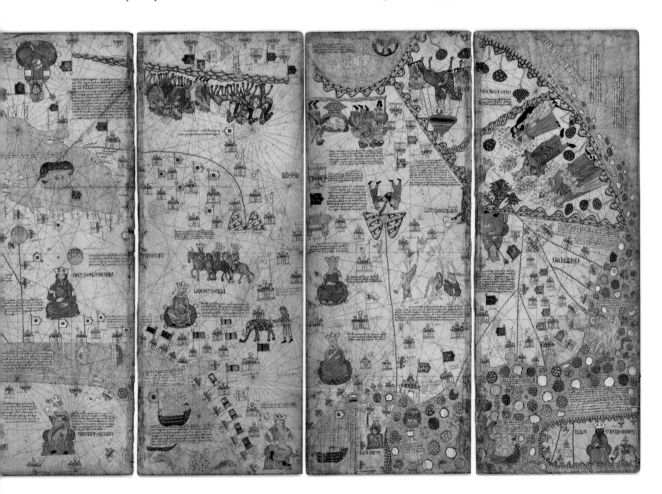

shown on the west coast where a small ship bobs, labelled as that of Jaume Ferrer 'who set sail on St Lawrence's Day [10 August] 1346, bound for the Rio de Oro'. Whether Ferrer found the river of gold he sought is unknown, since he vanished without trace and virtually all that is known of him is this note on the Catalan Atlas and that he was a native of Palma de Majorca.

Perhaps the Atlas's most famous image, however, is of 'Musse Melli', or Mansa Musa (d. 1337), who ruled Mali between 1312 and 1337. In his hands he holds what appears to be a huge nugget of gold, a reference to his vast wealth, as his kingdom sat astride the principal gold-trading route (the actual source of the gold, which the Malians scrupulously kept secret from the inquisitive gaze of Europeans and other outsiders, lay far to the south at Bure and Bambuk on the edge of the tropical forest). The rulers of Mali had converted to Islam and Mansa Musa's pilgrimage to Mecca in 1324 brought him resoundingly to the attention of the outside world (including Catalan cartographers). The trip's opulence has left him marooned in the popular imagination in the limbo between fable and fact. His caravan across North Africa was virtually a mobile city, composed of 60,000 pilgrims, guards, porters, cooks, camp-followers and 12,000 young slaves clad in robes of silk, 500 of whom rode ahead of the main party bearing rods of gold to alert settlements in his path of the Mansa's approach. When the multitude finally made it to Cairo, the Malian king's spending was on such an epic scale that it caused a sudden inflationary surge and a crash in the price of gold. It also depleted his seemingly inexhaustible resources to such an extent that he was forced to borrow extensively from money-lenders (a sum which, when he finally returned to Mali in 1325, he promptly paid back all at once, causing another wave of instability on Cairo's financial market).

Dotted amid the fables and hard geographical information are doses of wishful thinking. To the south-east of Egypt, a label on the map refers to the 'emperor of Ethiopia and of the land of Prester John', who is said to hold sway over the Christians of Nubia. The search for this elusive ruler, whom western European monarchs and

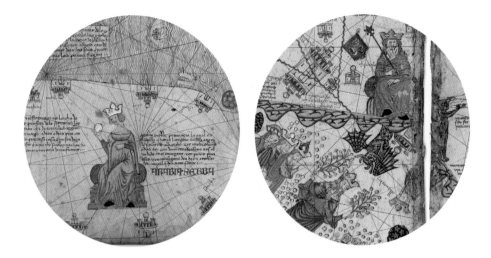

adventurers thought might be a useful ally against the growing might of the Muslim states on Europe's border, was in part the motive that prompted the missions of John of Plano Carpini and William of Rubruck (p.40). It also inspired the travels of the Franciscan Odoric of Pordenone in the 1320s, who travelled via Tabriz and Hormuz in Persia, India, Ceylon, southeast Asia and ultimately to Zaitun in China. He claimed to have visited along the way both the kingdom of Prester John and Hell itself. In truth, Prester John remained elusive: a letter, which came to light in 1165, claiming to be from him and describing his kingdom as an Earthly Paradise with 72 provinces in which the rivers flow with precious stones and his palace, roofed with ebony, is studded with gold, sapphires and amethyst, continued both to tantalize and disappoint.

The baggage of one traveller who came from the East bore an item which was destined to have a far greater influence on the course of European scholarship and map-making than fevered dreams of locating Prester John. Whereas in the thirteenth century, western Europeans had thought they might find military support in the East, a hundred years later the situation was reversed and, as the Ottoman Empire expanded and the Byzantine Empire – the defiantly long-lived successor to Rome – receded, the latter's rulers sent ever more desperate pleas to their western cousins to launch a new crusade, or indeed any kind of expedition, no matter how small, to relieve the pressure. They even went so far as to suggest a reunion of the Greek Orthodox and Roman Catholic Churches, which had been sundered in the Great Schism of 1054; given the ecclesiastical vitriol which had always accompanied any suggestion of compromise on either side, this was no mean offer.

The Byzantine scholar Manuel Chrysoloras (*c.* 1350–1415) was sent on one such embassy in 1390 by the Emperor Manuel II Palaiologos (who would a few years later come himself to try some in-person but fruitless diplomacy with King Charles VI of France, who proved unfortunately to be insane, and Henry IV of England, who made polite noises and put on a tournament in his honour, but offered little concrete support). Chrysoloras made such an impression during his equally barren diplomatic effort that in 1396 he received an invitation from Coluccio Salutati, the chancellor of Florence and a cultivated man whose interest in ancient manuscripts earned him the unkind nickname 'the ape of Cicero', to become a professor of Greek at the city's university. It was a bold move, as no one had been able to learn the classical language in the north of Italy for more than 700 years, but Chrysoloras nurtured a group of talented students, including men of the stature of Leonardo Bruni, who played a key role in stoking the fires of the Florentine Renaissance. More importantly, however, he brought with him a copy of Ptolemy's *Geography*.

As already noted (p.24), Ptolemy's work had disappeared from western Europe during the early Middle Ages (though never from the Islamic World, nor from the Greek-speaking Byzantine Empire). The particular manuscript that Chrysoloras carried with him also contained a world map and 26 regional maps, which had been put together around 1295 using Ptolemy's latitude and longitude instructions. The effect on western mapping was electrifying, at least once the text had been translated into Latin in 1406 and the maps received equivalent treatment about a decade later. No longer were map-makers bound by the medieval conventions of the *mappae mundi* (although arguably they found themselves now bound by the equally constraining conventions of the ancient Alexandrian).

The first fruit of this work was a map by the Danish cartographer Claudius Clavus (or as he was known back home on the island of Funen, Klaus Swart; b. 1388). This was produced around 1425 and appended to a manuscript of the *Geography* owned by the French Cardinal Fillastre (1348–1428), who had in turn acquired it in 1414 during the Council of Constance (called to deal with the growing challenge to the church of the Hussite heresy in Bohemia and which infamously burnt its leader Jan Hus at the stake, despite his having received a safe conduct). The Clavus map concentrated, as befitted a Scandinavian, on the far north, correcting Ptolemy's somewhat hazy and frequently mistaken conception of what lay in the far northern lands about which he knew little and had not even second-hand accounts to go on. Fillastre, who also wrote a commentary on the *Geography*, noted approvingly of the work of Claudius Cymbricus (as he calls Clavus, after the Latin for a tribe that originated in Denmark) that 'Beyond that which Ptolemy put here, there are Norway, Sweden, Russia and the Baltic Sea . . . beyond this sea is Greenland and the island Thule more to the east . . . Ptolemy made no mention of these places, and it is believed that he had no knowledge of them.'[1]

Ground-breaking in so many ways, Clavus's map included a proper outline of Scandinavia for the first time, including in it an observation that at high latitudes the day in summer is 24 hours long. It also gave the first cartographic representation of Greenland, the last contact with whose Viking colony, nominally under the suzerainty of Denmark, had been not long before, in 1408. Although he draws it incorrectly as a landmass attached to Scandinavia, its presence is a sign that for all the excitement over the discovery of Ptolemy, fifteenth-century cartographers were aware that the Alexandrian had his limitations, not least at the edges of his known world.

Before long, Ptolemaic-style atlases were proliferating, although until the 1450s they largely reproduced the maps found in Chrysoloras's manuscript, with almost fifty examples known. The intervening period did at least produce a final flourishing of the medieval *mappa mundi* tradition with some of its most extravagant, and its most curious, productions.

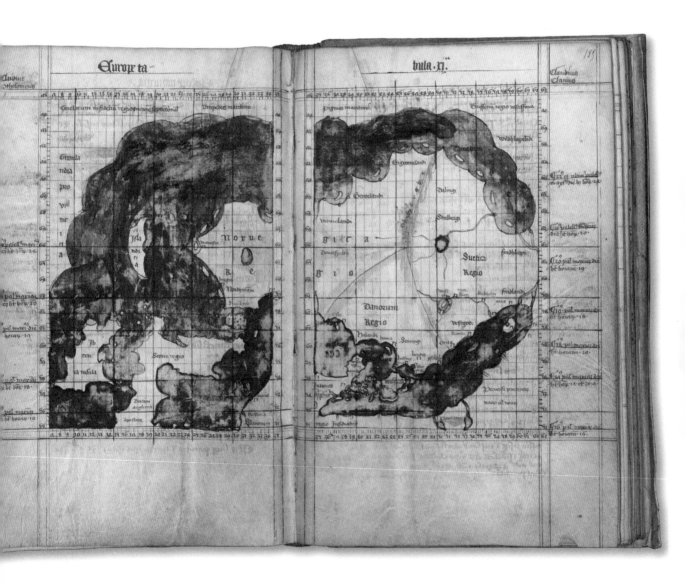

The most splendid is that of Fra Mauro (*c.* 1400–64), produced some time around 1450. Despite being a monk of the Camaldolensian Order at their house at San Michele di Murano (on a small island off Venice, which now houses the city's main cemetery), he had access to the work of the Italian humanists, scholars who had assiduously sought to recover ancient Greek and Roman manuscripts to supplement the thin selection of classical works approved by the Church. He also had a collaborator, Andrea Bianco, who had travelled extensively throughout the Mediterranean world and was himself a cartographer.

Fra Mauro compiled a first world map for King Afonso V of Portugal, who was able to share information gleaned from the voyages of discovery sponsored by his uncle Prince Henry the Navigator in the 1420s, but this has not survived. The second version, however, made shortly before Fra Mauro's death in 1459 bursts with energy. He rather needlessly apologizes for not showing the world exactly as Ptolemy had described it in his tables of co-ordinates, but the near-2-m/6-ft-diameter round map depicts the Indian Ocean as open, rather than enclosed by land, as Ptolemy had suggested, and his outlines of the continents, in particular Europe, is more refined than previous Ptolemaic imitators. Yet, in the grand medieval tradition and still a century before Copernicus, Mauro includes information on the heavenly spheres within which the planets orbited, and includes such traditional elements as Adam and Eve being expelled from the Garden of Eden (though no longer sited in the east, as older maps would have it, but instead ambiguously out of the frame since, despite all those missions to the Mongols and China, no hint of the earthly paradise had ever been found). He also shows Gog and Magog, Noah's Ark atop Mount Ararat, and Alexander the Great engaged on his conquests. Jerusalem, though, is no longer situated in the centre of the map for, although a Christian monk and the author of an ostensibly traditional-style *mappa mundi*, Fra Mauro is not concerned to present a map of the world as a symbol and a focus for faith. He wanted to show it, as best he was able, as it really is.

As part of this, he discarded the time-hallowed tradition in European maps of being oriented with east at the top (which somewhat inconveniently gave pride of place to rather unknown regions of Europe) in favour of a south-north orientation (similar to that of traditional Arabic cartography). He was also, presumably on the basis of intelligence received from King Afonso, able to include the very latest information on Africa. So, as well as Prester John, whom Mauro situates in Central Africa, and the large mountain with three lakes that Ptolemy asserted was the source of the Nile, Mauro includes a series of place-names along the west coast which had only just been reached by the Portuguese, such as Cape Rosso, south of the Gambia River, discovered by Dinis Dias in 1445.

Claudius Clavus's presentation of Ptolemy's maps was further refined by Nicolas Germanus (*c.* 1420–*c.* 1490), who may also have been a Benedictine monk, and whose atlas in 1482 included a better outline of Scandinavia and pushed Iceland into the far west of the *Mare Congelatum* ('Frozen Sea') as he labelled the North Atlantic. He also showed Greenland correctly, not as an appendage to Scandinavia.

Yet these and other *tabulae novae* ('new tables') intended to supplement and correct Ptolemy were still overshadowed by rather conservative productions, like the tiny Olmütz map drawn around 1450, which still shows Paradise in the east, and the traditional four

rivers flowing out from it, with Gog and Magog still bestriding northern India. Even the Catalan World map produced around 1450 (which ended up in the Biblioteca Estense in Modena by 1488) showing the Portuguese discoveries in West Africa since the 1440s (including Cape Verde) still includes the traditional caste of Adam and Eve, Gog and Magog and Alexander the Great. Another *mappa mundi* of the Venetian cartographer Andrea Bianco, produced in 1456, appears in an atlas that also incorporates a set of sea charts. The map shows the Garden of Eden, too, although it goes against Ptolemy in depicting the Indian Ocean open to navigation. In the furthest south, the South Pole is uninvitingly labelled as *nidus alli malium* ('the nest of all evils') and, for anyone not deterred by that, it is illustrated with an image of a hanged man.

As well as world maps, regional maps, maps of the Holy Land and those maps of towns which found their way into works such as Vesconte's *Liber Secretorum*, the later Middle Ages saw the rise of a particular genre of atlas that incorporated collections of maps of islands. Sometimes scarcely more than compilations of charts, but in their most developed form lavishly produced atlases, they were born of a tradition of Mediterranean navigation and travel and were known collectively as *isolarii*. Although the bulk of them date from the late fifteenth or sixteenth century, one of the most notable, the *Liber insularum arcipelagi*, was compiled by the Franciscan friar Cristoforo Buondelmonti (*c.* 1385–1430). A native of Florence, with access to the humanist circle that grew up there during the early Renaissance, in 1406 he moved to Rhodes. This perhaps gave him a taste for the island life, as in 1415 he travelled to Crete.

This, and his other travels around the Aegean, provided Buondelmonti with the information to put together his 'illustrated books of the islands of the Cyclades and of other islands scattered around them', which amounted to an atlas with 79 maps of islands and some locations on the coastlines of the mainlands opposite them. Although the geographical information provided in his text is something of a hotch-potch of hearsay spiced with historical fact, the maps are a visual delight, dotted with artistic representations of the key sites he wished to illustrate, such as the medieval fort of Neratzia on Kos, remote mountain monasteries and, most splendid of all, the Byzantine capital of Constantinople, with its age-old imperial palaces, churches, hippodrome and imposing city-walls; this was the last detailed representation of the city we have before its capture by the Ottoman Turks in 1453.

The disappearance of the Byzantine Empire marked the end of a political entity that had endured for more than two thousand years, since the traditional date of Rome's foundation in 753 BC. It sent a new wave of Greek-speaking refugees westward to join Cardinal Bessarion (1403–72), who had moved in 1437 to attend a church council and ended up in the employ of the Papacy. They brought with them manuscripts to join the *Metaphysics* of Aristotle which Bessarion had translated, but already the day of the hand-produced, illuminated manuscripts of the Middle Ages was drawing to a close, the hard-graft and beauty of the monastic scriptorium or humanistic copying room replaced by the solid utility of the printing press with movable type, an innovation devised by the German

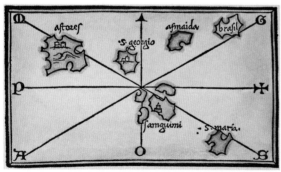

66.   95

SEPTEMTRIO

sydere clara foret Sumptam de fronte coronam sumisit celo
tenues uolat illa pauras. habet hec insula promontorium Ar-
uisium apriseis dictum, a quo aruisia uina optima denomina-
ta sunt, de qbs maro i Daphni, Vina nouum fundam calathis
aruisia nectar, & horatius et meminit insermonibus.

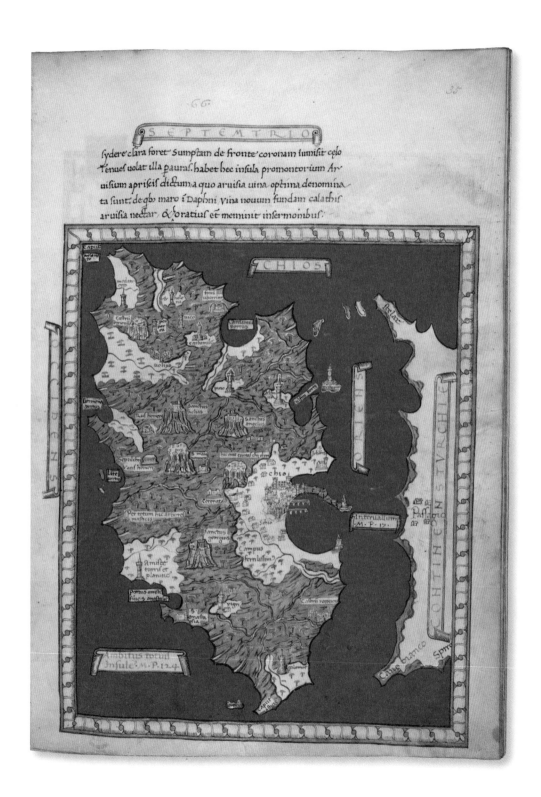

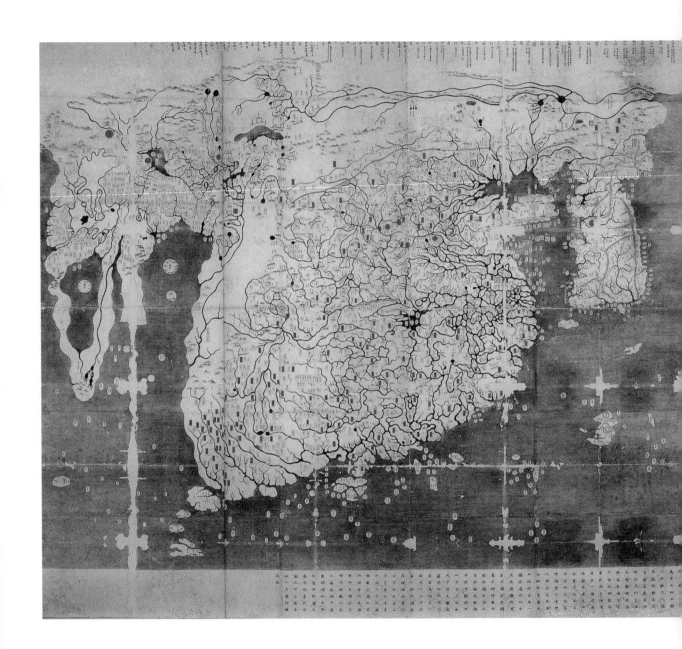

inventor Johannes Gutenberg in Mainz in the 1440s. Printing took a little time to catch on for maps – the very first printed map is a T–O *mappa mundi* included in a 1472 edition of Isidore of Seville's *Etymologiae* (p.39), but once it did, maps soon began to proliferate: from an estimated 56,000 in circulation by 1500, to several million a century later.

Printing with movable metal type was no novelty in other parts of the world. In Korea the first books printed using the technology appeared in 1234, although its use became more widespread once King Sejong the Great (*r.* 1418–50) reformed the Korean written language and introduced the simplified *hangul* alphabet, initially with 28 characters, rather than the 24 in the modern version. The Koreans, like their Chinese neighbours, developed a sophisticated administration which in turn required mapping. As well as a celestial map, completed in 1395, senior bureaucrat Kwon Kun (1352–1409), Assistant Councillor of the State Council, devised a world map, which he finished in 1402. Entitled the *Honil kangni yoktae kukto chi to* ('Map of the Integrated Regions and Terrain, and of the Historic Countries and Capitals'), and known as the Kangnido for short, it has the distinction of being the first map produced in Asia to show an outline of Europe. Delicately painted on silk rather than the vellum of its European counterparts, it depicts an enlarged version of the peninsula of Korea (unsurprising considering the interest of the cartographer in showing its importance), while a multiplicity of islands are shown as simple circles dotting the South China Sea and the Indian Ocean, the bodies of water depicted in a very striking ochre-green. It is China, though, and not Korea which sits firmly at the centre of the map, with Japan, the other major power of the region, looming menacingly to the south. Africa is shown as circumnavigable – clearly the Koreans were not bound, as European map-makers were, to Ptolemy's assertion that it was not.

In terms of its sophistication, the Kangnido map is a warning not to assume that European cartography was the only advanced mapping tradition to emerge by the fifteenth century, and a reminder that many of the areas 'discovered' by Europeans had themselves been host for many centuries to advanced civilisations, whose geographical knowledge about areas such as Central Asia and the east coast of Africa far surpassed that of the first generations of European explorers. As Kwon Kun says in his explanatory text placed at the bottom of the map, his was 'a new map entirely, nicely organized and well worth admiration. One can indeed know the world without going out of his door. By looking at maps one can know terrestrial distances and get help in the work of government.' A more succinct and compelling manifesto for cartography could hardly be imagined!

By the time, though, that the first printed map of the world in the modern style, attributed to a Florentine copper engraver named Francesco Rosselli (1448–*c.* 1513), was published in the late 1480s, the world, and mapping, stood on the brink of change in more fundamental ways. Although Rosselli knew of the Portuguese discoveries down the coast of Africa, right down to its southern tip, the Cape of Good Hope, discovered in 1488, he was working a decade too early to incorporate the findings made by Vasco da Gama on his circumnavigation of the continent, which brought him into the Indian Ocean and finally to the Indian port of Calicut in May 1498. More importantly, however, he was four years too soon to include the even more startling news brought back by Christopher Columbus from his voyage west across the Atlantic in 1492. That, and the new age of European discovery it heralded, marked a new epoch in the history of the atlas.

OPPOSITE
Kangnido map, 1402

NEW HORIZONS

(1500–1550)

The sixteenth century was when maps became ubiquitous. The Age of Exploration provoked not only an interest in maps but also a supply that made them available to a wide audience where previously they had been within the purview only of elites, explorers and merchants. As a result, the first half of the sixteenth century saw a huge change in the number of maps being produced. The ease of rapid production that the new technology of printing allowed meant that these reached into the millions by the end of the century.

Maps became more widespread and accessible to a larger public. They were embedded in chronicles, geographical works, as standalone sheets or in atlases, and in some cases even painted on walls. More importantly, the world they depicted was a radically different one from that which their predecessors had portrayed just decades before. The voyages of Christopher Columbus (1451–1506), Vasco da Gama (c. 1460–1524) and those who came after them opened up new worlds to European colonizers and merchants, but it also made those worlds available to being mapped by outsiders. Christopher Columbus's pioneering voyage to the Caribbean in 1492 brought knowledge of lands that were wholly unsuspected by Ptolemy or the creator of the Hereford *mappa mundi*. The Portuguese captain Vasco da Gama, who in 1497–98 rounded the coastline of Africa to re-emerge in the Indian Ocean, created an entirely separate set of routes for European navigators, and proved once and for all that Ptolemy was wrong about the Indian Ocean being landlocked. The three-year voyage of Ferdinand Magellan (1480–1521) in 1519–22, or more precisely that of Sebastian Elcano, who survived the death of the expedition leader during an altercation with indigenous people in the Philippines, connected all these worlds by circumnavigating the Earth for the first time, providing the first hard evidence that it really was a sphere.

These journeys, and the maps and atlases that followed, were made possible by a series of misunderstandings which arose from the maps the Genoese navigator Christopher Columbus chose to use to plan the expedition he proposed to make west into the Atlantic. He and his brother were both chart-makers, well aware of their home city's long-standing cartographic tradition. They also had access to a letter written by the Florentine Renaissance scholar Paulo dal Pozzo Toscanelli (1397–1482), who in 1474 had analysed a set of maps at the request of Afonso of Portugal. Toscanelli had come to the conclusion that China and Japan could be easily reached across the Atlantic, since Lisbon lay only 6,500 miles distant from the Chinese coast, and Japan was even closer at 2,500 miles from the (mythical) island of Antilia. Much of this was a combination of hearsay, information derived from the *Travels* of Marco Polo and an underestimate of the distance between each line of longitude, but it made the pitch that Christopher and his brother made for financial support for their voyages more convincing. Even so, it was rejected by King John II of Portugal in 1484 and 1488; he may have been distracted on the latter occasion by the more immediately enticing news that Bartolomeu Dias (c. 1450–1500) had just rounded the Cape of Good Hope. A second approach, to King Ferdinand of Aragon and Queen Isabella of Castile in 1486, became mired for almost six years in a series of bureaucratic scrutinizing committees. The Spanish monarchs were cautious enough to make a series of small grants totalling around 12,000 maravedis (equivalent to six-months' pay for a ship's pilot) to stop them taking their proposals elsewhere. But that did not prevent a frustrated Bartholomew Columbus travelling to London in 1491 to offer his services to King Henry VII. In a move that didn't augur well for the English rather than the Spanish discovering the New World, he was refused even an audience.

When Columbus set out with his three caravels, the *Niña*, *Pinta* and *Santa Maria* on 3 August 1492, he did so with confidence that it would be a short voyage: that is, after all, what all the maps he had consulted told him. Candidates for the actual 'Columbus Map', which may have been among those Columbus referred to in an annotation to the *Imago Mundi* (a 1410 work by the French cleric and theologian Pierre d'Ailly which had included the assertion that 'the sea is narrow which separates the extreme west of the habitable world from its eastern edge'),[1] include the diminutive 'Paris' map which came to light in 1848. This was a small sheet just 80cm long by 40cm wide (31½ x 16in), and it includes Portuguese discoveries as far as the Cape of Good Hope as well as Iceland in the North Atlantic, but nothing further to the west. Another possible candidate is some version of the world map produced by Henricus Martellus Germanus, a German map-maker who worked in Florence in the 1480s and 1490s, and who produced two editions of Ptolemy's *Geography*

BELOW
Nautical chart of the Mediterranean (detail), possibly produced in the workshop of Christopher and Bartholomew Columbus, 1490s

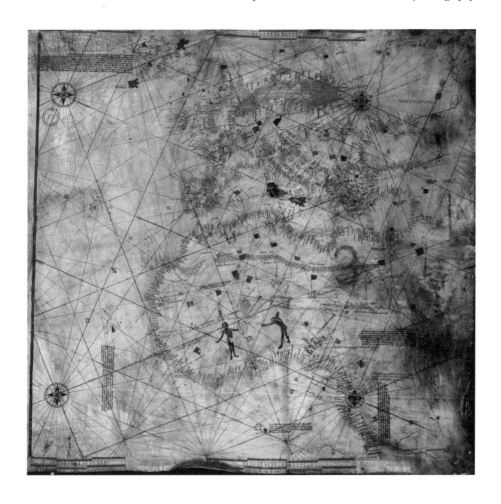

and a number of versions of Buondelmonti's *Isolario*. One of the latter includes a world map showing the discoveries made by Bartolomeu Dias on his way to rounding the Cape of Good Hope, though in Asia Martellus includes a long projecting peninsula to its east he calls Cattigara. In general, the inhabited world – from the west coast of Europe to the east coast of Asia – is shown as larger in extent in Martellus's map than in classical Ptolemaic cartography, extending to 220 degrees or more.

These maps were part of a cartographic milieu which minimized the distance between Asia and Europe, all of which served only to encourage Columbus in his quest. Perhaps also implicated was the Behaim Globe, the very earliest surviving globe map of the world which just predates Columbus's voyage. The globe was constructed from 1490–92 by Martin Behaim (1459–1507), a Nuremberg cloth merchant whose commercial travels took him to Portugal and possibly down the west coast of Africa. Made with the help of the artist Georg Glockendon, it is capably and brightly drawn, full of traditional illustrations and annotations about the history and culture of the regions shown, mixing tall tales from medieval travellers such as John Mandeville, with the slightly more credible stories of Marco Polo, and the hard geographical information derived from the Portuguese voyages. In a nod to Ptolemy and the Roman naturalist Pliny, Behaim even places on North Africa two sciapods, mythical human-like creatures who were reputed to have just one enormous foot, under whose shade they could shelter from the beating sun. He also extends Asia even further into the Pacific than Germanus had, in particular the island of Zipangu (or Japan), which is shown sitting a long distance east of the coast of China, and only around the 2,400 nautical miles distant from Europe which Columbus claimed was the true distance.

After fending off a mutiny by his crew, who were heartily fed up of his promises and the 36 days they had spent at sea – far longer than their captain had indicated – Columbus finally made landfall in one of the Lesser Antilles (probably somewhere in the Bahamas). He had not found Japan, China, the Spice Island, nor even the fabled Antilia. He never quite came to terms with what he had found (the Americas), not believing, even when he landed on the South American mainland during his third voyage in 1498, that he had encountered a new continent. The only map we have from the voyage is an indistinct sketch of the coastline of the island of Hispaniola, whose scrawled lines, made by Columbus himself, tell us very little. Others on his voyages, though, were more forthcoming. The first world map to incorporate their discoveries and usher in the new era both

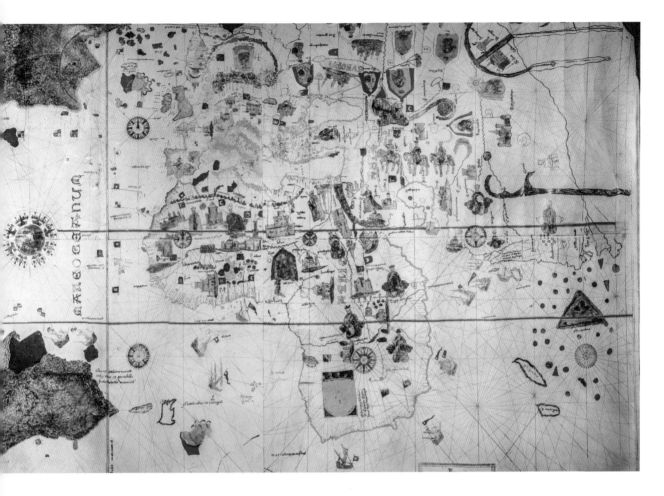

of mapping and discovery was made by Juan de la Cosa (1460–1510), who was the owner of the *Santa Maria* and came on Columbus's first three voyages, and who also managed to include information from the explorer John Cabot (or Giovanni Caboto, another Italian, *c.* 1450–1500), who had succeeded in interesting Henry VII in a transatlantic expedition and so had stumbled across the coast of North America in 1497. Made in 1500, it is the first map to include anything like the extent of the world as we know it today, though of course it is still missing the Antarctic and Australia, which were both yet to be discovered by Europeans. Made of two ox-hides stitched together, it is at first sight very much the traditional portolan world map, but in a fit of exuberance, de la Cosa has coloured the Americas a deep green (while the rest of the world is left unshaded), highlighting the breathtaking extent of the new discoveries. The coastline of North America is rather rough and jagged and that of South America rather indistinct, but the islands of the Caribbean show the high level of knowledge gleaned in less than a decade of exploration.

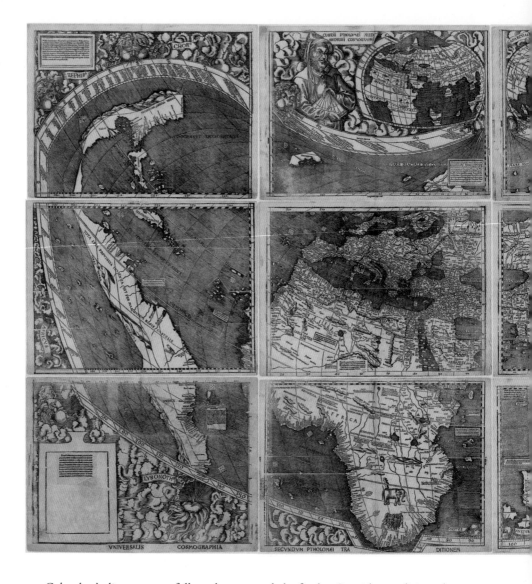

Columbus's discovery was followed up not only by further Spanish expeditions, but with attempts by the Portuguese to assert ownership of at least part of the New World. They claimed that the Treaty of Alcaçovas, signed in 1479, gave them a right to any lands south of the Canaries (which would include all the territory in the Americas the Spanish had just begun to colonize). The Spanish vigorously disagreed, and the row between the two maritime superpowers was only settled by the Treaty of Tordesillas, agreed in 1494 under the auspices of Pope Alexander VI, which determined that a line 270 leagues west of the Azores should be the dividing line between their respective domains, with all newly discovered lands to the west of it falling to the Spanish, and any to the east of it being

allocated to Portuguese rule. It was possibly no coincidence, therefore, when the Portuguese navigator Pedro Álvares Cabral (1467–1520) made landfall in Brazil in April 1500, a region which turned out to fall on the Portuguese side of the Tordesillas Line. Their easy accession to its terms might have been on the basis that they already *knew* a land mass lay there.

Other rulers became jealous of, or at least concerned about, the potentially vast new territorial gains being made by Spain and Portugal. It is to a piece of enterprising espionage on behalf of one of these that we owe another of the very earliest maps to show the New World. Venice, in particular, felt that its commercial position was threatened. It had, after all, profited more than most from the spice trade, and stood to lose most

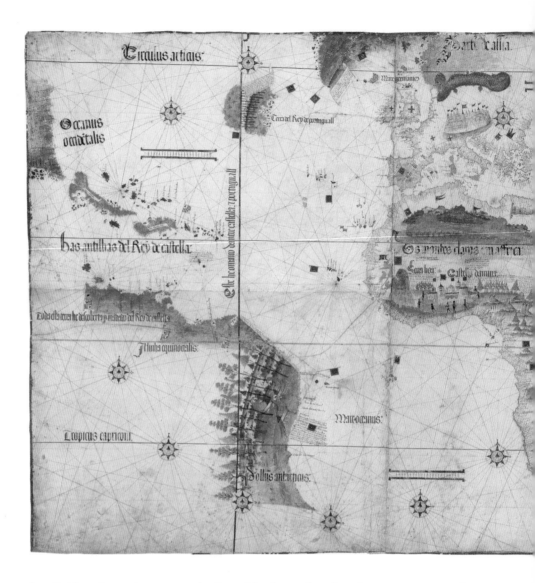

heavily if an alternative route to the Spice Islands was found, and worse, one not under Venetian control. In August 1501, a Venetian diplomat in Castile, Angelo Trevisan wrote to a contact in Lisbon, Domenico Malipiero, suggesting he acquire maps of the Portuguese discoveries. Although initially Malipiero warned that being caught trying to obtain these would risk the death penalty, before long he promised maps that would reveal the route to Calicut in India. Similarly, in 1502, Ercole d'Este, Duke of Ferrara, sent his agent Alberto Cantino to Lisbon where, for the price of 12 ducats, he suborned a Portuguese map-maker into creating a world map incorporating the supposedly secret outline of South America.

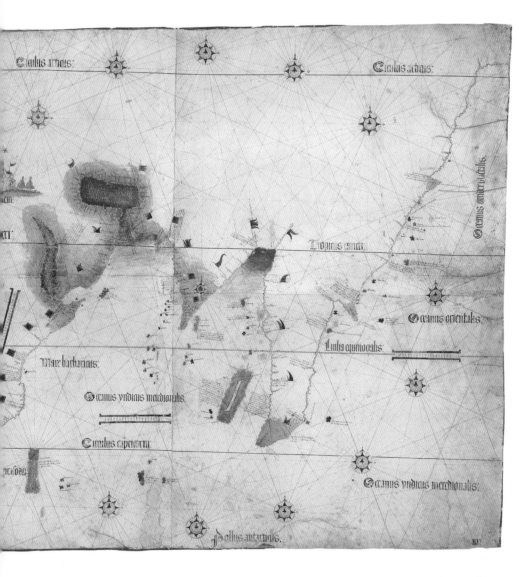

The result, the *Cantino Planisphere*, seems to be a map of Portuguese spheres of influence, with their territory in South America and the coastlines that they had explored in West Africa, together with parts of India and the Malay peninsula, all highlighted in deep green, while the rest of the world subsides into a sombre neutral yellow. Most strikingly, the Tordesillas Line is marked in as a deep red gash which scores across the Atlantic, plunging into South America just to the north of Brazil.

The *Cantino Planisphere* neither shows the Americas as two continents – no one was quite sure that they were – nor names them as the Americas. Initially, apart from the hopefuls who insisted that they had found Asia, the discoveries were labelled on maps as something like 'Novus Mundus' (New World). We owe the name 'America' to a series of chances and the keenness of the growing printing industry in Germany to produce editions of Ptolemy that reflected the new discoveries. The Florentine merchant Amerigo Vespucci (1454–1512) certainly provided them with ammunition. An able self-publicist, he claimed to have participated in a voyage to the Americas as early as 1497, and definitely took part in one headed by the conquistador Alonso de Ojeda in 1499. The chief navigator on this voyage was Juan de la Cosa, and it explored the coastline of Venezuela (which Vespucci named *Veneziola*, or 'little Venice', from the indigenous houses built on stilts that he observed). Vespucci also headed an expedition in 1501–02 commissioned by King Manuel I of Portugal to garner more information about his new territory in Brazil; during this voyage he explored and named the region that later became Rio de Janeiro.

Back home, Vespucci wrote a series of letters describing the 'Novus Mundus', clearly intended for publication and to steal some of Columbus's glory. When one of them was published in 1503 it achieved rapid notoriety, a fame which influenced the Alsatian scholar Matthias Ringmann (1482–1511), who had been tasked by René II, Duke of Lorraine, with producing a new edition of the *Geography*. He teamed up with the German cartographer Martin Waldseemüller (1470–1520), and together the pair not only reworked the 27 maps of the canonical Ptolemy tradition, but added 20 new maps, including most importantly those showing the New World. To this they appended the *Cosmographiae Introductio*, a guide to cosmography, and a translation of Vespucci's letters. In the first of these, alongside a host of conventional material relating to Ptolemy's world

scheme and the division of the world into climatic zones, they include the statement that 'The fourth part of the earth, we have decided to call Amerige, the land of Amerigo . . . because it was discovered by Amerigo'.

This first use of the term was followed up in the most extravagant part of the project, the *Universalis Cosmographiae Descriptio in Plano* (or 'Description on a Map of the Universal Cosmography), a world map printed on 12 sheets, each 62 x 45cm (24½ x 17¾in), which together produced a gargantuan 3.3m² (36ft²) chart – large enough for a wall map, but supposedly folded as an insert into the *Introductio*. As normally reproduced, with the joins between the sheets showing, and in the rather sepia-tinted monochrome of the original, the key part of the map could be easily overlooked – the labelling of the interior of Brazil as 'America' in the middle left-hand sheet covering the north of South America. Waldseemüller backtracked somewhat, or more likely reassessed the veracity of his key source, Vespucci, and in his later maps removed the reference to Vespucci but by then it was too late; the progress of 'America' as the universally accepted name for the new continents was unstoppable.

For all the work done by the bodies set up by the Iberian monarchies to stem the flow of information leaking out into the public domain – the Casa da India in Portugal and the Casa de Contratación, founded in Seville in 1503, to handle matters relating to what had by then become known as the 'Indies' – it was impossible to halt it completely. All pilots returning from the Americas were supposed to be examined on their return by the Spanish 'pilot-major', an office held by Vespucci between 1508 and 1512, and then by Juan Díaz de Solis for the next four years, followed by the Englishman Sebastian Cabot, who supervized the office for three decades until 1548. No chart could be issued without being authenticated by this official, but this did not stop a procession of New World maps and editions of Ptolemy. One of these was by the Italian cartographer, Bernardus Sylvanus, whose edition published in Venice in 1511 included an innovative cordiform map (drawn somewhat in the shape of a heart, with extended wings and an indentation in the centre), which has the distinction of being the second Ptolemy-style map to include the Americas.

Cartographers continued, too, to produce portolan-style collections of charts of the Mediterranean, including the Genoese map-maker Vesconte Maggiolo (1478–1530). Together with his children Jacopo and Baldassare, he ran a cartographic workshop responsible for over 20 maps and atlases over the first half of the sixteenth century. One of them, part of a small atlas published in 1516, again shows the insistent progress of the New World into the map-maker sights, as it includes the eastern seaboard of Central and South America, with a world map that incorporates the Americas squashed in on the left with a bare dozen or so placenames. It also includes a scale in the form of lines of latitude for the first time as an easy means of dividing up and navigating around the map. Although Ptolemy had specified the latitude and longitude of cities and other geographical features, he had not suggested that lines linking places of equal latitude or longitude should be included on maps.

It was perhaps the line drawn by the Treaty of Tordesillas that had concentrated minds on the very real effects of imaginary lines set down on a map. The neat supposition that the Americas were largely to be the domain of Spain, and that the discoveries made by Portugal in Africa and (after Vasco da Gama's pioneering voyage to India in 1497–98) the Indian Ocean were to be Lisbon's prize, was rather ruined by the cupidity that the lure of spices inspired. The problem was that while the Treaty of Tordesillas drew a clear line in the Atlantic, it had nothing to say about whether this should be extended around the Poles and similarly divide the two powers' marine territories somewhere in the Pacific and, if it was, where exactly that line should lie.

By 1511, the Portuguese had captured the key stronghold of Malacca on the Malay peninsula from its indigenous sultan. From there, the Moluccas, the source of the cloves, nutmeg and mace (made from the seed covering of nutmeg) that collectively formed the most valuable spices, seemed within their grasp. Two years later, however, the Spanish crossed the Darien Peninsula in Central America, providing a rapid transit route from the Caribbean to the Pacific and the prospect that a westward thrust might finally reach the Spice Islands (which, after all, had been Columbus's aim all along). To head off the seemingly inexorable Portuguese progress to total domination of the spice trade, it occurred to the Spanish that perhaps a case could be made that the Moluccas in fact lay on their side of the line.

Support came from an unlikely source: a Portuguese navigator who had actually taken part in his nation's successful attack on Malacca. By now, though, Fernão de Magalhães, as he was born in Sabrosa in Portugal in 1480, had become Fernando de Magallanes (or Ferdinand Magellan), basing himself at Seville in Spain after his persistent pleas to be allowed to head up a Portuguese expedition to the Spice Islands had all been turned down. In partnership with his countryman, the cosmographer Rui Faleiro, who had made calculations indicating that the Moluccas were, indeed, by rights Spanish, he tried to persuade anyone who would listen that he should be appointed to lead a fleet to assert Madrid's claim.

These entreaties fell on the receptive ears of the Habsburg Emperor Charles V, who as Charles I ruled Spain, an inheritance from his mother, the mentally unstable Juana, the daughter of Columbus's sponsors Ferdinand and Isabella. Having convinced the Emperor and his advisers that not only did the Spice Islands belong to Spain, Magellan also persuaded them that he could find a navigable passage around the tip of South America (which had never been located, let alone traversed), from where he could sail west to the Moluccas. Magellan seems to have derived his confidence from the Behaim Globe (p.86), but its underestimate of the width of the Pacific almost proved catastrophic. Having set off in September 1519 with five ships, and after a succession of mutinies and the loss of one vessel (the *Santiago*), it was only in November 1520 that Magellan found a way through the storm-lashed strait that later came to bear his name and entered the Pacific. Instead of a relaxed stretch of a couple of weeks, his crews were then faced with five gruelling months out of sight of land before they came to the Philippines in March 1521.

This stretch of the voyage proved to be the end of Magellan, too, as he died on the island of Mactan after he intervened in a quarrel between local tribal leaders and was killed during a skirmish. It was left to his deputy, the Basque pilot Sebastián Elcano (1476–1526), in command of the remaining 200 sailors and two ships, to make their way to the Moluccas. There, they loaded a small quantity of pepper and nutmeg and began the long voyage home. When finally he limped into port in Seville, all save he and 17 other crew members had died, deserted or been detained by the Portuguese. Elcano had completed the first ever circumnavigation of the globe (and was rewarded by a grateful Charles V with a coat-of-arms eccentrically embellished with cloves and sticks of nutmeg), but he had not proven Spain's claim. Arguments over the Tordesillas Line's extension continued in a series of meetings at which maps and counter-maps were presented, with the Spanish generally having the best of it, and once again employing the services of a Portuguese specialist, this time the cartographer Diogo Ribeiro (d. 1533). Finally, in 1529, with the pressing need for allies against a coalition of England and France, Charles V gave up on the Moluccas and signed the Treaty of Zaragoza, which extended the Tordesillas Line to the other side of the world, but safely (as far as the Portuguese were concerned) to the east of the Moluccas. To celebrate the occasion, Diogo Ribeiro created a world map, blazoned with the statement that it was a 'Universal Chart in which is contained all that has been discovered in the world until now . . . Which is

BELOW

World map,
Diogo Ribeiro, 1529

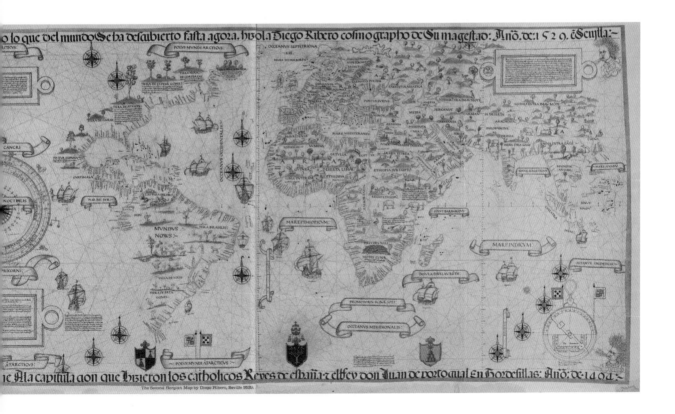

The Second Borgian Map by Diogo Ribeiro, Seville 1529.

divided into two parts according to the capitulation which took place between the Catholic Kings of Spain and King John of Portugal at the city of Tordesillas in 1494.'

The Portuguese, then, still held the Spice Islands, and ultimately a worse threat to their commercial empire would come not from the Spanish, but from the Dutch and English in the seventeenth century. They had Brazil, where their growing knowledge was demonstrated in the 1519 atlas compiled by the cartographers Lopo Homem (1497–1572) and the father-and-son team of Pedro (*fl.* 1485–1540) and Jorge Reinel (*c.* 1502–after 1572). The richly illustrated section depicting Brazil, includes an illustration of indigenous Americans working on a brazilwood plantation, a small, but ominous, indication of the exploitation that would characterize the future history of the region.

Just as the political duopoly between Spain and Portugal suffered its first cracks (with the expeditions of John Cabot to North America on behalf of England in 1497 and that of Jacques Cartier, who surveyed the coastline of Newfoundland and the St Lawrence River for France in 1534), so modern map-making techniques were beginning to spread outwards from the Mediterranean. The French map-maker Oronce Finé (1494–1555) produced a fine heart-shaped map of the world in 1519, but it was in the Netherlands where a more important hub of cartography became established.

The first impetus to this was given by the work of Dutch mathematician Gemma Frisius (1508–55), who turned his hand to the making of globes, but whose main contributions to the map-making art were his mentoring of one of the greatest cartographers of all-time, Gerardus Mercator (p.106) and his mapmaking manual the *Libellus de locorum describendorum ratione* ('A Pamphlet on the logic of describing places'), published in 1533, which set out for the first time the principle of triangulation. This is where a fixed baseline is established and then angles to a third point are measured with surveying instruments creating a 'triangle'; the length of its perpendicular is calculated through trigonometry, which in turn determines the precise location of that point. This process proved invaluable to surveyors and led to a survey of Frisius's native Flanders in 1540, and to the first provincial maps of the Netherlands. These included those by Jacob van Deventer (1505–1575), who produced a set which included Brabant (1536) and Holland and Utrecht (1542) and Gelderland (1543). This last one included the instruction given to the map-maker by the Emperor Charles V to create it 'by order and at the expense of His Imperial Majesty as there are towns, villages, monasteries, castles, with all the fine and excellent rivers, measured plotted according to the true art of Geography'. From these small beginnings, the need for mapping grew greater after the Dutch revolt against Spain in 1568 resulted in an 80-year war between the rebels and Madrid and created the independent United Provinces of the Netherlands. The new nation's dependence on maritime trade for its prosperity in turn led to an increased demand for both local maps and those of the regions, particularly in the Baltic and the Indian Ocean to which Dutch fleets sailed.

In time, the Dutch would become famous for their 'Rutters', or route-maps, and 'Wagoneers', maritime atlases named for the Dutch cartographer Lucas Janszoon Waghenaer (*c.* 1533–1606), whose *Spieghel der Zeevaerdt* ('The Mariner's Mirror'), published in 1584, became the best-known and most imitated example (p.122). These were the lineal descendants of both the old *periploi* and the portolan charts, combining details of local conditions with drawing of coastlines which gradually turned into maps. The oldest known printed example is, in fact, French: *Le Grand Routier de la mer* compiled by Pierre Garcie Ferrande between 1502 and 1510, which described the English, Welsh, French and Portuguese coastlines. But it was the Dutch who made the genre their own, providing guides that ensured that ships were no longer entirely dependent on the availability and vagaries of local pilots in navigating regions with which they were not familiar. At first dealing with the coastline of Flanders, Holland and Friesland, and then venturing into the Baltic (where Dutch seamen were muscling in on the valuable herring trade), they began to appear in printed form in the first half of the sixteenth century, often including an additional section on the Law of Wisby, a form of international maritime law, which in the absence of an overarching political authority to enforce order on the seas was generally accepted by maritime states and their merchants.

The earliest versions were produced by cartographers whose work helped the Netherlands become the most renowned map-making centre of Europe: Jan Severszoon created the first printed rutter there, the *De kaert vander zee*, in 1532. Jan Jacobszoon, who acquired Severszoon's workshop and printers, brought out new editions, including a section on the Zuiderzee, the great inland sea in the north-east of the Netherlands, whose capricious waters had caused frequent floods (one of which, the St Lucia Flood of December 1287, inundated large parts of the north of the country, killing over 50,000 people). By the 1550s, these rutters had become more sophisticated. Among them was a 76-page version in 1558 assembled by Cornelis Anthonisz that included a guide to navigation as well as useful drawings of coastal features, and what would become the most widespread rutter of all, the *Leeskaartboeck van Wisbuy*, which became known by

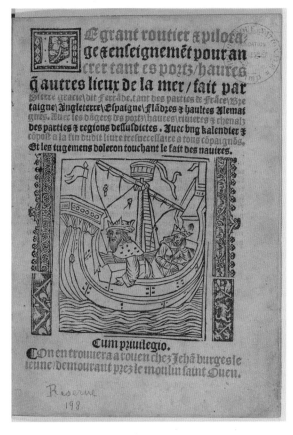

ABOVE

Frontispiece, *Le Grand Routier de la mer*, compiled by Pierre Garcie Ferrande, 1502–10

foreigners who found it hard to get their tongues around the Dutch language as the 'Wisbuy Rutter'. Including a guide to navigation both in the Baltic and off the Netherlands coast, and extending as far as the French Atlantic coast, it was frequently reprinted, adapted and pirated, and was still in use in the 1580s, long after the original information on which it was based had been superseded.

The Netherlands also became the centre of a thriving trade in maps. Unconstrained by the legal threats of royal monopolies such as Spain's Casa de Contratación, their benchmark was not what was allowed by the authorities, but what would sell. First in workshops in Antwerp and then after Dutch independence in Utrecht, The Hague, Deventer and Amsterdam, publishers made use of the ever more refined etching and engraving skills – which had in turn been honed by the techniques of the Italian Renaissance as they filtered north and inspired an artistic flowering in the Low Countries. As well as the advances in knowledge, both local and global, which their customers eagerly consumed, their engraving techniques advanced from the previously revolutionary woodblocks on which maps were etched, to the introduction of copper plates, on which the map image was produced by the action of acid. Such plates began to be available in the middle of the century and were more robust, meaning that more copies could be impressed without the plates wearing out, but also, potentially, that the longevity of the plates meant that maps remained 'in print' long after their information had become out-of-date.

The increased diversity of maps, and books in general that the advent of printing had brought and which the burgeoning middle classes and comparative intellectual freedom of the Dutch cities fostered, together with reduced prices, led to a widening of the field in all areas of publishing. As well as traditional world maps (either in manuscript, books or as wall maps, globes, the first regional, provincial and national maps, and collections that approached the status of atlases), maps began to appear in larger quantities in other works, such as the *Nuremberg Chronicle*. First published in the German city in 1493, it was intended as a history of the world with text by the German historian and humanist Hartmann Schedel (1440–1514). Its glory, though, is the collection of more than 1,800 woodcut illustrations, many of them depicting contemporary towns like Nuremberg itself, but also cities further afield, such as Constantinople, providing an invaluable resource for the late-medieval topography of Europe's principal urban settlements. Many of the townscapes may have been drawn by no lesser an artist than the young Albrecht Dürer, who learnt his art in the studio of Michael Wolgemut, who supervised and produced most of the engravings for the work.

Not long after, another form of itinerary map appeared, which in some ways constitutes Europe's first road map. The *Das ist der Rom Weg* ('This is the road to Rome') map by Erhard Etzlaub (*c*. 1460–1532) was produced as part of the celebrations for the Holy Year of 1500, when a special indulgence, or reduction of the time the faithful might spent in purgatory to atone for their sins, was available for all visiting Rome. Oriented with northern Europe (and Germany, where Etzlaub's hometown of Nuremberg lay) at the bottom and Italy at the top, the map becomes ever more crowded with towns and cities as the longed-for pilgrims' destination of Rome comes close.

In a similar vein to the *Nuremberg Chronicle*, but coming just over half a century later, in 1544, is the *Cosmographia* of the cartographer and Hebrew scholar Sebastian Münster (1488–1552). He was born in Ingelheim, and his career reflected the turbulent times in which he lived. Beginning as a Franciscan friar, he defected to Lutheranism as the Reformation gathered strength, an act which secured him a post as professor of Hebrew at the University of Basel in reformed Switzerland. The *Cosmographia*, which combined modern geography and historical accounts with a potpourri of classical sources, including Pliny, remained in print for around a century.

BELOW

Buda (part of modern Budapest), *Nuremberg Chronicle*, 1493

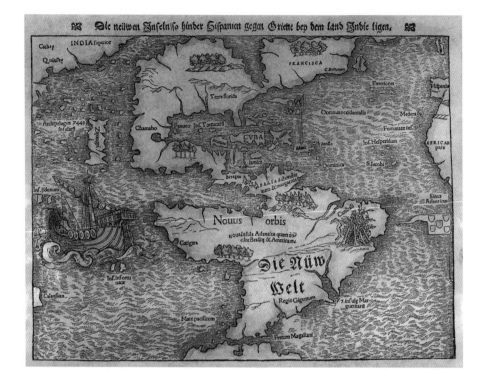

Its carefully drawn outlines of the continents including the New World mingled with the text concerning India, which faithfully recounted battles between dragons and elephants as though they were entirely factual.

Mapping by 1550 still stood equally balanced between the medieval and the modern. While world maps such as that of Fra Mauro (p.76) still harked back to the era of Ptolemy and had a touch of the *mappa mundi* about them, crowded with fabulous beasts and mythical figures such as Gog and Magog, works such as the *Boke of Idrogaphie* by the Dieppe cartographer Jean Rotz (b. 1505) show how mapping was increasingly a tool of ambitious royal administrations. Presented to Henry VIII in 1542, Rotz's work shows an unparalleled level of detail of the British coastline, at a time when the English were increasingly concerned about French raids on the south coast (a French fleet had burnt the fledgling town of Brighton to the ground in 1514, highlighting the woeful lack of mapping which could assist in planning coastal defence).

Rotz was rewarded for his labours with the position of Royal Hydrographer; he was the first to hold the grand-sounding title and his professional descendants, the Royal Navy's Hydrographer of the Navy, continued to be responsible for producing the service's marine charts until 2001. His atlas, which included a total of 11 regional nautical charts, also included sheets covering North and South America. Its northern part is illustrated with smiling and apparently peaceable indigenous Americans, and the south by threatening native peoples with large bows who are seen attacking settlements, as though an inducement to the king to promote English exploration of the north and a condemnation of the Spanish and Portuguese for the violence and lawlessness of the areas which they had colonized.

Yet no matter how innovative, conservative, inward- or outward-looking a map-maker might be, by 1550 none could (or did) ignore the reality of the New World. Ptolemy had been proven wrong (or at least lacking) and, emboldened by the success of the Spanish in conquering the Aztec Empire of Mexico by 1521 and reducing the Inca realm in Peru to a rump by 1533, Europeans were beginning to press out into the world, occupying and colonizing where the resistance was least, alternating violent confrontation with unequal trade where it was greater. The next half-century, though, would in many respects bring even greater changes.

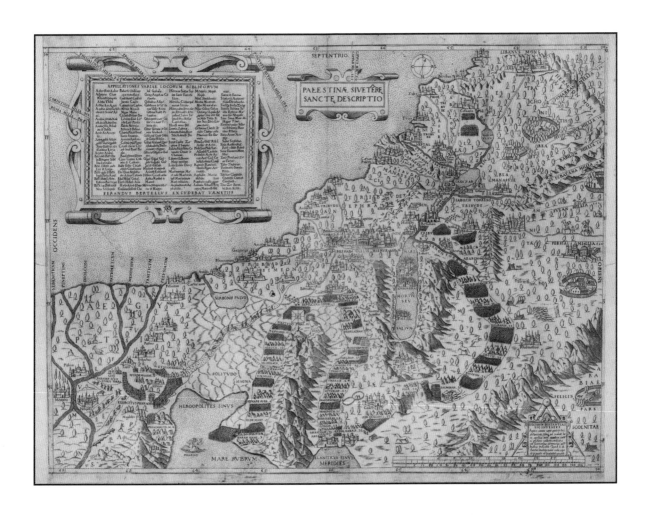

RIGHT

East coast of South
America, oriented with south
at the top, *Boke of Idrographie*,
Jean Rotz, *c.* 1535–42

OPPOSITE

Das ist der Rom Weg,
Erhard Etzlaub, 1500

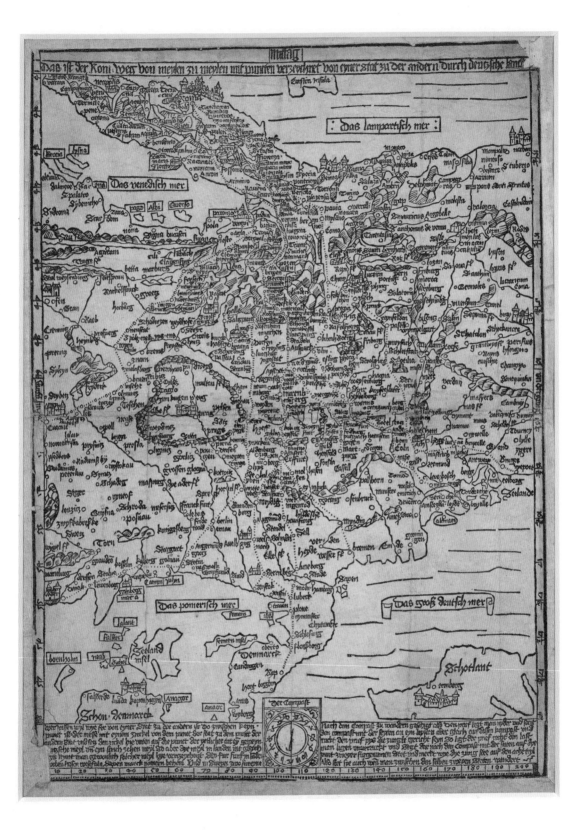

THE GOLDEN AGE OF THE ATLAS

(1550–1600)

The half-century after 1550 was the golden age of the atlas. It was a period in which some of the greatest cartographers in history worked, producing maps that set new standards in terms of accuracy, in the innovation of the projections they used, in their presentation and in their inclusion of ever more refined geographical knowledge of the world, the fruit of both further European exploratory expeditions and the beginnings of European colonialism which wrought changes on the ground, including the decimation of indigenous peoples and the establishment of new European-style towns and cities, all of which had to be mapped. It saw the careers of men such as Gerardus Mercator and Abraham Ortelius, whose maps and atlases became the benchmark of cartographic excellence.

Gerardus Mercator, who was born as Gerhard Kremer in 1512 (d. 1594) in a small village south-west of Antwerp, began unassumingly enough. He acquired the Latin version of his name (which is a simple translation of the Dutch *kremer*, meaning 'merchant') in his late teens – a common-enough affectation among would-be humanists or savants at a time when Latin was the language of international learning and Rome the yardstick against which almost every endeavour was measured. His first known map, drawn when he was only 25, was a small-scale one of Palestine, the *Terrae Sanctae descriptio* ('Description of the Holy Land'), followed up with a regional map of Flanders commissioned by a group of local Flemish dignitaries which he published in Louvain, where he was by then based. This brought the aspirant cartographer a certain amount of positive attention, and he was employed to make a terrestrial globe for Emperor Charles V. He diplomatically dedicated it to the imperial chief minister Cardinal de Granvelle, and it perhaps sparked his interest in the distortions caused by transferring the image of the Earth shown on a globe (where the relative size of regions and their proportional distance from each other could be true) onto a flat surface where there was always bound to be some distortion.

In 1538, Mercator tried his hand at a map of the world, using the very distinct cordiform heart-shaped projection earlier pioneered by Oronce Finé (p.96), and for the first time labelling North and South America as distinct continents. His clearly questioning nature was encouraged by his education at the humanist school of 's-Hertogenbosch and survived the University of Louvain, which had made a promising start at a reformed curriculum a few decades earlier, but by Mercator's time had descended into stultifying conformity and sterile debate over the finer points in Aristotle. Yet his enquiring mind was to get him into serious trouble. It was a Protestant, a follower of the Swiss reformer Huldrych Zwingli (1484–1531), who had produced the first ever map published in a Bible (of the Israelites' Exodus from Egypt). Lutherans in common with members of other reformed churches tended to favour a more literal Biblical geography, illustrating Biblical episodes and providing a topographic guide to places in the Holy Land instead of the almost mystical theology embodied in the Catholic *mappae mundi*. It was a model that Mercator followed on his 1538 map and the cordiform project, too, had become associated with Lutherans, who saw in the shape of the heart a sign of the grace of God, which might assist in contemplation and prayer.

Mercator's growing reputation brought him to the attention of the authorities and the faint whiff of Lutheranism that seemed to emanate from his activities caused Pierre Dufief, the procurer-general of Brabant, to issue a warrant for his arrest (along with fifty-one others). Queen Maria of Hungary, the regent for the Emperor Charles V in the Netherlands, on whose authority the warrant had been issued, kept a firm grip on hints of heresy in her domains during her twenty-five-year rule. Hundreds of people were condemned to death for their religious beliefs, and a revolt in 1539 had been severely crushed. Dufief, too, was a dangerous man to have angered; he was an inveterate heretic hunter who in 1535 engineered the arrest of William Tyndale, one of the leading English Protestant reformers, whose translation of the Bible into English was the first widely

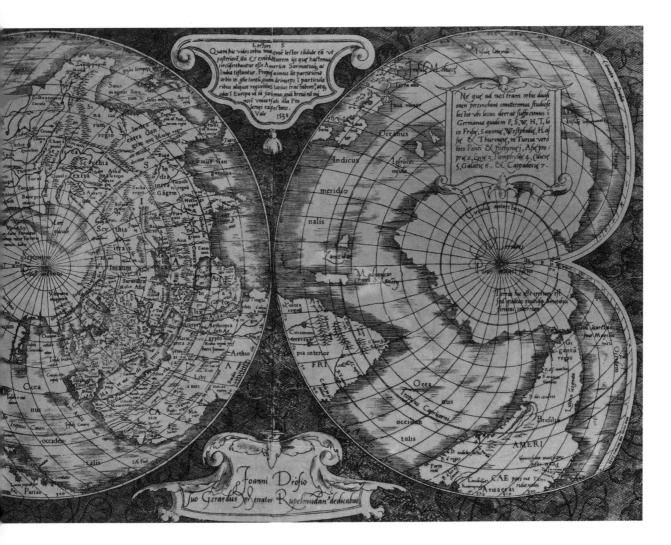

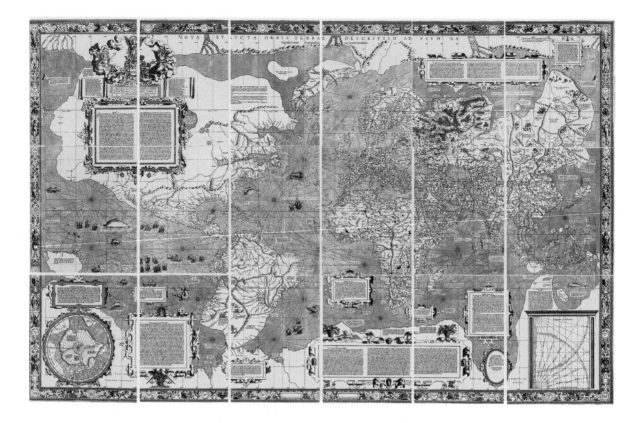

distributed printed version, but cost him his life when he was tried, condemned and executed in October the following year at Louvain.

Given the prevailing climate, Mercator was ultimately lucky. Listed on the warrant as 'Geert Schellekens' (the latter was his wife's maiden name), Mercator languished in the dungeons of Rupelmonde Castle for eight months before his release after the intercession of his local parish priest and the university authorities at Louvain. The taint of heresy, however, made him cautious and he received no significant further cartographic commissions before finally, in 1552, transferring to the much more tolerant atmosphere of Duisburg in the Rhineland, at the invitation of its ruler Duke Wilhelm of Jülich-Cleves-Berg.

Here, Mercator produced his finest work, beginning in 1554 with a 15-sheet large-scale map of Europe, whose improvements on the continent's outline (shortening the width of the Mediterranean, for example, by nine degrees compared to Ptolemy's estimate) made it the best available. He also embarked on a much more ambitious project, no less than an entirely new cosmography, 'of the whole universal scheme uniting the heaven and the earth'. The first part of this was a chronology of the world since the creation; with the need to make definite statements about such tricky matters as the date of the Creation or that of the Crucifixion, this also ran the risk of upsetting various Church authorities. Using a tabular format that owed something to Easter computational tables and which allowed the comparison of dates across various calendrical systems such as the Roman, Greek, Hebrew and Christian, it was innovative, but it was not a success.

Undeterred, Mercator embarked on the part of his project for which he is perhaps best known: a world map, published in Duisburg in 1569, with the daunting Latin title of *Nova et aucta orbis terrae descriptio et usum navigantium emendate accommodata* ('A New and Augmented Description of the Earth With Corrections Included for the Navigational Use'). Produced in 18 sheets, it was a mammoth 2 x 1.25m (6½ x 4ft) in total, more suited to a wall hanging than handling on a desk. In some ways the map does not look much like progress. North America is mostly obscured by a cartouche, is labelled as 'India Nova' and its northern and western coastlines, as well as the southern outline of South America, are distinctly sketchy. Meanwhile, the Arctic and Antarctic run the whole length of the top and bottom of the map, including annotations that confidently repeat assertions made by one Nicholas of Lynn, a fourteenth-century Oxford monk and the possible author of a travelogue called the *Inventio Fortunata* ('The Fortunate Discovery') which recounted his alleged voyages to the Arctic, a region which he says is broken into 19 islands; he also alleges that Greenland is inhabited by pygmies. Mercator also derived some information and encouragement in his beliefs from a correspondence with John Dee, an alchemist and alleged magician who was Queen Elizabeth I's court astronomer (and whose own interest in cartography was linked to his promotion of the establishment of English colonies in North America). This says much about the cross-over between solid geography, scientific cartography and the frankly esoteric during the late Renaissance.

Mercator's map seems somewhat backward-looking in other ways, with other annotations discussing the existence and location of Prester John (who despite centuries of looking had never revealed himself, let alone come to the aid of Christian monarchs; p.72) and such hoary legends from Pliny as the tribe who dig out gold from ant's nests. Yet it contains one startling new development, that was to shape cartography right until the present day. Map-makers ever since Ptolemy had struggled with the question of the type of projection they should use, in other words how to cast on a flat surface the image of an Earth whose surface in reality sat on a sphere (and to which the rhumb lines on portolans were a partial solution). The cartouche that sat on North America on this map explained Mercator's approach, beginning with the wholly anodyne intention 'to represent the positions and dimensions of the lands, as much in conformity with the truth as it is possible to do'. His solution, which was to make the meridians, or lines of longitude, parallel to each other rather than curving and drawing close together as they approached the Poles, was novel. In addition, the lines of latitude were stretched apart in proportion to the distortion of the longitude meridians. It was a bit like stretching a balloon across the surface of a cylinder, and caused the land masses to be distorted and enlarged the closer to the Poles they were, but it did mean that a straight line drawn across the surface of the map would be true to the direction on the sphere of the Earth, which was a very useful advance (and without the maze-like mesh of the rhumb lines to confuse the eye).

The result, though convenient for navigators, has had significant political effects ever since. Greenland is enlarged massively to the point where it is as large as the entire continent of South America (whereas in truth, at just under 2.2 million km²/ *c.* 850,000 mi², it is only roughly one-ninth the size) and Africa, particularly its equatorial

regions, is diminished in visual importance compared to Europe. Many of what would later become the most impoverished and heavily colonized regions of the Earth found themselves as poor relations on Mercator Projection maps, which, as global power balances began to shift, led to a clamour for a 'fairer' projection (p.251).

Although Mercator's intentions were good, he was on shaky ground when it came to explaining the mathematics behind his calculations that would back up his projection. The matter was only clarified, and not by Mercator, in the 1599 work *Certaine Errors in Navigation*. Written by the Cambridge mathematician Edward Wright (*c.* 1561–1615), who took a sabbatical from his academic post at the request of Elizabeth I to join a raiding party on the Spanish-held Azores in 1589 and to take scientific measurements during the otherwise piratical expedition. His publication allowed other cartographers and pilots to make their own maps using Mercator's projection (and perhaps to pause a moment to smile at the rather unfortunate pseudonym Wright assumed during the Azores voyage: Captain Edward Careless).

Mercator, meanwhile, continued to work away in the background at his grand cosmographic project, first producing, as so many of his predecessors had done, an edition of Ptolemy's *Geography*, complete with a set of 28 maps. He followed this up with sets of modern mapping (called the *Tabulae Geographicae*), which were issued in a series of instalments: in 1585 France, the Low Countries and Germany in 51 sheets; and Italy and the Balkans in 22 maps published in 1589. Mercator never quite finished his labours. Much like Magellan (p.84), a fair degree of his fame has become attached to an achievement that was completed posthumously by others, in this case by his son Rumold (*c.* 1545–99), who had returned to Duisburg in 1587 from London, where he had been running his own lucrative map-publishing operation. In 1595, just a year after his father's death, the younger Mercator gathered together unpublished maps by his father of Iceland, the British Isles, Scandinavia and Eastern Europe, added his own world map, and included three specially engraved continental maps drawn by his own nephews Gerardus Junior and Michael (cartography was very much a business of family dynasties in its early stages!). He published the whole as the *Atlas sive cosmographicae meditationes*

de fabrica mundi et fabricati figura ('Atlas or Cosmographic Meditations on the Structure and Shape of the World'). Here, finally, was the first collection of maps which explicitly described itself as an atlas.

Oddly, the world map included did not employ Mercator's 1569 projection (a sign, perhaps, that the Mercator family themselves did not expect its subsequent ubiquity), and it was nothing like a comprehensive world atlas, even in the terms of the day, as there were not yet any regional maps of Spain or Portugal. But the foreword, which Gerardus had written some years before and which his son included in the final publication, explains the genesis of the Atlas and how it relates to his 1569 world map, quoting the words of the Scottish historian and poet George Buchanan: 'May you perceive how small a portion of the universe it is/That we carve out with magnificent words into proud realms.' From (though he never knew it) one of the most famous cartographers of all, it is an appealing call for humility.

Mercator's subsequent fame has somewhat eclipsed the reputation of another cartographer from the Low Countries. Abraham Ortelius was born in Antwerp in 1527 and, unlike Mercator, remained in his home town until his death 71 years later in 1598. In 1547, he became a member of the town's guild of St Luke, where he found employment as an illuminator of maps, an indication that by then cartography was already a profession in which its practitioners might expect to find lifetime employment. It was not enough, however, to support him, since the young Ortelius's father had died in about 1537 and he was faced with having to provide for his mother and two sisters, and so turned to trading in maps, mounting them on boards, embellishing them with his illumination and engraving skills and selling them to the increasingly prosperous Flemish middle class. One of these, Aegidius Hooftman, a merchant and fellow Antwerper, complained of the inconvenience of having to assemble a collection of miscellaneous charts and maps to conduct his business overseas, and how much better it would be if all these maps were available in one place and at some sort of consistent scale.

The message got through to Ortelius via Hooftman's assistant Radermaker, and the cartographer began to assemble a group of maps that could all be printed and bound

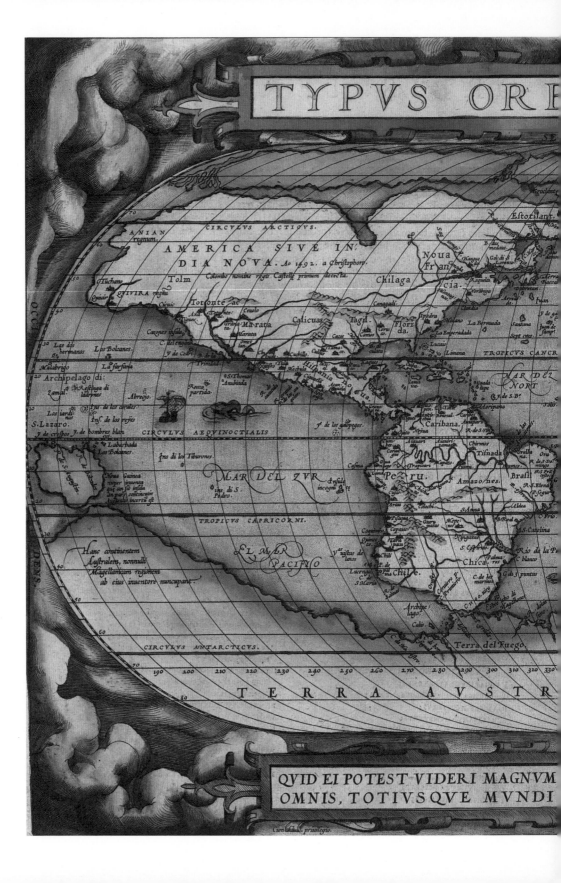

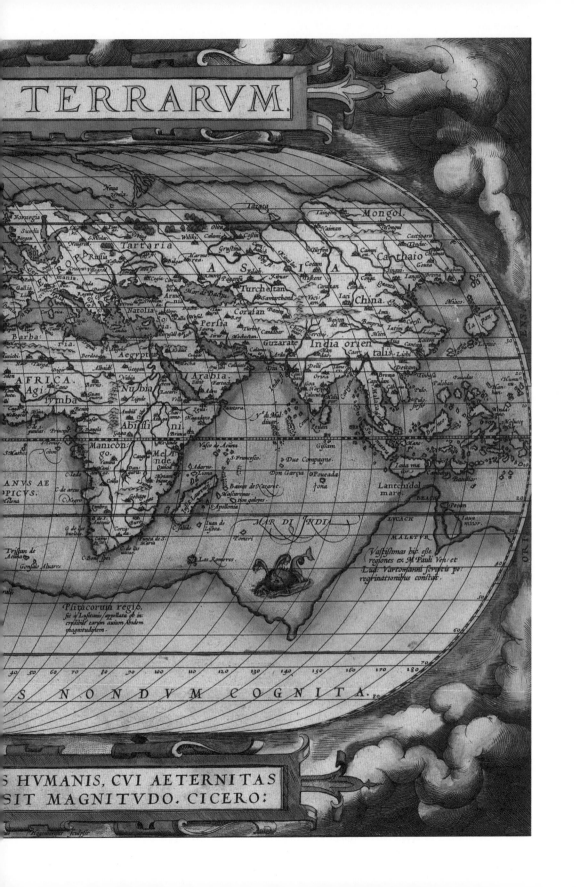

together in a single volume large enough to contain useful detail but small enough to handle easily in a mercantile office or aboard ship. Ortelius was friendly with Mercator and apparently discussed his idea for the project; Mercator encouraged him, even though he was working on his own atlas (albeit on a much grander scale). It took about 10 years of hard labour and meticulous fine-tuning to complete the work and in 1570 the flamboyantly named *Theatrum Orbis Terrarum* ('Theatre of the Globe of the World') was published. Although it did not include the word 'atlas' in its title, that is in effect what it was, and it trumped his friend Mercator by 25 years. The *Theatrum* included the latest state of knowledge on all the continents (although with some wobbles along the west coast of South America, which is also shown separated from a vast Antarctic continent, while a large, and totally imaginary, landmass appears in the Pacific just south of the Equator). The Antarctic itself is labelled *Terra Australis Nondum Cognita* ('The southern land not yet known'), in the hopeful expectation that it soon would be and Ptolemy, at least in this respect, thus vindicated.

In other ways, Ortelius was more cautious than Mercator. He had – sensibly given the accusation of heresy levelled against his friend – understood that he must not include any engravings that offended the Church, or include maps that had the coats-of-arms of rebel families or of monarchs unfriendly to Spain. To bolster his credentials, he included a list of 87 predecessor geographers whose works he had used in compiling the *Theatrum*, a catalogue that lengthened with each new edition.

The results were highly satisfactory. The *Theatrum* also achieved far greater immediate commercial success than Mercator's; Ortelius's atlas was, after all, designed with a very particular market in mind, and it met that market's needs. It went through 28 editions during his lifetime and was translated (and pirated) into a range of languages, including Dutch, German, French, Spanish and Italian editions. Exhibiting great shrewdness, Ortelius also offered his markets something new in the updated editions, so that by the time the Italian edition came out in 1612, it had more than 100 maps, almost double the 53 of the original edition. Letters of praise flooded in, including one from the Italian humanist and Protestant exile Petrus Bizarus who gushed: 'You are therefore to be exalted with the greatest of praises, learned Ortelius, you who, adorned with the greatest gifts of the mind, have worked hard both to secure the immortality of your name and to deserve the very best from humanity.'[1] Mercator was rather more measured in his language, writing to 'compliment you on the care and elegance with which you have embellished the labours of the authors, and the faithfulness with which you have preserved the production of each individual'.

One of Ortelius's correspondents had even grander designs. Born to a family of barber-surgeons in Angoulême in central France, André Thevet (1516–90) was forced to become a novice in a Franciscan monastery, before escaping and travelling widely in the Levant, including a pilgrimage to Jerusalem. This set of journeys inspired his debut in geographical writing, the *Cosmographie de Levant* in 1554. The following year he took part in the expedition to Brazil led by Nicolas Durand de Villegaignon (1510–71), the man who in 1548 had been entrusted with the delicate task of providing a naval escort for the infant Mary, Queen of Scots as she was whisked to safety in France. The expedition's quixotic attempt to establish a colony, which became known as France Antarctique, under the noses of the Portuguese was doomed to failure, particularly as it became a haven for French Huguenot refugees, making it a nest of heretics the Lisbon authorities felt they could not ignore and which in 1567 was finally extinguished. Thevet, however, used his ephemeral stay there (of just ten weeks) to produce a new work, *Les singularitez de la France Antarctique* ('The New Found World, or Antarctike').

His publishing career now established, Thevet had managed to get Papal dispensation from his vows as a Franciscan in 1558, leaving him free for even more ambitious projects. These culminated in *Le grand insulaire* ('The Great Book of Islands'), in some ways a homage to the *Isolarii* of the previous century, and borrowing heavily on the works of others to produce what Thevet hoped would be a compilation of 350 maps of the world's principal islands. Sadly, though, political instability in France, which forced King Henri III to flee Paris in 1588, hampered the project. With Thevet bankrupt, and his work impounded, it seems only 131 of the maps were ever completed and they were never published.

PREVIOUS SPREAD AND OPPOSITE

World map (previous spread);
The Americas (opposite),
Theatrum Orbis Terrarum,
Abraham Ortelius, 1570

BELOW

Portrait of André Thevet, 1586

Other would-be imitators of Mercator and Ortelius were more successful, particularly in the Netherlands. The Nijmegen cartographer Gerard de Jode (1509–91), who moved to Antwerp to ply his trade and, like Ortelius, was a member of the Guild of St Luke, spent much of his early career printing the maps of others, including the world map of the Venetian map-maker Giacomo Gastaldi (1500–66). Commissioned by Venice's ruling Council of Ten to draw a series of maps on walls in the Ducal Place where a previous version had been destroyed in a catastrophic fire in 1485, Gastaldi's first version was rejected (perhaps he baulked at the brief to include the kingdom of Prester John, which of course did not exist). Though his work, too, was subsequently lost from the *Sala delle due Mappe* ('Chamber of the Two Maps') which they adorned, they survived long enough to be copied, disseminated and then reprinted by de Jode.

De Jode had in the meantime been working away at his own atlas, which was planned with the novel twist of printing maps with accompanying text on the back, a device that

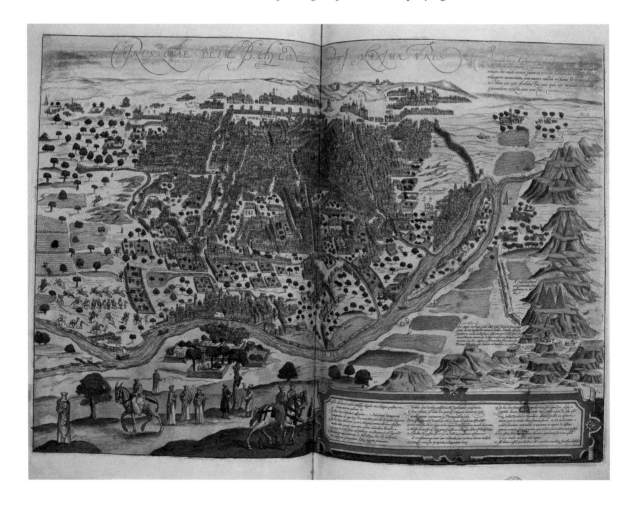

enabled him to sell the maps individually before the actual atlas was complete. By 1573, the collection was complete and ready to be bound together and published in atlas form. But there was then a five-year delay, which may have been caused by Ortelius getting wind of the project and obstructing the permits de Jode needed to have it printed. By then, the Ortelius atlas had come out and so, when it was finally issued in 1578, de Jode's *Speculum orbis terrarum* ('Mirror of the World') had to accept the consolation prize of the second world atlas to be published. Even at the bargain price of six guilders (half the price of Ortelius's *Theatrum*), it consistently undersold its rival. Even a new edition, produced by his son Cornelis in 1593 (Gerard had died two years before) was something of a flop, and in 1600 all the copperplates were bought by a rival Antwerp publisher Joan Baptista Vrients, who had also just purchased those for the *Theatrum Orbis Terrarum*. Such was the cut-throat nature of Dutch cartographic publishing.

All of the main three atlases were expensive – the twelve guilders of the *Theatrum* represented about a month's salary for a printer, and so those who produced the atlases may well not have been in a position to afford to buy them. To resolve this problem, Ortelius commissioned a reduced format version of his atlas, called the *Spieghel der werelt* ('Mirror of the World') when first published in 1577, but which then acquired the more convenient title, the *Epitome*. A mere 20 x 28cm (8 x 11in) in size, it deserves the title of the first pocket atlas ever published. Its text, which was not only written in Dutch, rather than the Latin of the original, but also in rhyme (translated by the humanist Peter Heyns), made it even more appealing to the popular market. It went through a number of editions, including in 1596 a French translation (as *Le miroir du monde*) in a somewhat larger format. By then, Heyns, a Protestant, had been forced by the exigencies of the Dutch Revolt to move to the safer northern Netherlands (his past association causing Ortelius to be interviewed by the authorities in 1588 on suspicion of heresy).

As well as pocket atlases, town atlases began their long popularity in the sixteenth century. Sebastian Münster's *Cosmographia* (p.99) had included views of cities, but these were of little use in navigating the labyrinths that made up most medieval urban centres. Long-distance travel (and certainly tourism) was in its infancy, but the growing European economy (with the Netherlands increasingly at its epicentre) provided a market for those who wanted to find their way around. The first attempt at this was made by the Flemish engraver Franz Hogenberg (1535–90) and his partner, the German geographer Georg Braun (1541–1622). Hogenberg was yet another victim of the political and religious turmoil of the time; he was expelled from the Netherlands in 1568 by the Duke of Alba, who had been sent by Philip II of Spain to stifle rising dissent, but whose execution of the Dukes of Egmont and Hoorn instead provoked the uprising that ultimately destroyed Spanish rule.

In exile, Hogenberg established a flourishing engraving business in Cologne, which among more its conventional output, such as single-sheet maps and illustrations for a history of his adopted city, included some striking innovations. In 1579, he published the *Itinerarium orbis christiani* ('Itinerary of the Christian World'), a very early form of road atlas, which included 84 maps. By then, though, the first volume in what would prove his most famous work had been issued. The *Civitates Orbis Terrarum* ('Cities of the World') came out in six volumes between 1572 and 1617, by which time Hogenberg himself had been dead for 27 years and the business was being run by his son Abraham. The finished version included 543 plans of cities, mainly in Europe, but also including Cairo and Casablanca in North Africa and Mexico City and Cusco from the Spanish possessions in the Americas, providing invaluable resources for historians of the urban layouts of the time.

To assist in managing the mammoth project, Hogenberg turned to the Catholic cleric and geographer Georg Braun, who wrote the accompanying text and helped hire the team of cartographers and engravers needed to bring it to fulfilment. Men such as Joris Hoefnagel (1542–1600) and his son (also called Joris) provided illustrations for the *Civitates*, and helped secure Cologne a place as a centre of cartography. This was aided by its proximity as an easy haven for those fleeing the religious tumults in the Netherlands. Among them was Christiaan van Andrichem, a priest from Delft, whose work included the *Theatrum Terrae Sanctae* ('Theatre of the Holy Land'), published in Cologne in 1590, whose plans of the Holy Land, Jerusalem and the areas settled by the 12 tribes of Israel make it the first proper historical atlas of the Bible.

Map-publishing houses were appearing in other regions too, not just in the traditional cartographic centres in Italy and the Netherlands, producing their own regional maps. In Switzerland, Aegidius Tschudi (1505–72), a pupil of the great Protestant reformer Ulrich Zwingli, as well as a friend of Sebastian Münster, had in 1538 already produced the *Nova Rhaetiae atque totius Helvetiae descriptio* ('New Raetia and a Description of All of Switzerland'), a nine-sheet map which was the first to show the country in such detail. Here, Basel and Zurich emerged as the main hubs and in the latter the Protestant clergyman Johannes Stumpf (1500–78), who was in turn a friend of Tschudi, in 1548 published a chronicle of Swiss history, the *Gemeiner loblicher Eydgnoschafft Stetten, Landen und Völkeren Chronick wirdiger Thaaten Beschreybung* ('A Description of the Cities, Provinces and Peoples of the Swiss Confederation along with a Chronicle of their Worthy Doings'), which as well as featuring the first historical map of the country, showing its development in the Roman period, contained eight maps of the Swiss cantons, making it the first regional atlas of the country.

The advances in topography over the previous decades that heralded the beginnings of scientific surveying were eagerly taken up in Germany, where Philipp Apian (1531–89; the son of Peter, who had produced an early cordiform world map in 1524), was commissioned by Duke Albrecht V of Bavaria in 1554 to undertake a topographic survey of the duchy. As a professor of mathematics at Ingolstadt University (a role also filled by his father), Apian was meticulous in his attention to the conduct of the triangulations, so that it was not until 1568 that the map was complete, with its 23 sheets bound into an atlas (the *Bairische Landtafeln XXIII* ('The Bavarian Land Table in 23 parts') that remained more or less the definitive map of Bavaria into the eighteenth century and spawned similar topographic surveys in other German states such as Württemberg, Trier and Saxony.

In England map-making had, perhaps more than in any other European country, been seen as an extension of royal power, or at least as a means of establishing its limits and where its defence might most usefully be directed. The great cartographic survey ordered by Henry VIII in 1539, when invasion from France, ever a peril, seemed imminent, consumed £376,500 by the time it was complete (which is actually more than the king spent on the lavish showiness of his various palaces such as Whitehall and Hampton Court). Although this provided the material for a number of partial maps of the south coast and plans for sites where new fortifications might be built to fend off the French, it was nothing like a consistent set of regional maps, let alone an atlas. Although the great antiquary John Leland (*c.* 1506–52), whose *Itineraries*, produced after a series of tours of England and Wales between 1535 and 1543, constituted a detailed prose portrait of Henry's realm, had promised the king that he would follow up with a map (setting 'this yowr worlde and impery of England . . . sette forth yn a quadrate table of silver' [2]), nothing was produced. Driven to despair by the magnitude of the task and overwhelmed by an obsessive personality that compulsively collected both books and facts, Leland simply slipped into insanity.

It took almost 30 more years before a similar enterprise was undertaken, this time by Christopher Saxton (*c.* 1540–1610), a Yorkshire map-maker. Saxton was fortunate enough to have been employed as an apprentice by the local vicar John Rudd, in 1570, who happened to be a keen cartographer. Rudd's work became known to Thomas Seckford, an official at the royal treasury and then, in turn, to William Cecil, Lord Burghley, Elizabeth I's chief adviser, who saw the merits of undertaking a national survey and producing a national map. So it was, by this circuitous route, that Saxton was commissioned in July 1573 to begin the arduous task of mapping the whole country. The process was a little stop-start, suffering from significant delays, probably caused by interruptions in raising the financing. From its beginning with Norfolk, the first county to be surveyed (which was ready in 1574), the task was complete within five years. The scale varies throughout: Norfolk came out at 1:235,000; Kent, Surrey, Sussex and Middlesex

BELOW

Sketch from *Bairische Landtafeln XXIII*, Philipp Apian, 1568

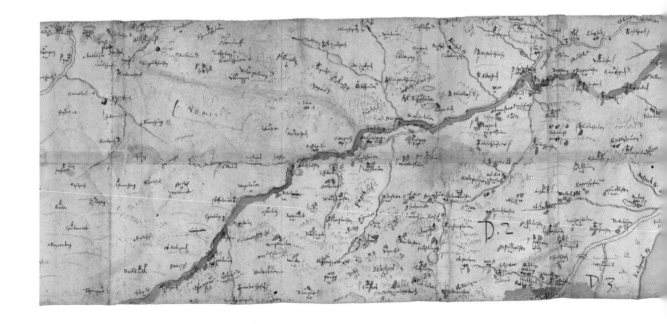

were shown at 1:314,000; Devon and Cornwall had to settle for even less and, curiously, Saxton's home county of Yorkshire got the worst scale of all. The result, though, by 1578 was a complete 'County Atlas' of all 52 counties of England and Wales. Some counties had to share their sheets, with only 25 receiving individual treatment. The bulk of the individual ones were coastal, as opposed to inland counties, and in many cases the internal parish boundaries within the county were not included; all vagaries probably explained by a prime motivation for Burghley's willingness to fund the project being a continued preoccupation with coastal defence.

With their bright colours and surprising level of detail, including even a single tree where he found it noteworthy (such as the 'Knigtons Ashe' he depicted on his 1576 map of Wiltshire), Saxton's maps were not to be surpassed as a collection until John Speed's *The Theatre of the Empire of Great Britain* in 1611 (p.149). In the meantime, single-county surveys continued to be carried out, such as that in William Lambarde's *Perambulation of Kent* in 1570, a pioneer county history, and more comprehensively by John Norden (*c*. 1547–1625), a member of the Somerset gentry who conceived the grand plan to produce a set of county guides, complete with an index of places, a history of notable locations and their sights, and an accompanying county map. Norden's *Speculum Britanniae* (or 'Mirror of Britain') was planned to cover the whole country, but the project was beyond any single individual and certainly beyond the resources of someone who (as he vociferously complained) received no official financial support. Even so, he managed to publish the volume for Middlesex in 1593 and that for Hertfordshire five years later, with separate maps

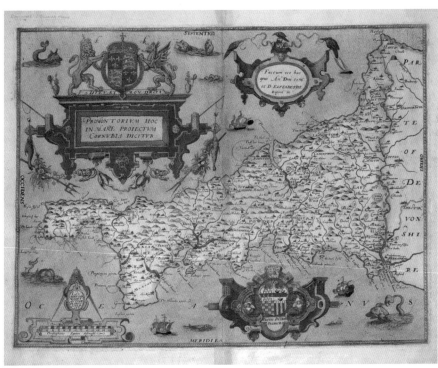

of 10 other counties (though shorn of their projected accompanying material). Despite all his travails, Norden's level of detail still exceeds that of Saxton and he cannily – in a failed bid to attract the attention of ministers and perhaps that of the Queen herself – included details likely to appeal to the court such as royal palaces, as well as the locations of the houses of the gentry, the country's principal roads, some indication of economic resources (such as Cornish tin mines) as well as a liberal deployment of the royal coat of arms. For all this, though, the *Speculum Britanniae* remains Britain's greatest atlas that never was.

While late Tudor England remained a comparative novice in cartographic terms, Dutch map-makers continued to be at the forefront of practical mapping. The real pioneer and most notable exponent of maritime cartography was Lucas Janszoon Waghenaer (*c.* 1533–1606), who spent his whole life in the fishing port of Enkhuizen. This was a town that had grown rich on the revenues of the herring fishery, monies which, after the Dutch declaration of independence in 1568, flowed to the local burghers rather than to the coffers of the Habsburg imperial authorities, and during Waghenaer's lifetime it quadrupled in size to around 16,000 inhabitants. An instinctive feeling for the water that surrounded the town is already clear in Waghenaer's first cartographic endeavour, a map of Enkhuizen riven with waterways and dikes, all carefully labelled. He spent time at sea himself, as a pilot, probably plying the route carrying herring into the Baltic and grain back to the Netherlands in return, gaining on those trips a familiarity with the ports, coastline and maritime hazards along the way. From 1579, when he retired to a more comfortable and predictable life as the inspector in charge of licence fees for the demarcation of sea lanes, he began to work on his life's great project, the *Spieghel der Zeevaerdt* ('The Mariner's Mirror'). The first published sea atlas, its format appealed to pilots, although its bulk made it a less practical proposition. The book was organized in four-page sections, each of them beginning with a page of description and sailing instructions, followed by a double-page chart and then a blank page. The cost of engraving the plates caused Waghenaer significant financial difficulties, but he managed to publish the first part, covering the western Netherlands, in 1584, cannily dedicating it to Prince William of Orange, the Dutch rebels' chief political leader.

Perhaps as a result, Waghenaer obtained a subvention of 600 guilders to help him publish the second volume, which covered the eastern trade. Together they amounted to a finely engraved set of coastal charts which could carry Dutch mariners as far south as the Canaries and as far east as the Baltic as well as helping them navigate the tortuous labyrinths of Dutch waters. The fame the *Spieghel* brought him helped Waghenaer finance a second sea atlas in 1592 (the original had already undergone revision and been published in Latin in 1586 as the *Speculum Nauticum*, dedicated to Queen Elizabeth I of England and King Frederick of Denmark). This, the *Thresoor der Zeevaerdt* ('The Treasure of the Sea') benefited from the research of men such as Dirck Gerritszoon Pomp (1544–1608), the first Dutchman to visit China and Japan in the 1580s. His enthusiasm for the orient led him to be nicknamed 'Dirck China' and, indirectly, to the Dutch voyages to the Spice Islands that prompted the foundation of the Dutch East India Company in 1602 and the subsequent establishment of a Dutch maritime empire.

Still the seaman at heart, Waghenaer turned later in his career to less ambitious projects, producing a pilot guide in a smaller, octavo format that could be of practical use to pilots on board ship rather than being pored over in offices or admired in the houses of the well-to-do. The *Enchuyser Zee-caert-boeck* ('Enkhuizen Sea Atlas'), which came out in 1598, included fine detail on the Zuiderzee, as well as charts for the routes to West Africa and Brazil, but it also incorporated nearly 350 pages of sailing instructions for pilots.

Waghenaer had his rivals and collaborators in the small, overlapping and presumably somewhat claustrophobic world of Dutch cartographic publishing. Cornelis Claeszoon (*c.* 1546–1609) was the principal one, whose acquisition of the rights to publish Waghenaer's work gave him something of a stranglehold. Waghenaer died in poverty in 1606, never knowing that he would achieve a kind of immortality by having the genre of maritime atlases come to be known as 'wagoneers' in his honour. This was despite the widespread admiration for his pilot guide, and two sea atlases, and the translation of the *Spieghel* into other languages (including German, Spanish and French editions overseen by Cornelis Claeszoon), as well as a grant of an annual pension of 100 guilders by a grateful States-General of the United Provinces (the name by which the independent Netherlands became known).

BELOW

Stavanger–Bergen, *Spieghel der Zeevaerdt*, Lucas Janszoon Waghenaer, 1584

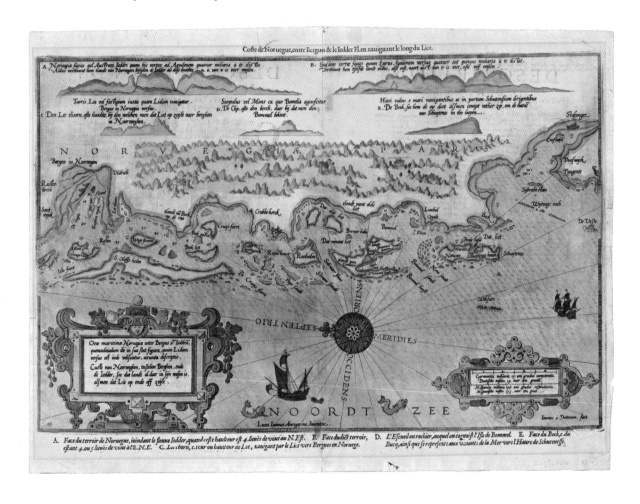

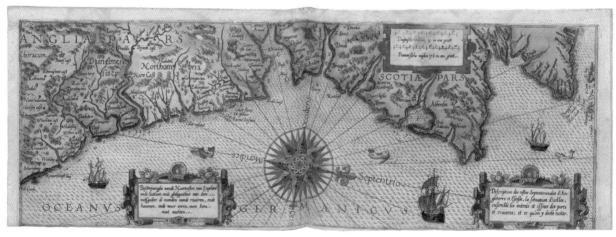

It was only towards the end of the sixteenth century that the Dutch cartographic houses that would provide charts for its emerging empire began to appear, fronted by men such as Jodocus Hondius (1563–1612), who revised Mercator and who worked with Anthony Ashley to produce the *Mariner's Mirrour*, the first English-language version of the *Spieghel*; Willem Barentsz (*c.* 1550–97), who in 1595 created the *Nieuwe beschryvinge caertboeck van de Midlantsche Zee* ('The New Pilot Guide to the Mediterranean'). This last guide was a reflection of the increasing level of Dutch trade with southern Europe, and with its attractive frontispiece of ships at anchor in Genoa, was an enticing piece of work, containing fuller descriptions of ports and coastlines than Waghenaer had been able to include (though not all from Barentz's personal experience, as the text for the eastern Mediterranean is largely lifted from an Italian source).

Despite his clear interest in the Mediterranean, Barentz was to find fame as the Dutch pioneer of attempts to find the North-East Passage, a fabled route north over Russia that it was hoped would provide access to the Spice Islands, in much the same way that there was supposed to be a shortcut around the Canadian Arctic (but a practical navigable version of this 'North-West Passage' eluded generations of explorers). His three voyages were eventful: on the first in 1594 the crew made the mistake of capturing a polar bear, which caused havoc aboard ship and had to be killed, and on the third, which discovered Novaya Zemlya in 1597, Barentz's boat was held fast by the ice for months, and he died on an open boat as the surviving mariners tried to make it through the ice-choked sea to the Kola Peninsula.

A more practical route to the East was taken by Jan Huygen van Linschoten (1563–1611), who sailed there in Portuguese service in 1583, and spent time in Goa, the capital of Portugal's spice empire. His return voyage in 1589 was interrupted by an attack by English privateers, intent on getting their hands on the fleet's cargo of spices, and van Linschoten ended up stranded for two years on Terceira in the Azores. He made use of the time to compose a history of the island, illustrated with a plan of its capital Angra. This, together with the copious notes he had made during his time in the East constituted a valuable trove of information, which Waghenaer tapped into for his *Thresoor*. Van Linschoten was persuaded by friends to gather the material together and produce it as the *Itinerario*, a work which was published by none other than the ubiquitous Cornelis Claeszoon. Bound in with it was the *Reys-Gheschrift van de navigatien*, a compilation of maps and accounts of areas which van Linschoten had not visited, such as South America, which was becoming of increasing interest to the Dutch, and for whose exploration and exploitation they founded a West India Company in 1621. Included in the whole sumptuous work was a world map by Petrus Plancius (1552–1622) and five regional maps of the world outside Europe (engraved by Arnold van Langren and his brother Hendrik, the second generation of yet another dynasty of Dutch cartographers).

Van Linschoten's work and his enthusiasm for disseminating news of the riches to be had in the East had an even longer-term effect, as it helped inspire the voyage of Cornelis de Houtman (1565–99) to the Spice Islands in 1595. Already with a track record in the field, Houtman had been sent by a consortium of Amsterdam merchants to Lisbon to obtain, by fair means or subterfuge, Portuguese charts of the East which would allow Dutch merchants to trade there, Portuguese-owned ports having been closed to them

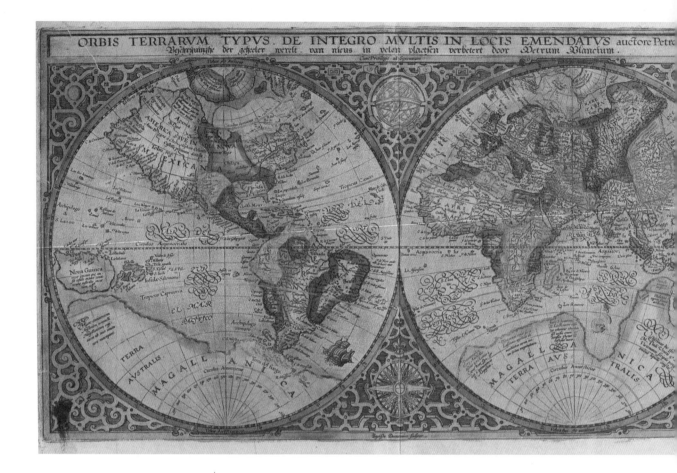

ORBIS TERRARVM TYPVS. DE INTEGRO MVLTIS IN LOCIS EMENDATVS auctore Petro

Orbis Terrarum Typus De Integro Multis In Locis Emendatus, Petrus Plancius, *c.* 1594

Notable for the wide North-West Passage shown (erroneously) to the north of mainland North America.

since the Union of the Portuguese and Spanish thrones in 1580 made Portugal as much an enemy as Spain was. When the Portuguese authorities found out about his activities, Cornelis and his brother Frederik were arrested, but released and allowed to return to Amsterdam. With a set of instructions compiled by van Linschoten to hand, Houtman then set out in April 1595 with a fleet of four ships bound for the East Indies. The voyage was a mixed success. Van Linschoten landed near the Cape of Good Hope and on Madagascar, but scurvy had ravaged the crew and he had to bury 70 of them there. The fleet never even made it to the Moluccas, the ostensible destination of the voyage, giving up at Bali, where van Linschoten was able to acquire a small cargo of peppercorns. By the time he reached home two years and four months after setting out, only around a third of the original crew of 248 was left alive.

Despite its apparent lack of commercial success, which must have disappointed his investors in the *Compagnie van Verre* (Distant Lands Company) which had financed it to the tune of 290,000 guilders, de Houtman's voyage sparked a spice rush from the Netherlands and before long regular expeditions were setting out (with 14 Dutch fleets making the journey to the East Indies between 1595 and 1601). The uncontrolled competition between rival ventures drove up the price of pepper and other spices so much that it threatened to throttle the Dutch trade to the Spice Islands before it had really even started. It took the intervention of the States General in 1602 to force the companies to merge into one single *Verenigde Nederlandsche Geoŝtroyeerde Ooŝtindische Compagnie* (the United Netherlands Chartered East India Company), the VOC, which was to be the main vehicle for Dutch trading and political expansion in the East for the next two centuries (p.134).

The Italian states had been completely left behind by the Spanish and Portuguese in the rush to colonize the Americas and dominate the spice trade. The trade had in its overland form been one of the life-bloods of Venetian and Genoese commercial dominance, and Italian map-makers continued to produced mapping which harked back to their glory days. Antonio Lafreri (who was in faŝt an immigrant, born in Burgundy in 1512 as Antoine du Pérac Lafrery, but who transferred to Rome in 1544) produced one of the finest examples. He collaborated with some of the finest Italian cartographers of his time, including the Venetian Giacomo Gastaldi (1500–66), Battista Agnese (*c.* 1500–64) and the engraver Antonio Salamanca (1478–1562) to produce a series of *Lafreri Atlases*, which seem to have been produced to order, including a slightly varying seleŝtion of maps, all made up in the enterprise's workshops near Rome's Piazza Navona, a distriŝt which had attraŝted a large community of goldsmiths, engravers and sellers of prints and books.

Italy also saw the publication of a number of specialized atlases, some in the spirit of earlier works such as Sebastian Münster's *Cosmographia* (p.99) or the *Isolario* of Cristoforo Buondelmonti (p.78). In 1568, Giulio Ballino produced his *De' disegni delle piu illuŝtri città e fortezze del mondo* ('On the Designs of the Most Famous Cities and Fortresses of the World') which contained more than 50 town views and plans as well as maps of battles, making it another early example of a historical atlas. It inspired a series of 'town books' which became a popular genre in later sixteenth-century Italy, some of which contained in addition maps of islands. These, though, were most often

illustrated and mapped in specialist *isolarii*, notably *L'Isole piu famose del mondo* ('The Most Famous Islands of the World') by the Venetian cartographer Tomasso Porcacchi (*c.* 1530–85) and the *Isole Famose, Porti, Fortezze e Terre Maritime* ('Famous Islands, Ports, Fortresses and Coastlines'), traditionally attributed to Giovanni Francesco Camocio (*fl.* 1560–75) and published between 1571 and 1574. No longer really intended as a praŝtical atlas, Camocio's *isolario* was published at a time of intense fighting between Venice and other Christian powers and the Ottoman Empire in the eastern Mediterranean and so it principally includes islands which sat within the theatre of confliŝt, though sequencing them in no particular order, geographical or otherwise.

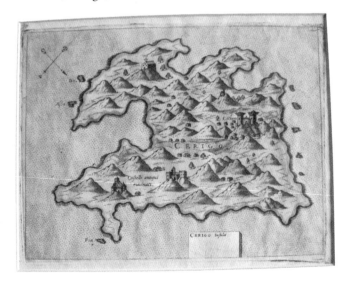

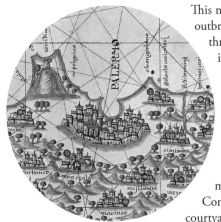

This mini-Renaissance of Venetian cartography was rather disrupted by an outbreak of bubonic plague which struck the city in summer 1576 and swept through it for a year, killing 46,000 people, or over a third of its inhabitants, including the painter Titian. A public procession held on the Feast of Saint Roch on 14 August 1576, and a vow by the city's senate to build a new church to the Redeemer (whose dedication is celebrated annually to this day as a thanksgiving for the end of the epidemic), were both said to have helped stem the plague's progress, but among the casualties it could do nothing about was the city's map industry as many of the precious copperplates were sold off or made their way to Rome.

There, another type of atlas was being produced, and one both less mobile and more robust, in the forms of series of painted wall maps. Commissioned by Pope Gregory XII to decorate one side of the Belvedere courtyard in the Vatican, the *Galleria delle Carte Geografiche* ('Gallery of Geographical Maps'), they were painted by the Dominican friar and cosmographer Ignazio Danti (1536–86). A true Renaissance man, Danti came from a talented family (his brother Vincenzo had written an important work on artistic theory) and among his achievements were the design of the Dominican monastery of Santa Croce at Marengo, and a stint as professor of mathematics at Pisa from 1571. Almost a decade earlier, in 1562, when Danti was just 25, Duke Cosimo de' Medici had asked him to paint a series of large cupboard doors in Florence's Guardaroba Nova, which housed the ducal artistic and literary collections. The chosen theme was to be 57 maps of the world, with the ceiling additionally painted with a star map on Ptolemaic lines. Although the whole scheme was planned out by Giorgio Vasari (the author of *The Lives of the Artists* and the Medici court artist), the first set of maps was painted between 1563 and 1575 by Danti, covering regions including Indonesia, Indochina, China and Japan, showing the latest discoveries of the Portuguese, but symbolically asserting Florentine and Medici dominance over areas which in practice they had no hope of penetrating.

Danti took time out to make astronomical observations which revealed the 11-day error that had accumulated in the calendar since Roman times; this ultimately led to the Gregorian Reform of 1582, when 11 days were omitted to allow the seasons to catch up, to much general confusion. His labours at the Guardaroba were brought to an abrupt end, however, when Cosimo's son, Francesco, succeeded to the ducal throne on the death of his father in April 1574. Danti had been appointed Francesco's mathematics tutor in 1571, but pupil and teacher had clearly not got on at all well, for within a year the new duke had expelled Danti, giving him only 24 hours' notice to quit the duchy.

Danti made his way to Rome via Bologna, where he again served as professor of mathematics, and Perugia, where he conducted a survey and made a map on behalf of the Pope – within whose domains the city lay. From 1580 in Rome, he

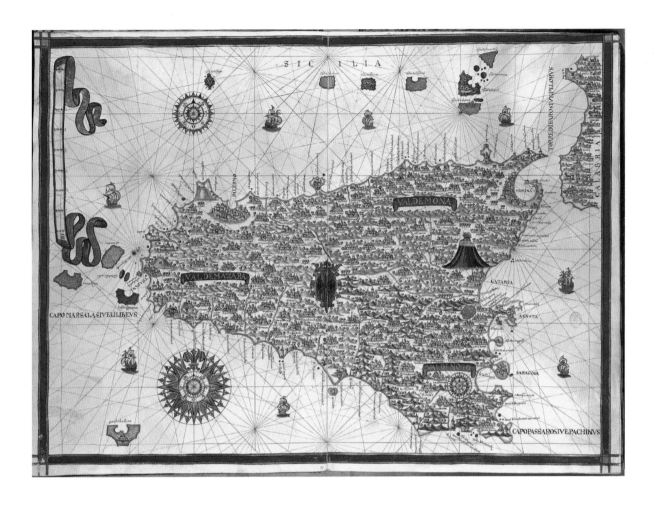

designed the 32 map panels that made up the *Galleria delle Carte Geographiche*, which depict the various regions of Italy. These are replete with historical and geographical vignettes, including the marking out of the lands allegedly given by the Roman Emperor Constantine to Pope Sylvester in AD 315, which was used to justify the Pope's secular rule over the Papal States. Although it was a mid-eighth-century forgery (as had long been suspected, including by the humanist Eneo Piccolomini, who wrote as much in 1453 but then chose to do nothing when he became Pope Pius II in 1458), the Donation of Constantine was still a useful piece of propaganda, even in the late-sixteenth century when Danti incorporated it in his scheme.

As a reward for his work on the *Galleria*, Danti was appointed Papal mathematician and cosmographer, and he oversaw the completion of the maps of the Terza Loggia – begun as long ago as 1560 by the French cartographer Étienne du Pérac (*c.* 1525–1604) – rounding them off with a world map in two hemispheres and 10 regional maps of Africa, Asia and the Americas. Although it proved to be his last major cartographic commission – he was appointed a bishop in 1583, though still finding time to write a treatise on surveying published in 1586, the year of his death – Danti's cycles of painted maps are a fitting testament and coda to the great age of atlases, a kind of enormous installation and homage to both Ptolemy and Mercator, the two giants of cartographic history. They also marked the point where Italy, Spain and Portugal were giving way to new political powers in the north – England, France and the Netherlands – who, while already making their mark on the world of atlases, would soon come to conquer the world they first had mapped.

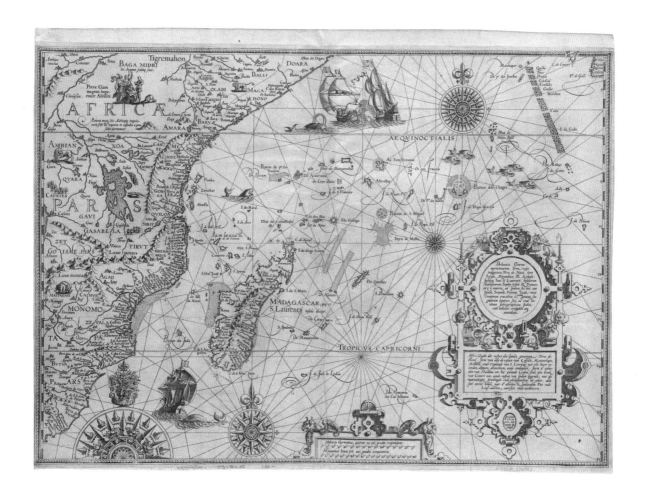

THE ATLAS DIVERSIFIES

(1600–1700)

The seventeenth century saw maps come more and more into the mainstream of life for the growing educated urban middle-classes of European cities. Competing publishers pumped out an increasing amount of information, which was now freely available rather than being guarded in the hydrographic offices of the main maritime nations. The Netherlands continued to be a principal centre of map-production, as the Dutch Empire impinged on territories in the Indian Ocean previously held by the Spanish and Portuguese, such as Malacca on the Malay peninsula, and the overseas expansion of England and France got underway (most especially in North America and in the slave trade down the west coast of Africa).

A further consolidation in the Dutch map-publishing industry took place in 1604 when Gerardus Mercator's son, Gerardus Jr, sold the copperplates for his father's atlas to Cornelis Claeszoon (1546–1609). He was working with Joan Vrients (1552–1612), the acquirer of the rights to both Ortelius's and de Jode's atlases (pp.114–17), giving the duo something of a monopoly position in the field. This pair continued to produce versions of the Mercator Atlas, playing on its creator's great fame in the 1606 edition entitled *Gerardi Mercatoris Atlas sive Cosmographicae meditatitones* ('The Atlas of Gerard Mercator, or Cosmographic Meditations'), which included 37 new maps in addition to Mercator's 107 originals, filling in gaps in Africa, Asia and the Americas to make it finally a truly comprehensive world atlas. The atlas was produced jointly with another titan of the Dutch cartographic community, Jodocus Hondius (1563–1612), who seems to have acquired all the copperplates after Claeszoon died in 1609, and he and his family then held a monopoly, giving them little incentive to improve or expand what became known as the Hondius-Mercator atlas for the next 25 years.

Around the time that Hondius died in 1612, map-making began to reach a new peak in Amsterdam, a phenomenon largely attributable to a rising star in the city's cartographic firmament. The career of Willem Janszoon Blaeu (1571–1638) began unpromisingly enough in the family herring business, a profession in which he might have remained marooned, had it not been for a chance visit to the island of Hven in Denmark. This happened to be the home of the astronomer Tycho Brahe, who had built his great observatory of Uranianberg there, and from which – astonishingly without the use of the yet-to-be-invented telescope – he made a series of accurate observations that helped correct existing astronomical tables and map nearly 800 fixed stars. The young Blaeu remained at Hven for two years and when he returned to Amsterdam, his head filled with the latest knowledge of astronomy, geography and precision instruments, he dedicated himself to selling and, ultimately, to making maps. By 1606, he had turned from globes, his earliest cartographic venture, to sea charts, with the publication that year of the *Generale Pascaerte*, adorned with the golden sun-dial which became his trademark. Within a year he had also further diversified, producing a map of Europe and a (now-lost) four-sheet world map.

Blaeu worked in Amsterdam, which if not yet at the zenith of its power, was certainly near the height of its self-confidence, having virtually secured its independence from Spain (although this was only finally recognized by the Peace of Westphalia in 1648). The Dutch East India Company (VOC), chartered in 1602, was sending out its first fleets to the East, and men such as Petrus Plancius (p.125), a Protestant minister who fled to the United Provinces to join the exodus of those escaping the religious persecution in the southern Netherlands, provided both new capital – he was an investor in the VOC – and their expertise. As an accomplished mathematician, Plancius did important work on attempting to devise a system for determining longitude as well as working alongside cartographers such as Cornelis Claeszoon and Blaeu).

The beginnings of Blaeu's career coincided with the tail-end of that of that other great Dutch cartographer, Jodocus Hondius, whose *Atlas Minor*, yet another revision of the Mercator Atlas, was issued in 1607. Competition was fierce, and the rival firms of Hondius and Blaeu vigorously pursued claims of infringement against each other, with Blaeu registering a plea in 1608 to the Estates of Holland and Friesland for protection against pirates who were copying his maps even 'before the ink on them was dry'[1]. Confusion was probably increased among perfectly innocent clients because of the practice of Dutch cartographers of sharing or borrowing plates, while Blaeu's original version of his own name, Willem Janszoon, caused him to be muddled with a competitor, Willem Janssonius, who just happened to live next door to him. Finally, in about 1621, when he was in his early 50s, Willem Janszoon took on the additional surname 'Blaeu' to make the difference with his less-illustrious rival clear.

Blaeu's early cartographic endeavours depended on the good offices of the political authorities in the Netherlands. In 1608, he was awarded 200 guilders to produce a new set of sea charts, *Het Licht der Zeevaerdt* ('The Light of Navigation'), a fairly

BELOW AND PAGE 136

Frontispiece (left); Africa (p.136), *Atlas Minor*, Jodocus Hondius, 1607

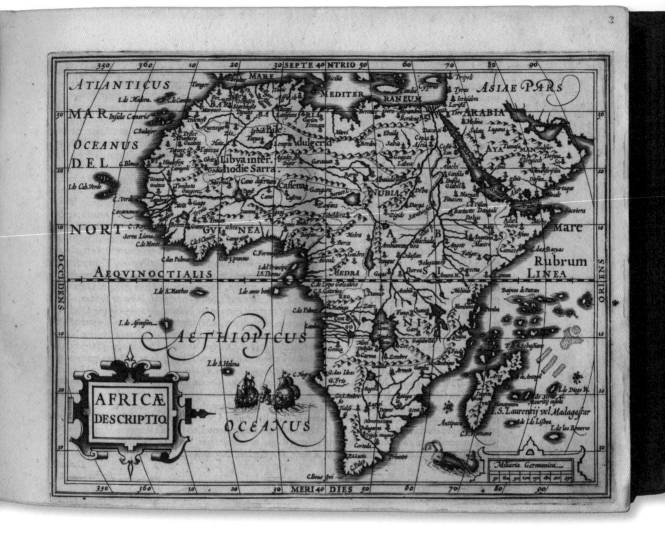

conventional wagoneer, which borrowed extensively from Waghenaer's originals but benefited from his access to the astronomical observations of Tycho Brahe. Blaeu's ambitions, however, were far greater, though it took him decades to achieve them, aided by his son Joan, who joined the family business in the 1620s. Together they published hundreds of maps, most of them reproductions of the works of others, aimed squarely at a burgeoning commercial market for maps in Amsterdam.

A few of them, though, were Blaeu originals, like the 1606 four-sheet world map on a Mercator projection. Though the original was lost during the Second World War, reproductions show that its borders contained a wealth of information of interest to the Dutch mercantile and ruling classes of the time, including an equestrian parade, showing what Blaeu labelled the 10 most powerful rulers of the age on horseback, with the King of Spain in first position and the King of France second, while the King of England came in tenth, after the rulers of Tartary and China. Making it a mini-atlas in its own right, the map also includes town plans of 28 urban centres, most of them taken from Frans Hogenberg's *Civitates Orbis Terrarum* (p.117), ranging from nearby Cologne to commercially important (to the Dutch) places such as Danzig, Stockholm, Goa, Bantam (on Java) and 'Gammalamma' (the Dutch-controlled fort of Kastela on Ternate in the Moluccas, from which the VOC controlled the hugely lucrative trade in cloves). The whole was rounded out with a series of illustrations of the natives of various countries, from Sumatrans, Brazilians, natives of the Congo and Arabs, to Lapps, Hungarians, Spanish and Germans. The Eurocentric (or rather Dutch-centric) viewpoint of the explanatory text is underlined by the description of 'Europe, enthroned on high, the supreme ruler with the world at her feet' to whom 'Africa offers you costly spices and fragrant balsam and also enriches you with shining white ivory, to which the dark coloured peopled of Guinea add a great weight in gold.'[3]

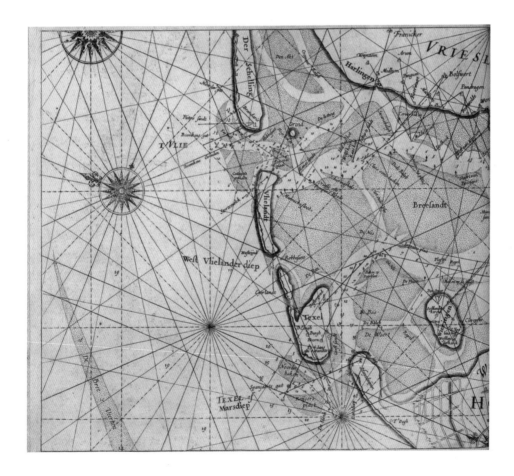

Blaeu was clearly making a name for himself and one of his early sea charts, from 1605, makes an appearance in Johannes Vermeer's 1668–69 work *De geograaf* ('The Geographer'), clearly identifiable hanging on a wall behind the young cartographer who is the principal figure in the painting. Blaeu's progress, though, suffered a setback in the 1620s when bitter arguments over the wisdom of signing an 11-year truce with Spain in 1609 became entangled with religious differences between hard-line Calvinists and the more moderate Arminians or Remonstrants. After the arrest and execution of no lesser a figure than Johan van Oldenbarnevelt, the Land's Advocate of Holland (the official who presided over meetings of the States General) and a leading Remonstrant, life for those, such as Blaeu, who had been sympathetic to the Arminian cause became distinctly uncomfortable.

At just this time, the VOC decided to take a firmer control of the cartographic information leaking out after Dutch voyages to the East returned home. As well as imposing a massive fine of 6,000 guilders on anyone publishing unauthorized maps, they decided to appoint an official cartographer. William Blaeu, who should have been the leading candidate, was overlooked in favour of Hessel Gerritsz (1581–1632), one of his employees in the cartographic workshop in Amsterdam. Gerritsz made the most of his opportunity, allegedly confining the work on new sea charts to four assistants who operated from his home. Among the secret intelligence that came his way, and which he incorporated into his maps, was the growing Dutch awareness of the coastline of Australia, Ptolemy's great unknown southern continent which had finally been encountered by a Dutch explorer, also called Willem Janszoon (1570–1630), who landed somewhere on the Cape York peninsula in northern Australia in 1606. In 1612, Gerritsz published a translation of the account of the Portuguese navigator Pedro Fernandez de Quiros (1565–1615), at the time working for the Spanish, of his exploration of New Guinea, in which he refers to 'Australia Incognita'. By 1627, when Gerritsz produced his *Caert van't Landt van d'Eendracht* ('Chart of the Land of Eendracht'), Australia was considerably less 'incognita' since a large part of its west coast had been charted by Dutch voyages (and is included on Gerritsz's map), most notably by Dirk Hartog (1580–1621), who in 1616 became the second European to land in Australia (on an island near Shark Bay). Hartog named his discovery 'Eendrachtsland' after his ship, the *Eendracht*, whose name meant 'agreement', although the rather poetic name did not in the end stick.

While Gerritsz's cartography benefited from the cutting edge of Dutch exploration and the patronage of the VOC, Blaeu plodded along, prosperously enough, publishing a vast range of sheet maps, wall maps and globes. Then, in 1629, he achieved the coup of purchasing the surviving plates for Mercator's old atlas. Jodocus Hondius, who had acquired them in 1609, had benefited considerably from the publication of increasing numbers of variants. After his death in 1612, his family had proved less adept at business,

and certainly less innovative, with the reprint of an unchanged version of Hondius's last atlas coming out between 1612 and 1619. The death of his son Jodocus the Younger in 1629 persuaded them to cut their losses and sell around 40 of the copperplates to Blaeu, who put them to almost immediate use, publishing an atlas the following year under the title *Atlas Appendix, sive pars altera* ('Supplement to the Atlas, or Part Two'), using 37 of the Hondius plates in a modestly scoped atlas of 60 maps.

Blaeu did not rest there, however. Fully aware of the almost magical power of the Ortelius and Mercator names (on both of whose works his rivals had previously held a publishing monopoly), in 1631, he struck another blow at the house of Hondius, producing an *Appendix Theatri A. Ortelii et Atlantis G Mercatoris* ('Supplement to the Theatre of Ortelius and Atlas of Mercator') with 103 maps. The response was the fevered production of new atlases by Henricus Hondius, the surviving senior member of the family, and Johannes Janssonius (who had been the co-publisher of the Mercator atlases with Jodocus Hondius the Elder), including, in 1633, a new version pointedly entitled *Gerardi Mercatoris et I. Hondii Atlas* and new versions and appendices to the standard Mercator-Hondius atlas in French, Dutch and German.

Not to be outdone, Blaeu shot out yet another salvo in the atlas war. This one was an entirely revised atlas, with 150–160 maps, which he called the *Novus Atlas* ('New Atlas') and which he enlarged further with a 49-map supplement in 1635. If that were not enough, he then divided this into two parts, to produce a two-volume atlas in Dutch, French and Latin. His ambition for this was grandiose: in the preface he claimed that, 'It is our intention to describe the whole world, that is the heavens and the earth, in other volumes such as these two of which two about the earth will shortly follow.' [3]

His confidence was well-founded, for the prize that had eluded his grasp in 1612 had now fallen to him. After Hessel Gerritsz's death in September 1632, the position of chief cartographer to the VOC lay vacant. Twenty years had calmed the fighting between Remonstrants and their Contra-Remonstrant enemies that had denied him the coveted appointment, and he now had an important ally in the Company in Laurens Reael, a former Governor-General of the Dutch East Indies. Early in 1633, Blaeu received word that he now held the most prestigious position in the Dutch map-making world. The salary of 300 guilders a year might have been more significant at an earlier stage in his career, but it was the prestige and the unparalleled access to the information sources of the VOC that mattered more. He was even able to use some its supposedly secret copperplates in the *Novus Atlas*.

By 1637, Blaeu was doing so well commercially that he was able to move into larger premises on Amsterdam's Blumengracht, together with his sons Cornelis and Joan, who had already worked with their father on the *Novus Atlas*. They installed the latest printing technology and recruited the most talented engravers (much to the chagrin, one presumes, of the Hondius and Janssonius businesses). In a fit of whimsy, Blaeu even named his nine huge flat-bed printing presses after the Nine Muses (though it is not known whether Urania, the muse of astronomy, whose symbols were the globe and the compass, had pride of place).

At the height of his power, Willem Janszoon Blaeu died in October 1638, leaving the business to Joan (1596–1673) and Cornelis (1610–44). They had a stroke of luck at this vulnerable moment, as Henricus Hondius finally gave up on publishing atlases, leaving Janssonius as the last rival standing to the Blaeus. Their cause was further boosted by the appointment of Joan as his father's replacement as chief cartographer to the VOC, a position that was only growing in importance as the company sent around 100,000 tons of shipping east each year, and was the principal underpinning of the Dutch economy. All of their masters required charts, and Joan Blaeu provided them, in return being able to inspect all of their logs and journals for any new information he could incorporate into his mapping. The profit he extracted from his position as monopoly supplier to the VOC was considerable – in 1668 alone he charged them 21,135 guilders (more than 100 times the salary his father had been awarded by the company in 1632). He also cannily prevented the company from promoting a uniform manual of navigation (from which he would have profited considerably less).

Janssonius responded to this barrage of setbacks with his own blockbuster atlas, confusingly entitled the *Atlas Novus*, which was published in three volumes in 1636 and contained over 300 maps, to which he added steadily over time, as Joan Blaeu's rival works gained ground. He brought out a historical atlas in 1658 and then began to issue an even larger 11-part atlas, the title of whose German edition, modestly, was the *Novus atlas absolutissimus* ('The Most Perfect New Atlas'). By 1675, an even more mammoth version, entitled the *Atlas Major* was available, which included over 500 town plans for those customers who chose to pay a supplement.

All this time, Joan Blaeu was issuing volumes of a new project, the *Theatrum orbis terrarum* (its name, so similar to that of Ortelius's work, cannot have been an accident), which by 1655 amounted to six volumes, the fourth of which was dedicated to King Charles I of England. This was unfortunate timing, as it came out in 1645, just as the royalist cause in the English Civil War descended to the status of forlorn hope. The final volume that covered China in 16 maps, with one of Japan, (as opposed to the 113 which Britain had merited, a sign of the relative paucity of information still hampering mapping of the East), still did not provide Blaeu with the advantage he craved. He had long planned a comprehensive work that would provide as complete a description (and set of maps) as was possible of the earth, the oceans and the heavens.

The appearance of Janssonius's *Atlas Major* prompted Joan to accelerate his project. Setting aside the marine and astronomical sides of the project, Blaeu concentrated on the geographical atlas. The scale of the work needed to research, compile and engrave all the maps was vast and he was forced to pull out of the book and map-selling trade, selling off his considerable stock to raise funds. The first volume of the result of all this work appeared in 1662. The *Atlas maior* – or to give it its full title, the *Atlas maior sive cosmographia Blaviana, qua solum, salum, coelum, accuratissime describuntur* ('The Great Atlas, or Cosmography of Blaeu, in which Land, Sea and Heavens are most accurately described') was a prodigious piece of work. In its final 11-volume form (completed in 1665 in its Latin edition), it contained 593 maps, spread over 4,608 pages. The French edition, which was finished by 1667, was a touch larger, with 596, while the 'home' edition in Dutch, published two years earlier, had 600. Add to this the German and Spanish editions (the latter being the last to be finished, in 1672) and the entire print-run of probably about 1,550 copies contained over 5 million pages of text. It is estimated that

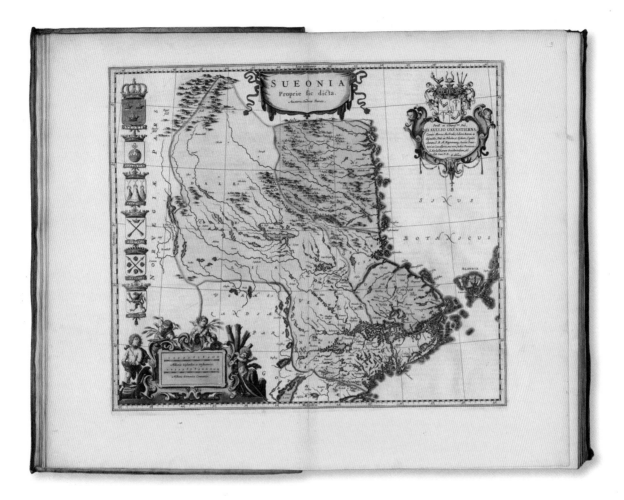

ABOVE

Sueonia [Sweden], *Atlas Maior*, Joan Blaeu, 1662–65

typesetting all the editions would have kept his team of compositors busy for more than six years, and that those nine printing presses would have had to operate for four-and-a-half years. To make things worse, some of the maps had to be hand-tinted, adding even further to the workload and the delays.

The result was an atlas both sumptuous and impossibly expensive, which none of his rivals could possibly hope to compete with, and very few people could afford to buy. The black-and-white version of the *Atlas Maior* cost 350 guilders, while the hand-coloured version carried the price tag of 450 guilders, at a time when humble book-trade assistants were paid but two guilders a week; to afford the deluxe version, they would have to fork out nearly four-and-a-half years of their wages.

Although a gigantic operation, the *Atlas Maior* was not particularly innovative, with the majority of the maps being printed using copperplates that were decades old, and with a heavy concentration on mapping of Britain, Germany and the Netherlands (which was allocated 63 maps, around an eighth of the total). It even reverted in its very first map to a

stereographic projection of the world on two hemispheres, rather than the by-then well-established Mercator projection. Even so, it proved a handsome commercial success: with an eye to diplomacy, the translated editions are dedicated to powerful sovereigns, including Emperor Leopold I of Austria (for the Latin version) and Louis XIV of France (for the French edition). Blaeu also had a copy sent to the Ottoman sultan Mehmed IV, who was said to have been mightily impressed and ordered a personal translation into Turkish. The atlas itself was so large that copies often had their own individually carved walnut cabinet for their transportation and suitable display after arrival.

By now the business was beginning to pass into the hands of a third generation of Blaeus, Joan's sons Joan II (1650–1712), Willem (1635–1701) and Pieter (1637–1706). But the dynasty's era of prosperity and the Dutch dominance of the cartographic trade was also coming to an end. A disastrous fire ripped through the Blaeu printing works on 23 February 1672, causing over half a million guilders of damage. The elder Joan died the following December, and his children struggled to rebuild the operation. By now the Dutch were facing growing competition from the English (with whom they fought three maritime wars between 1652 and 1674) and the French, whose closure of their ports to Dutch shipping in 1672 caused considerable commercial damage.

In this more difficult atmosphere, people were less willing to take risks, and investing in (or even buying) expensive large-format atlases became less fashionable. A number of the copperplates had already been destroyed in the 1672 fire, and between 1674 and 1694 the rest of the *Atlas Maior* plates were sold off, compromising the Blaeus' ability to produce any new products. In 1696, the business was wound up and seven years' later the VOC removed the Blaeu name from its remaining mapping.

The mania for producing ever larger atlases reached its final conclusion in the 1660s with the binding up of Dutch wall maps into giant atlases. The very largest of these was the *Klencke Atlas*, presented by the Amsterdam merchant Johannes Klencke to Charles II on the occasion of his restoration to the British throne. Measuring an impressive 176cm x 231cm (5ft 9in x 7ft 6in) when open, it contained 41 plates showcasing the finest cartographic and engraving skills of the golden age of Dutch map-making. At around 200kg (440lbs) in weight, its sheer bulk must have made regular consultation difficult, although one of the maps it contains, by Hugo Allard of the British Isles, has significant wear damage, suggesting that its particular interest to the British court did cause it to be examined more frequently. It took six librarians at the British Library, where it has been lodged since 1828, to move the elephantine volume when it was first put on public display in a 2010 exhibition. Similar giant wall atlases were put together for Johan Maurits van Nassau, who gave his in 1664 to the 'Great Elector', Friedrich Wilhelm of Brandenberg, and for Duke Christian I of Mecklenburg for his own use. Perhaps unsurprisingly, the huge cost and effort required to create such mammoth map books meant that they did not become commonplace. The three that do survive have preserved valuable wall-maps, whereas those that were actually hung on walls often perished through the effects of light, damp, overuse and sheer neglect.

The concentration on producing ever larger versions of essentially the same thing (an expanded version of the Mercator atlas with the addition of a leavening of new material) had reaped short-term dividends for those able to invest in the race. Yet it had not entirely stifled other forms of map-making in the Netherlands, or crowded out competitors abroad.

At the other end of the scale, Dutch cartographers continued to produce pocket atlases for a more general market and Jodocus Hondius himself published an *Atlas Minor* in 1607 with 152 maps reduced from his larger Mercator atlas, and an atlas under the same name (but with 146 specially produced maps) was brought out by Johannes Janssonius (1588–1664) in 1628. Specialists works, such as historical atlases, also continued to gain ground, with one entitled *Theatrum geographiae veteris* ('The Theatre of Old Geography') compiled by Petrus Bertius, which included a reproduction of the Roman *Peutinger Table* (p.31), coming out in 1618. A more comprehensive *Accuratissima orbis antiqui delineatio* ('A Most accurate Description of the Ancient World') came out in 1652 which used some plates taken from Ortelius's *Parergon*, but added a selection of maps covering the Biblical and classical worlds, as well as a four-sheet version of the *Peutinger Table*, all researched by Georg Horn, a professor of geography and history at the University of Leiden.

Of more immediately practical use, the Dutch shipping industry's need for navigational charts meant that the market for Waghenaers (or wagoneers) and rutters (p.97) continued to be healthy. Willem Janszoon Blaeu's own *Het Licht der Zeevaerdt* underwent no fewer than six editions between 1608 and 1629, facing off rivalry from Claeszoon's new edition of Waghenaer's original pilot guide (published as *Nieuwe thresoor der zee-vaert* in 1609), but suffering the occupational hazard of plagiarism, this time by his perennial rival Janssonius. As a result, in 1623 Blaeu published yet another pilot guide, the *Zeespiegel* ('Sea Mirror'), which his publishing house guided through 15 editions between then and 1653.

Further versions followed, each seemingly with a more outlandish name than its competitors, all intended, no doubt, to gain attention in a crowded market. Jacob Colom (1600–73) produced the *De Vyerighe Colom* ('The Sea Column') in 1632, its title a playful reference to his own name, which earned its own counter-reference when Pieter Goos published the *Zeespiegel* in 1650, which in its English edition was entitled 'The Lightning Column' (and included an inscription charmingly giving Goos's address as 'on the water at the Sign of the Golden Sea Mirror'). Colom rather provocatively challenged Blaeu in *De Vyerighe Colom*, when he explained that his purpose was to ensure 'The defects and errors of the previous Light or Mirror of the Sea are exposed and corrected'. He nevertheless managed to survive in the cut-throat world of Amsterdam map publishing, bringing out over twenty editions of the Fiery Column (including in English and French) and also issuing two alternative versions, one in portrait form, called *Oprecht Fyrie Columne* ('The Upright Fyrie Columne'), the other in a larger folio format (as *De Groote Lichte ofte Vyerighe Colom*) in 1651.

By the end of the seventeenth century, the baton of leading cartographer had been taken up in the Netherlands by Johannes van Keulen (1654–1715). His *De groote nieuwe vermeerderde zee-atlas ofte water-werelt* ('Great New Enlarged Sea Atlas of the Water World'), published in 1680, was supplemented the following year with a substantial five-volume pilot guide entitled *De nieuwe Groote lichtende zee-fakkel* ('The New Great Shining Sea Beacon'), completed in 1681, which provided the first truly global pilot guide for the Dutch market.

Van Keulen's sea atlas was part of a new genre, a somewhat different stream of atlases to the grand Mercator-style productions of the Blaeus. Unlike the wagoneers and rutters, these covered all the world's coastlines (rather than merely local routes and ports described by the pilot guides) and could be used on board ship for more general planning, as well as on land by merchants or as a prestige item. Somewhat in the spirit of the old portolans, the first maritime atlas appeared in 1650, published by Johannes Janssonius, appropriately enough under the name the *Waterwereld* ('Water world'). It led to a cascade of competitors, including Arnold Colom's (1624–68) *Zee-Atlas ofte waterwereldt* ('Sea Atlas of the Water World') in 1658 and his father Jacob Colom's *Atlas of werelts-water-deel* ('Atlas of the Watery Part of the World') in 1663.

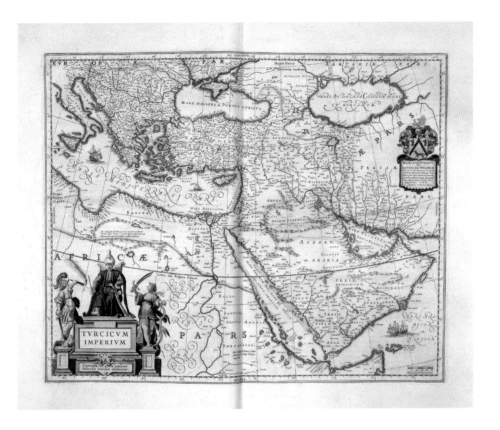

ABOVE

Turkish Empire, *Accuratissima orbis antiqui delineatio*, Georg Horn, published by Johannes Janssonius, 1654

Many of the charts that appeared in these publications had previously been restricted by the VOC. The inevitable plagiarism and rampant copying meant this information leaked out of the Netherlands, allowing foreigners such as England's John Seller (1632–97) to produce their own pilot guides. The chief hydrographer to Charles II, Seller was a mathematician-cartographer who was tasked with the project of producing a survey of the British coastline to match that which the Dutch authorities enjoyed. It resulted in a five-volume *English Pilot*, whose publication began in 1671, but which ultimately extended to the whole world (and featured a good number of copied Dutch charts, including those of Pieter Goos), fulfilling Seller's ambition of 'making a Sea Waggoner for the Whole World'. Seller had nearly not lived to reach such an exalted position, being arrested on charges of high treason in 1662 for allegedly having passed on rumours about a plot to assassinate the king. Although he was later released, his apparent co-conspirators were executed, and he dedicated The *English Pilot* to the Duke of York (later James II) to whom he had appealed from this prison cell in the Tower of London, and who may have had a hand in his release.

Seller also produced a more direct competitor to the Dutch sea atlases, with his *Atlas Maritimus* in 1675, but a plan to publish a comprehensive atlas of Britain, the *Atlas Anglicanus*, came to nothing. Mapping Britain had proved a troublesome task, not

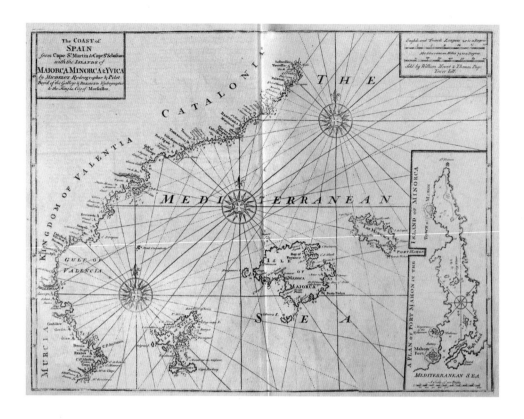

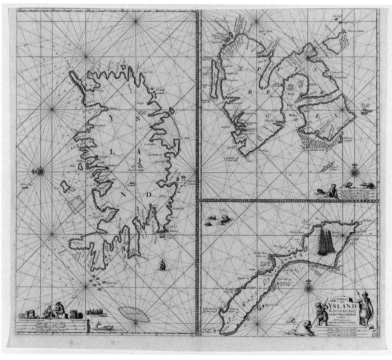

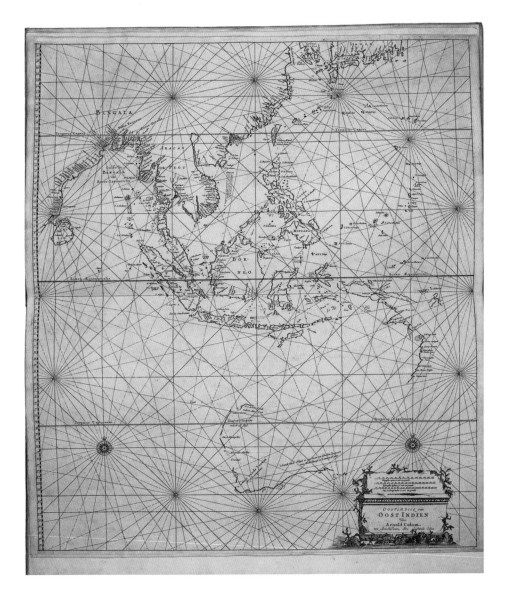

OPPOSITE, TOP

Spanish coast, *The English Pilot*, **John Seller, 1671 (1771 copy)**

OPPOSITE, BOTTOM

Iceland, Jan Mayen Island and Spitsbergen, *De nieuwe groote lichtende zee-fakkel*, **Johannes van Keulen, 1681**

LEFT

East Indies, *Atlas of werelts-water-deel*, **Jacob Colom, 1663**

It includes an outline of part of the coast of western Australia.

helped, as Christopher Saxton and John Norden had found to their cost (p.119), by the reluctance of successive monarchs to provide adequate finance. This task had fallen to John Speed (1552–1629), who began his career as a tailor in Cheshire before turning to cartography in the 1580s. He seems to have been something of a diplomat, since he attracted the attention of scholars such as Sir Robert Cotton (whose collection of manuscripts ultimately formed the core of the British Library) and William Camden, whose *Britannia*, a great topographical survey of the country providing an unparalleled collection of local histories and geographies, was published in 1586, and whose interest in a parallel project mapping Britain was clear. More importantly, perhaps, Speed secured the patronage of Sir Fulke Greville, a cultured courtier who combined literary ability (as the biographer of the poet Philip Sidney) with a certain quixotic chivalry (he asked the Queen to allow him to accompany Sir Francis Drake on an expedition against the Spanish West Indies in 1585) and hard-headed ability (he would later be

Treasurer of the Navy and Commissioner of the Treasury). He secured for Speed a comfortable position and salary in the Customs which, as Sidney later put it, freed him 'from the daily imployments of a manuall Trade . . . giving it full liberty thus to express the inclination of mind'.

Free from immediate financial worries, Speed embarked on a new survey of English counties, intended to match and surpass that of Saxton. He began with his home county of Cheshire and, the results proving satisfactory, he spent the next decade and a half surveying the rest of the country. He also added to his growing list of patrons the great Dutch cartographer Jodocus Hondius (p.125), who also seems to have contributed financially to the project and who lent his expertise by engraving a number of plates. The result, in 1611, was Speed's *Theatre of the Empire of Great Britaine*, the first atlas to be published that covered the whole of the British Isles, and which came just eight years after the personal Union of England and Scotland under Elizabeth I's cousin James I (or VI, as he had been in Scotland). The 67 maps in the atlas included an overall one of Great Britain and Ireland, a historical map of the Anglo-Saxon Heptarchy (in a distant echo of Matthew Paris's work, p.57), one of each of the constituent nations (England, Wales, Scotland and Ireland), 44 for the English counties, 13 for the Welsh and four for the provinces of Ireland (with Scotland having to make do with just its overall map). The level of information provided exceeded that of Saxton, with many locations omitted by his predecessor now included, and he rounded off the work with an array of town plans and a huge amount of antiquarian and topographic information (as befitted a protégé of Camden), so that the whole swarms with battle scenes, the coats of arms of local notables and pictures of local sites, such as that of Stonehenge, which adorns the county map of Wiltshire.

So successful was Speed's atlas and so high was the bar that it set for any future competitors, that it rather stifled any future such projects, a situation not helped by the chronic instability which gripped the country from the 1630s and led to a series of civil wars between 1639 and 1648, the execution of King Charles I the following year, and then the establishment of England's only period of republican rule, before the final restoration of the monarchy in 1660. In such turbulent times there was little room for map-makers. A few counties were resurveyed in the later seventeenth century, but nothing like the comprehensive surveys of Saxton and Norden was attempted. In some cases Saxton's plates were still being used into the eighteenth century, long after they had become out of date. The whole atlas was republished in 1676, with the addition of new maps of Massachusetts, New York, the Carolinas, Virginia, Florida, Jamaica and Barbados, a sign of Britain's fledgling empire, that would eventually help elevate it to the level of both political and a cartographic superpower.

Before that could happen, there was much work to be done at home. A rather colourful character, John Ogilby (1600–76) was Scottish born, and rescued his family from poverty (his father having been imprisoned for debt) through the unlikely recourse of buying a lottery ticket, which won him enough to both obtain his father's release and to set up his own dancing school. He then managed to secure a position as the tutor to the children of Thomas Wentworth, the Earl of Strafford and Charles I's principal favourite, whom he accompanied to Ireland when the Earl was appointed Lord Deputy there.

NOVISSIMA TOTIUS TERRARUM

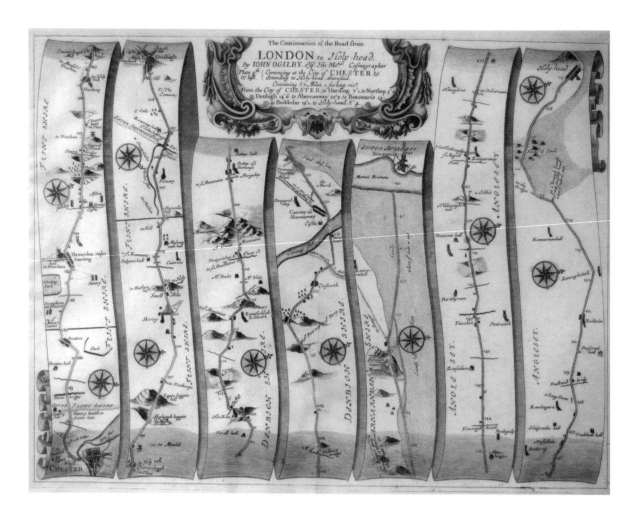

ABOVE

Continuation of the Road
from London to Holyhead,
Britannia, John Ogilby, 1675

Ogilby's stratospheric ascent seemed unstoppable. His connection to Strafford allowed him to establish Ireland's very first theatre, the Theatre Royal in Dublin, which turned him a handsome profit. Then, disaster struck. With the darkening of politics back in England, where Parliament had become first restive, and then downright rebellious, the Earl was recalled to help his king navigate his way out of trouble. When this failed, Parliament demanded his removal, and Charles, weak as ever, acceded and signed Strafford's death warrant, sending his former favourite to his execution by beheading on Tower Hill on 12 May 1641 before a crowd said to number in the hundreds of thousands.

Scarcely had Ogilby's patron met his end, than an Irish rebellion erupted, which both made life dangerous for those associated with the English monarchy and led to the bankruptcy of the Theatre Royal. Ogilby turned tail and fled for home, his discomfiture compounded by a shipwreck in the Irish Sea in which he nearly perished.

Destitute and without influential backers, most men would have subsided into quiet despair, but not Ogilby. He dedicated himself to learning Latin and Greek, then, on the back of his marriage to the heiress Christina Hunsdon, he set up a printing business in London, published a best-selling version of *The Fables of Aesop*, and by the time of the Restoration of Charles II in 1661, his star had risen again sufficiently to secure a role in the composition of speeches and odes for the royal coronation. To complete his triumphant return to fortune, he brought out a new translation of Homer's *Iliad* (though his parvenu credentials earned him the ridicule of Dryden in his *Mac Flecknoe*, where he archly wrote that 'from dusty shops neglected authors come'. Ogilby's *Iliad* did inspire Alexander Pope to his own, rather superior, translation, however).

With a safe sinecure as Master of the Royal Revels in Ireland from 1662, Ogilby finally turned his hand to cartography, a logical choice considering his connections in the printing industry, being appointed 'His Majesty's Cosmographer' in 1674. By that time he had published a number of atlases, some of them as a collaboration with the Dutch cartographer Jacob van Meurs (*c.* 1619–80), including volumes on Africa and Japan (1670) and an *Atlas Chinensis* (1671). Ogilby, however, had his sights set higher than these rather derivative ventures and, fired by the thought of further royal patronage, he had already begun on his most ambitious project yet, no less than an entirely new map of Britain. To achieve it, he took three years to survey the length and breadth of the land, travelling around 26,000 miles (nearly 42,000km) along the way.

The result, published in 1675, was striking, though perhaps not entirely what Charles II had in mind. Operating on the paltry salary of £13 6s and 8d a year, and with projected expenses amounting to over £20,000, Ogilby finally produced *Britannia*, which amounted to 300 pages, with 100 map plates, and weighed in at an impressive 6.8 kg (15 lbs). Crucially, it contained, not a simple topographical map of the country, but a series of strip maps, showing the principal roads and other routes between England's main towns (with a few sallies into Wales). All unnecessary material was stripped out, though he did include a number of decorative engravings, such as those of Neptune and the nymph Thetis (the mother of Achilles), who hold a banner-like scroll bearing the title of the plate showing the section from London to Flamborough Head in Yorkshire.

Britannia was, in short, the first real road atlas (a far more practical proposition than the *Peutinger Table*, p.31; or Matthew Paris's itinerary maps, p.57), and one which triumphantly fulfilled his stated aim 'to compleat within the space of two Years a Work . . . considering the Actual survey of the Kingdom, the Delineation and Dimensuration of the Roads, the Prospects and Ground plots of Cities, with other Ornamentals'. Though six volumes were projected, one of which was to be dedicated solely to London, he never got past the first in the set. Nonetheless, even though he could not benefit from the £34 for the six-volume set (equivalent to about £7,000 today) which he had hoped, Ogilby did very well indeed out of *Britannia* (though the king's contribution was far less than hoped for, as Charles II only in the end granted his royal cosmographer £1,000. The demand was so great that he had to produce four new editions within two years to keep up.

Britannia was innovative in other ways, too. Each of its plates, which between them mapped out 73 principal roads, was drawn at a uniform scale of an inch to a mile, the first time this had been achieved. It all added to the utility of the volume – if only it had not been too heavy to act as a practical guide. Others, though, saw the possibilities and before long Ogilby found himself suffering the fate of many of the early modern cartographers: he was pirated by others, including Thomas Bassett and Richard Chiswell who, much to Ogilby's fury, added in some maps derived from *Britannia* to their 1676 edition of Speed's *Theatrum Orbis Britanniae*.

Pocket editions, far more portable and suited to life on the road, began to come out and in 1719 a full miniature version of *Britannia* was published. By then, however, Ogilby was long dead and buried, far from his native Scotland in St Bride's churchyard in London. His true memorial, however, was *Britannia*, which finally enabled travellers in England and Wales to escape the haphazard nature of route finding which had in 1668 caused Samuel Pepys and his wife to have to pay a guide 22 shillings and sixpence to be shown the way along the short distance between Huntingdon and Oxford.

In some senses England still lay at the periphery of the cartographic world in Europe, where, as well as in the Netherlands, significant map publishers continued to produce atlases both in Italy and in Germany. In the latter in 1623, Matthäus Merian the Elder (1593–1650), a Swiss-born printer who learnt his trade in Zurich, took over the operation of the Frankfurt printing house of his father-in-law Johann Theodor de Bry, which had made a speciality of producing accounts of the exploration of the New World, complete with lavish engravings (such as those portraying Spanish atrocities against the indigenous population of Mexico, which illustrated the *Short Account of the Destruction of the Indies* by the Spanish friar Bartolomé de las Casas). Merian used this platform to produce a number of map-heavy works, including the *Theatrum Europaeum*, a 21-volume account of recent history, complete with maps and plans, and the more focused *Topographia Germaniae*, issued in 16 volumes between 1642 and 1654, which dealt with the development of the Holy Roman Empire, but also included a substantial number of plans of German towns. A more pointed sign of the times was the Merian press's production of *Amore Pacis* ('For the Love of Peace'), which was ordered by the Swedish court to show the battles fought by Swedish troops and the locations of garrisons involved in the Thirty Years' War (1618–48). Sweden's part in the war began with intervention by its king Gustavus Adolphus in north Germany to assist the beleaguered Protestant cause there and ended with a final invasion of Bavaria in 1648, costing in between the life of Gustavus himself, Sweden's most talented general, at the Battle of Lützen in 1632.

The nation that would emerge most strengthened out of that war, and the terms of the Peace of Westphalia which ended it, was France. Its main adversary, the Catholic Habsburgs who ruled both Spain and Austria (and the southern Netherlands, a running sore on France's borders), lost ground and military reputation and nearly bankrupted themselves. In cartographic terms, France was a comparative late-comer, its industry owing much to the Italian Catherine de Medici, the wife of Henri II, who had engineered the appointment of André Thevet (p.115) as the first *Cosmographe du roi* in 1561. In 1570, his successor Nicolas de Nicolay (1517–83) was commissioned to produce a work containing 'maps and descriptions of all the provinces in the kingdom'. Two years later, the outbreak in France of a series of religious wars (whose most notorious episode was the murder of 2,000 Huguenots – French Protestants – in Paris in the St Bartholomew's Day Massacre in August 1572) meant that for the next three decades there was little attention to be spared for cartography, and Nicolay's project was abandoned after he had completed work in just three provinces in central France. It was only in 1594 that Maurice Bouguereau (d. 1596) published *Le Theatre François,* the first atlas of France. Although its 14 regional maps did not quite cover the whole of France, the point that the nation was a unity (sorely needed after the fratricidal division of the Wars of Religion) was made by the inclusion of a portrait of Henri, Duke of Navarre. A popular figure, he had become King Henri IV in 1589, abjuring his Protestantism in 1593 in order to secure Catholic support (commenting notably that *'Paris vaut bien une Messe'* – 'Paris is well worth a Mass'), and finally bringing Peace to the nation by the 1598 Edict of Nantes which legally established toleration for Protestant worship.

Bouguereau's atlas was reissued in 1620 by the Paris engraver Jean Le Clerc, himself a Huguenot who had been forced to flee Paris during the Wars of Religion. No further comprehensive national atlas was attempted for over 50 years, even though Melchior Tavernier (1594–1665), from yet another Protestant family (and whose Antwerp-born

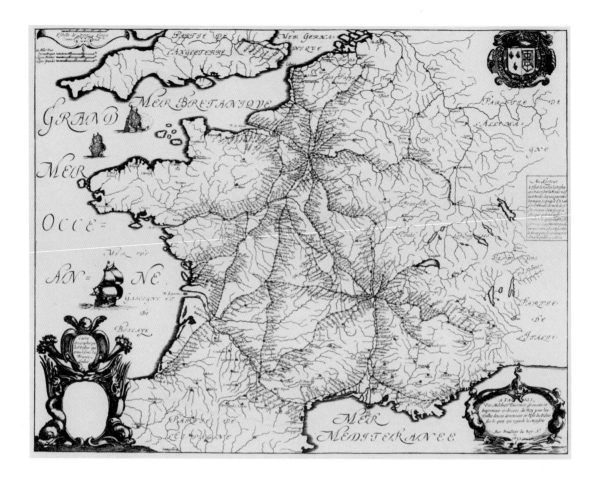

Post Roads of France,
Nicolas Sanson, 1632

father Gabriel had worked on Le Clerc's atlas), published a map of the post-roads of France (essentially the main routes), some of which extended as far as Brussels, or Turin, but which did not provide anything like a comprehensive new image of the French landscape.

The cartographer of this map was Nicolas Sanson (1600–67), who owed his success to a lucky stroke of fortune enabled by Cardinal Richelieu, Chief Minister to the young Louis XIII. Sanson's early love of maps had led him to devote himself to historical cartography, a career choice which led to nothing but penury until a map he had made of ancient Gaul came by chance to the attention of Richelieu in 1627. The Cardinal was impressed and, after an audience with the king, Sanson was appointed personal tutor to the king on geographical matters and also 'Geographer in Ordinary' with a stipend of 2,000 livres a year. As well as allowing him to work on the Post Roads map, the official salary gave him the breathing space to build a career in which he privileged scientific observation and research over artistic flourishes. He moved on from his partnership with Tavernier to an even more successful one with Pierre Mariette, which yielded the *Carte Generale de Toutes les Parties du Monde* ('General Map of all the Parts of the World') in 1658 and a series of

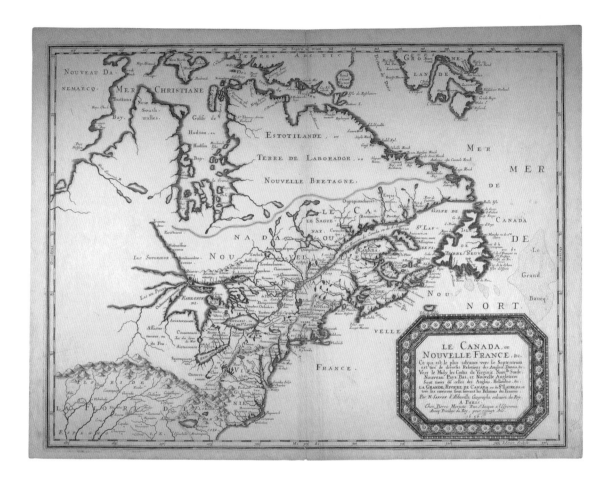

ABOVE

Le Canada ou Nouvelle France,
Nicolas Sanson, 1656

maps of the New World. Notable among these was *Le Canada ou Nouvelle France* in 1656, the first map of the new French territories in Canada since those produced following the original explorations of Samuel de Champlain almost half a century beforehand.

Sanson compiled a map for Richelieu around 1643 showing the boundaries of the *gouvernements-généraux*, the administrative regions into which France was divided, though the map has not survived. Then, in 1653, he compiled another large map of France, the modestly named *Carte et description general du tres-haut, tres-puissant et tres chrestien royaume de France* ('Map and general Description of the most high, most powerful and most Christian kingdom of France'). A project to develop this into 250 local maps, creating a truly comprehensive atlas of France, which Sanson himself admitted was 'among the most difficult of undertakings', proved beyond him and was abandoned. That task would have to await a new generation of cartographers, led by the Cassini family (p.166).

Sanson's work, though, did survive him. In 1695, Alexis-Hubert Jaillot (1632–1712) produced a large atlas of 95 maps, benefitting from his having taken over Sanson's

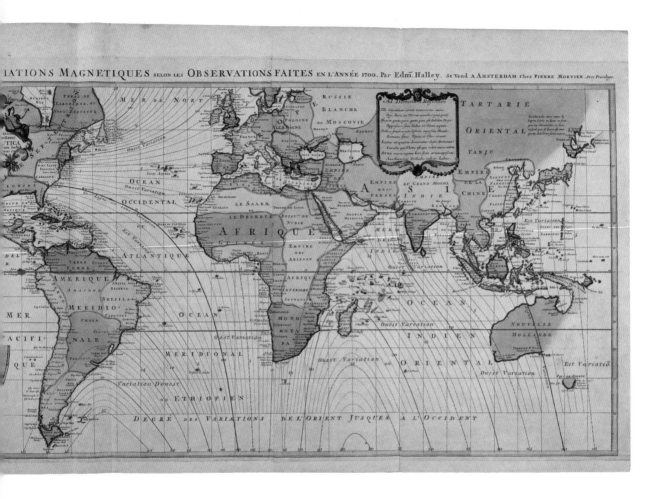

IATIONS MAGNETIQUES selon les OBSERVATIONS FAITES en l'Année 1700. Par Edm. Halley. Se Vend A AMSTERDAM chez PIERRE MORTIER. Avec Privilege.

materials and engraved copperplates. Yet another map-maker to achieve the position of *Geographe du roi*, this time to Louis XIV, Jaillot's prolific publishing and highly respected style led his name to be associated even with atlases that he did not produce, such as the *Neptune François*, a maritime atlas of the French coast which stemmed from the survey originally ordered by Colbert, the king's chief minster, in 1660, but whose results were kept secret until finally published in full in Paris in 1693 (with a frontispiece suitably glorifying the 'Sun King' with an image of the rising sun); it was later pirated by the Dutch publishers Pieter Mortier, whose French edition became attached to the name of Jaillot.

Sanson was not alone in his preoccupation with the historic and such antiquarian atlases appeared in increasing numbers as the seventeenth century progressed. Among the more remarkable was Michael Florent van Langren's Map of the Moon, published around 1645. Van Langren (1598–1675) was from a family of cartographers who, unusually, had fled Dutch Protestant territory for the Catholic Habsburg-controlled southern Netherlands rather than the more normal reverse migration. There he succeeded in securing the patronage of King Philip IV of Spain, to whom he became royal cartographer. As well as more conventional cartography, including drawing a map of Brabant, which appeared in Blaeu's *Novus Atlas* of 1635 (p.139), he pursued the interests of his grandfather, Jacob Floris van Langren, who had been a globemaker, and combined them with an intent to solve the problem of calculating longitude at sea. Van Langren's observations led him to create the first ever statistical graph in 1644, charting the difference in estimates of longitude between Toledo and Rome.[4] He also believed that the determination of longitude could be assisted by making observations of the Moon during its regular 28-day cycles (or during eclipses), taking note of the positions of craters or peaks on the Earth's satellite (a practice only recently made possible by the invention of the telescope by Hans Lippershey in 1608). The result was the first ever map of the Moon in 1645, including a variety of names for the various lunar features, most of which did not stick, with the notable exception of the Langrenus Crater on the *Mare Fecundatis* (Sea of Fertility), which he named for himself.

ABOVE

Map from *Les acquisitions*
de la France par la paix,
Pierre Duval, 1660

More conventional historical mapping was produced by Philippe Briet (1601–68), a French Jesuit, whose order demonstrated its dedication to the strengthening of Catholicism through education by using geography as a tool to shape young minds, including a set of maps of the classical world which he included in his *Parallela Geographiae Veteris et Novae* ('Parallels of Old and New Geography') in 1648–49. Religious sensibility also shaped the demand for atlases of the Holy Land, such as Philippe de la Rue's *La Terre sainte en six cartes géographiques* ('The Holy Land in Six Geographical Maps'), published in 1651. More connected to a growing sense of nation and of pride in conquest was Pierre Duval's *Les acquisitions de la France par la paix*, published in 1660, which chronicled the military gains of Louis XIV, and included for the first time a consistent series of fortification and battlefield maps.

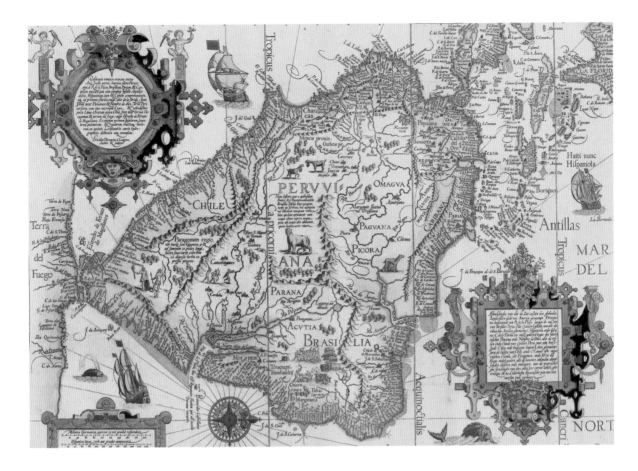

By the end of the century, Nicolas de Fer (1646–1720), from yet another cartographic dynasty (his father, Antoine de Fer, had also been a map publisher), produced *Les forces de l'Europe* (1690–95), which included dozens of maps of towns and their fortifications, largely in Europe, as the title suggests, but also extending to Batavia (Jakarta) in the East Indies, and Quebec in French North America. De Fer produced his first map, of the Canal du Midi, in his early twenties, and became official cartographer to Louis XIV's eldest son, Louis the Dauphin, in 1690. The prince's early death in 1711 meant he never became Louis XV and de Fer ultimately ended up as cartographer to Louis XIV's grandson, who would become Philip V of Spain. De Fer tapped into a sense of national pride and an interest in the type of fortifications designed by the great French military engineer Sébastien Le Prestre de Vauban. His was a cartography of national self-confidence. All that was lacking was a full, scientifically surveyed map of all those nations that had emerged from the furnace of the religious wars of the previous century and the testing grounds of royal absolutism and increasingly centralized (and to some extent efficient) bureaucracies. That mapping would be a matter for another century.

ABOVE

South America, the Caribbean, Florida and the Gulf Coast, Arnold Florent van Langren, 1596

On avertit que ce Livre est la Seconde partie de l'Introduction a la Fortification, dont la Premiere a été donnée L'Année derniere, et que le Sr. de Fer en donnera tous les Ans une partie composée de pareil nombre de Plans. Avec Privilege du Roy. 1693.

ABOVE AND RIGHT

Title page (left); fortifications of Valetta (right), *Les forces de l'Europe*, Nicolas de Fer, 1690–95

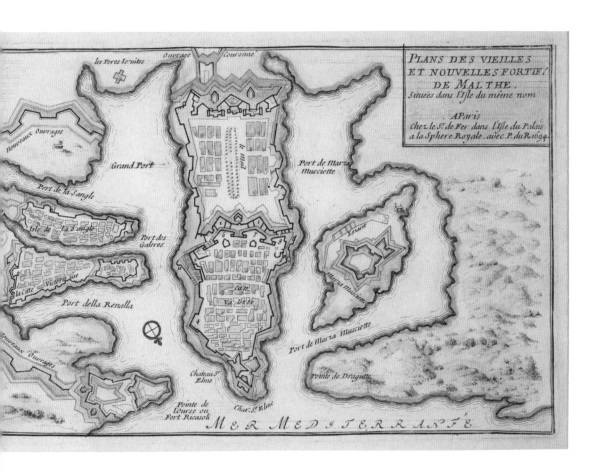

les Peres le uitres

Ouvrage Couronne

Nouveaux Ouvrages

Grand Port

Port de la S.angle

le mail

Port de Marza Musciette

Isle de la S.angle

Port des Galeres

la Citte Victorieuse

Port della Renalla

Marza Musciette

citte Va Lette

Nouueaux Ouvrages

Port de Marza Musciette

Chateau S. Elme

Pointe de Dragutte

Pointe de l'ourse ou Fort Ricasoli

Chat. S. Elme

MER MEDITERRANÉE

PLANS DES VIEILLES
ET NOUVELLES FORTIF.
DE MALTHE.
Situées dans l'Isle du même nom

A Paris
chez le S.r de Fer dans l'Isle du Palais
a la Sphere Royale. avec P. du R. 1694

MAPPING
THE NATION
(1700–1800)

By 1700, Europe had emerged from the turmoil of the previous century, with the religious wars in France and Germany, the civil wars in the British Isles and the Time of Troubles – a period of dynastic crisis and civil war that racked Russia from 1598 to 1613 – but distant memories. Increasingly self-confident monarchies, above all those in France and Britain, sought to harness scientific advances, most especially in military technology (such as the new *trace italienne* fortresses designed by the French engineer Sébastien Le Prestre de Vauban (1633–1707), star-shaped bastions built with overlapping fields of fire to mitigate the impact of gunpowder weaponry and artillery on the defenders), but also in cartography. This was put to use both to map the frontiers – the expanding ones in the case of Louis XIV's War of Devolution (1667–68) and other land grabs in the Netherlands – and to produce more comprehensive maps of the core of royal domains. What, in short, eighteenth-century governments and monarchs wanted was a map of the nation.

The surveys that produced these, and the atlases in which they were published, were a long time in the making. The survey of France consumed an astonishing century-and-a-half and became almost a personal crusade for the four generations of the Cassini family who undertook it. The first of these Cassinis, Giovanni Domenico (1625–1712), was born in Perinaldo, south-west of Genoa, a part of the Italian kingdom of Savoy. A talented astronomer, he moved to France in 1669 at the invitation of Louis XIV and helped set up the Paris Observatory, from where he discovered four satellites of Saturn (Iapetus, Rhea, Tethys and Dione) in the 1670s and 1680s, although he clung tenaciously to the outmoded notion that the Earth was at the centre of the Solar System. It was astronomy that would provide the kernel of the grand plan to map France along more consistent lines than had been achieved by Nicholas Sanson in the 1650s, p.156). Cassini's astronomical studies had included adapting a method described by Galileo for determining longitude by reference to an eclipse of Jupiter's Moons. In an echo of the technique employed two thousand years ago by Eratosthenes (p.20), Cassini realized that if the eclipse could be observed at precisely the same time in two different places and the time registered, this could be used to determine the relative longitude of those places. His insight fortuitously coincided with the initiative being developed by Louis XIV's exceptionally able finance minister, Jean-Baptiste Colbert (1619–83), who wished for a map for his master that would encompass 'the smallest hamlets and assarts, even chateaux, farms and private houses that stand alone and away from the parishes.'[1]

Yet to do so would be prohibitively time-consuming (and expensive) if undertaken by the time-honoured techniques of sending out large teams of surveyors to log the land painstaking yard by painful mile. To carry it out, Colbert instead brought together the expertise of Abbé Jean Picard (1620–82), a priest with a passion for topography and surveying (who was, like Cassini, a member of the Académie des Sciences, a society of elite scientists founded by Colbert in 1666) with that of Domenico Cassini. Using Cassini's methods to establish longitude, and then terrestrial measurement carried out with quadrants to calculate the latitude of points on the ground, Picard aimed to lay out an arc running north–south along a line of longitude, between Malvoisine (near Paris) and Sourdon (in the region of Amiens). From this meridian line, further triangulations could be made, ultimately creating a web right across the territory of France.

The initial stages did not go well. It turned out that the instruments being used by a certain David du Vivier, who had been tasked with the practical work on the ground, were not accurate enough. Adjustments were made and Picard took over much of the work, completing the projected meridian line by 1670. The result was the *Carte particulière des environs de Paris* ('Particular Map of the Environs of Paris'), based on Vivier's work and only finally published in 1674. Its scale at 1:86,400 represented one ligne (roughly a twelfth of an inch) to 100 toises (a toise was just under 1.95 m). The units reflected the old pre-Revolutionary measurements in France, before the Napoleonic regime introduced the metric system in the 1790s. The engravers, F. de la Pointe, also employed the innovation of using short stroke-lines or hachures to show elevation, so introducing the contour lines which came to appear on almost all modern maps.

The project was now extended to mapping the French coastlines in their entirety, a process that Picard began in Brittany in 1679, but which took him until 1684 to complete, and which was published as the *Carte de France corrigée* ('Corrected Map of France'). Much to the rather nervous surprise of everyone involved, the map revealed that the area of France,

BELOW

Carte particulière des environs de Paris, 1678

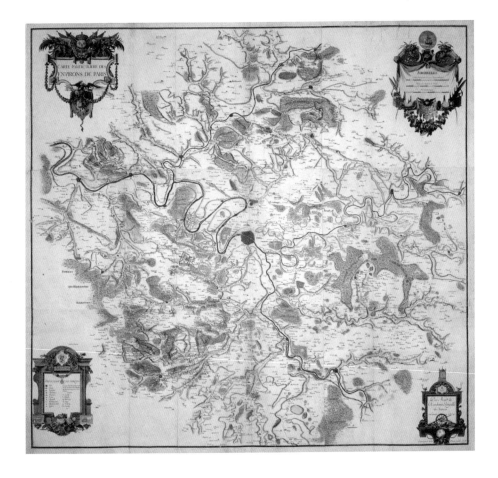

far from being 150,000km² (roughly 58,000mi²) in area, as previously estimated, was just 120,000km² (about 46,000mi²), a diminution of around a fifth. Fortunately, the king took it in good humour, jesting that the survey 'had brought him nothing but loss'. He could, after all, simply enlarge France again by conquering new territory. The wars that achieved this – an invasion of the Spanish Netherlands in 1683, and then the War of the Spanish Succession from 1703, sparked by Louis's ambitions to place his son Philippe on the throne of Spain, so ultimately effecting a union of the two crowns – nearly bankrupted France.

As well as undoing much of Colbert's good work on the reform of the economy, the cost of the war also hampered France's cartographic progress. Colbert himself had died in 1683, and in the absence of such a powerful patron, funds for what had come to seem like an inessential luxury dried up. Matters were rescued after a certain fashion by a seemingly abstruse argument over the shape of the Earth and whether it was a sphere, or an oblate spheroid, with bulges and flattenings at the Poles and the Equator. This mattered because if it turned out to be a spheroid, then the values of a degree of latitude and longitude would not be the same as if it were a perfect sphere, and all cartographic calculations based on that premise would have to be revised.

A new calculation was made, based on a survey by Jacques Cassini (1677–1756), Domenico's son, carried out between Bourges and Collioure in 1700–01, which strongly suggested that the Earth bulged at the Poles, making it shaped rather like a lemon (and also technically, a prolate, rather than an oblate spheroid). It also meant that the length of a degree diminished towards the Poles. The surveys staggered on fitfully: Jacques Cassini – now fully in control of the family business since his father had gone blind – made a northward extension to Picard's lines, running from the Observatory in Paris, all the way to Dunkirk (a distance of 56,960 toises).

There matters rested – enlivened by an argument between the supporters of the British mathematical genius Isaac Newton, who maintained that the Earth was an oblate spheroid, and those of the Cassinis, who defended the prolate cause, a debate which took on darkly nationalistic tones. In 1735, Louis XV was persuaded by his new finance minister, Philibert Orry, Comte de Vignori (1689–1747), a cultured man with a sharp tongue and an acute interest in the sciences, to sponsor an expedition to settle the argument once and for all. One party, including the mathematician and explorer Charles Marie de la Condamine (1701–74), was sent to Peru and slogged through appallingly difficult mountainous and jungle territory (where they were plagued by mosquitoes 'beyond the imagination') to lay out two base meridian lines, one on the Yaruqui plain near Quito, the other at Tarqui, near Cuença, and to survey the more than 300km (186 miles) of mountainous terrain between them. Although it achieved its purpose in establishing the length of the 'toise of Peru', inadequate funding from Paris resulted in Condamine being unable to return home for eight years (although as compensation he became the first European to encounter rubber and was able to carry out valuable work on the protective properties of the bark of the cinchona tree against malaria). A second group was dispatched north, to the Gulf of Bothnia, at the far northern end of the Baltic Sea, where Finland elbows round into Sweden. The icy conditions thwarted the original plan to use islands in the Gulf as the base line and so, paradoxically, the expedition had to head even further north to survey a line in the Lapland forest beginning at Torneå. Its

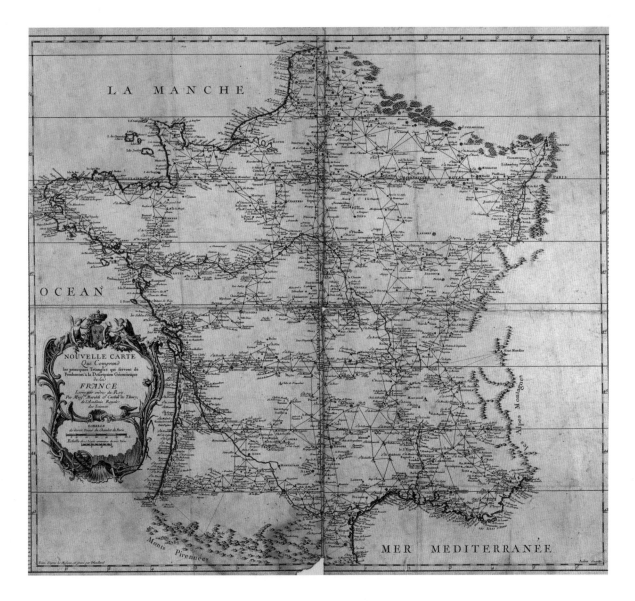

leader, Pierre-Louis Moreau de Maupertuis (1698–1759), had rather more luck than Condamine in returning home, and was able to report his results to the Académie des Sciences in August 1737.

Between them, the two sets of measurements confirmed that the Earth was flattened at the Poles, but bulged at the Equator (and that the planet was in fact really an oblate spheroid, as the British had maintained all along). It also meant that it was now necessary to reconduct the triangulation of the whole of France. The meridian through Paris came first, resurveyed by Jacques' son César-François Cassini de Thury (1714–84) in 1739–40,

and then new lines were laid out on France's eastern border around Nice and from Strasbourg to Speier. The work was arduous, as the terrain in the east of the country was mountainous and locals were suspicious of the outsiders – one group of surveyors was even murdered by villagers in Mézenc in the Ardèches region who confused their strange scientific surveying instruments for magical devices intended to do them harm.

Despite all the obstacles, by 1744 the survey was complete, having created 19 base lines with something like 800 subsidiary triangles in the network. Cassini de Thury published the whole thing in 1744 on 18 sheets, but anyone expecting a comprehensive map of France with 'all the smallest hamlets and assarts' as his grandfather had hoped almost a century before would have been disappointed. It was really just an outline map for future surveys, with much information that had not been directly relevant to the laying out of the triangles omitted, and with some of the areas surveyed by others (such as Languedoc, where the research was carried out by the local Royal Society of Sciences at Montpelier) so of uneven quality.

Other French cartographers did indeed step in to produce maps based around the skeleton which the Cassini de Thury map represented, such as Jean Baptiste Bourguignon d'Anville (1697–1782) and Didier Robert de Vaugondy (1723–86). D'Anville was a cartographic prodigy, helped by the fact that the curriculum at the College des Quatre-Nations in Paris, where he studied, included map-making. He produced his very first map, of ancient Greece, aged just fifteen, following it up with maps for Louis Dufour de Longuerue's *Descriptio historique et géographique de la France ancienne et moderne* ('Historical and Geographical Description of Ancient and Modern France') in 1719 and, with the sponsorship of the influential Duke of Orleans, the positions both of geography tutor to Louis XV and the title of royal geographer. He seems thereafter to have moonlighted for a few years for the Portuguese government (which the Duke was hoping to detach from its country's longstanding alliance with Britain) before returning to his regular duties. An assiduous researcher, he amassed no fewer than 10,500 sheet maps in his personal collection, which enabled him to fine-tune his own maps to an extent others with fewer resources had been unable to match, and produced lengthy memoranda detailing the precise reasoning for his cartographic choices. Although he did not himself publish a significant world atlas, his individual maps, including two general maps of the world, 27 European maps, 44 of Asia, 17 of Africa and 24 of the Americas were frequently bound together by other publishers to create bespoke atlases, and his *Nouvel Atlas de la Chine* ('New Atlas of China', 1737) became particularly popular.

Vaugondy took a more traditional approach. Following in the footsteps of his cartographer-father Gilles, he worked for 15 years to produce the massive *Atlas Universel*, published in 1757. The monumental folio edition and a rather less unwieldy three-quarter-size version were financed by subscription, an increasingly popular choice for such expensive ventures, as the end user received a premium product at a discount, and the publisher's risks were mitigated, knowing he had a guaranteed revenue. As well as the inclusion of a series of historical maps, the more than 100 geographical maps were also supplemented by a special set of five maps of postal roads in Britain, France, Germany, the Iberian Peninsula and Italy, for which subscribers had to pay out an extra six livres, and the whole atlas came in two sizes, 'petit papier' and 'grand papier', which were priced respectively at 96 and 120 livres for subscribers, a discount of 20 per cent off the post-publication price. The fame the *Atlas* brought Vaugondy led to his appointment as royal geographer in 1760, following in a distinguished line that included two of the Cassinis and Jean Baptiste d'Anville. He was particularly respected for the precision of his work, satisfying the aspiration expressed in his 1751 *Usage des Globes*, a work on world globes, that his 'principal aim has been to satisfy the mind with precision and exactitude, but since it is also necessary to please the eyes, I have taken every care possible to insure that the execution of my work corresponds in its beauty to its underlying design.'[2]

All this time, work on the Cassini survey and follow-up publications was proceeding at a snail's pace. Royal preoccupation with war held it up again, as France became embroiled in the Austrian War of Succession in the 1740s, including a number of engagements fought in the Austrian Netherlands. Yet it also piqued royal interest, allowing Cassini de Thury to embark on yet another topographic survey, this time intended to fulfil the original Cassini's ambition and to produce 180 maps on the uniform 1:86,400 scale. So from 1748, out went 20 surveyors organized in 10 teams with an annual budget of a substantial 40,000 livres. Cassini had calculated that if he could sell 2,500 copies of each sheet at a price tag of four livres he would turn a profit of over a million livres (much of which would go to the king as the project's principal investor). The survey was carried out on rigorous lines, with the engineer-surveyors each keeping

BELOW

Amerique Septentrionale (North America), *Atlas Universel*, Gilles Robert Vaugondy and Didier Robert de Vaugondy, 1752 (1757 edition)

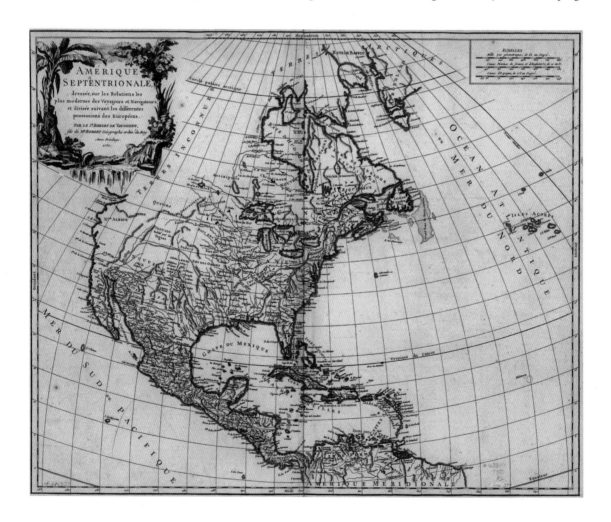

separate logs of the triangulation data they produced and of all the local topographic information they collected, which was supplemented by interviews with those who knew the localities, such as parish priests. Draft sketches of maps were sent to Paris to be assessed and, if necessary, corrected.

All of this was painstakingly slow, and after eight years just two of the 180 maps, including that of Paris where the survey began, were complete. As a result, royal patronage was withdrawn and Cassini de Thury turned to private investors to keep the work going. These included many leading members of the nobility (including the king's own mistress Madame de Pompadour) and Cassini did not disappoint them – fulfilling his promise of releasing one map a month by completing a further 37 over the following three years, and selling hundreds of copies of each. The production quality of the maps was of the highest order and the level of detail astounding for the time. Cassini's attention to detail is seen even in the symbology used, where he set down a standardized set of signs for towns, hamlets, abbeys (a tower with a bishop's crozier) and even the houses of the gentry, which would become standard in French mapping into the modern era.

As a further encouragement to potential investors, from 1758 Cassini offered subscribers the right to purchase the complete set of 180 maps for the discounted price of 562 livres, and more than 200 took up the inducement. Still, though, he did not regard the survey as complete and further financing had to be secured, including a royal decree in 1764 that forced regions to pay a portion of the cost of their own surveying. Despite this, by 1778 around a third of the projected maps had still to be finished. By the early 1780s, a fourth generation of Cassinis had joined the enterprise, with Cassini de Thury's son, Jean-Dominique (1748–1845; often referred to simply as Cassini IV). Tragically Cassini de Thury contracted smallpox and died in 1784, just when the map was on the point of completion. The number of map sheets was increased slightly to 182, and the survey finally concluded in 1789.

But then politics intervened. The outbreak of the French Revolution in July the same year had led to the overthrow of the monarchy and the installation of a National Assembly keen to show its credentials by sweeping away the rotten edifice of the Ancien Régime. Among its early actions was the reorganisation of the French provinces into a system of *départements*, and the Cassini map attracted the interest of one of the Assembly's more radical members, the poet and satirist Fabre d'Églantine (who came up with the names of the months of the French Revolutionary calendar, such as Vendémiaire in September/October, named for the grape harvest). As he pointed out, the information contained in it was of significant military interest and by rights should also belong to the people.

As a result of his urging, in September 1793 the Cassini map was nationalized and officials of the National Assembly seized all its plates. Although Cassini and his shareholders complained, the times were dangerous, as the eddies of the Terror unleashed by the most radical revolutionaries engulfed less nimble revolutionaries, anyone with the remotest of aristocratic connections and finally the radicals themselves, so anything more than muted protest was near suicidal. As many as 17,000 people were executed, largely by the newly invented guillotine, before the Terror's fury was spent. Among them were Maximilien Robespierre, the prime architect of the Terror and Fabre d'Églantine. Cassini IV might have allowed himself a wry smile, as, though arrested (as the director of the Royal

**Caspian Sea and Kamchatka,
Johann Baptist Homann,
1725**

This was one of the first
maps to show the Kamchatka
peninsula, based on a major
Russian naval survey of
1719–21, but still depicts a
mythical large land-mass just
to the east of the peninsula
(variously recorded elsewhere
as Compagnieland or Gama).

Observatory he was an obvious target for radical anger), he was somehow spared. He never returned to cartography, throwing himself instead into politics and achieving the distinction of receiving awards for his services to the nation both from Napoleon and from Louis XVIII.

The Cassini map, which had yielded a heavily cut-down version in 1790 to show the new revolutionary *départements*, was brought to its conclusion by the military, in the form of the Dépôt de la Guerre. The final sheets, of Brittany, were finally published in 1815, just before the fall of the Napoleonic regime. By then, more than 150 years after it had begun, the Cassini map and atlas of France was already becoming redundant, as in 1808 Napoleon had ordered a new survey to begin work on a map to supersede it.

The influence of the Cassinis extended further, however, than simply over their own prolonged journey towards the national map of France. French cartography continued to flourish, with successors not only to the Cassini dynasty, but to Nicolas Sanson (p.156) too.

A contemporary of Alexis-Hubert Jaillot (p.157), Guillaume Delisle (1675–1726) was born into map-making, his father Claude being a respected historian, publisher and cartographer, whose circles in late-eighteenth-century Paris included Sanson and the Cassinis. He collaborated with his father, producing a map of French North America in 1703 and appearing in a 1700 court-case in which a rival cartographer, Jean-Baptiste Nolin, was accused of copying a Delisle world map. By 1702, Delisle's reputation was already such that he was admitted to the Académie des Sciences at the age of just 27. By 1714 he had been appointed geography tutor to the Dauphin (the future Louis XV). Relations between Delisle and his pupil seem to have been cordial and in 1718 the king bestowed on him the newly minted title of *Premier Geographe du roi*, with an annual stipend of 1,200 livres. Sadly, he only enjoyed his elevated status for eight years as he suffered a fatal epileptic seizure one evening on his way home from his cartographic studio. His prolific output included hundreds of maps which were bound into other publishers' atlases, including the *Atlas Nouveau* published by Pieter Mortier (1661–1711) in Amsterdam in 1708, which achieved even greater fame in its Italian version, as the *Atlante Novissimo*, published in Venice in 1740–50.

Germany's long tradition of fine engraving (of which Albrecht Dürer's work from the 1490s was only the artistic peak) gave it an advantage in competing against the more established cartographic centres in Italy and the Netherlands. Foremost among its proponents was Johann Baptist Homann (1664–1724), who had trained to be a Dominican priest before a crisis and conversion to Protestantism caused him to move to Nuremberg, where he learned engraving and set up his own map-publishing business in 1702. By 1707 he had managed to publish his first atlas (the *Atlas bestehend in austerlesenen und allerneuesten Land-Charten über die gantze Welt* ('Atlas Comprising the Selected and Very Latest Country Maps of the Entire World'), with 33 maps, a number which was steadily increased until it became the *Grosser Atlas* in 1716. His success and fame were such that in the same year he was given the title of *Kaiserlicher Geograf* (royal geographer) to the Prussian court, putting him in the esteemed company of such French cartogaphers as Sanson and Vaugondy. His international connections enabled him to gain rapid access to up-to-date surveys rather than relying on endless reprints of decades-old maps, and so his

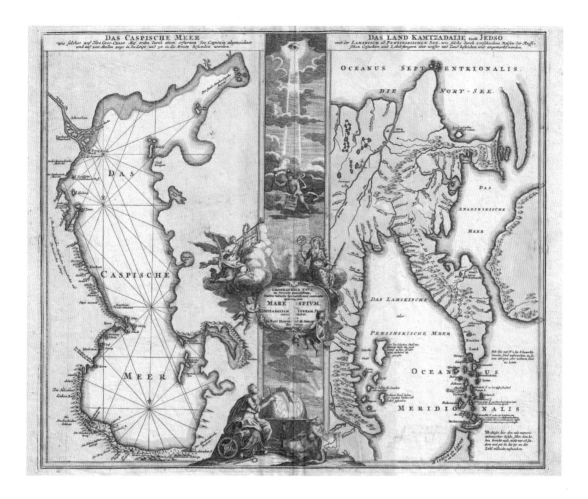

Grosser Atlas contained one of the first modern printed maps of Kamchatka in Russia. He made other innovations, too, and in 1719 published his *Methodischer Atlas* ('Methodical Atlas'), with just 18 maps specially supplied by the geographer Johann Hübner (1668–1731), which was specifically aimed at children. A pioneer in geographical education, Hübner had been rector of prestigious schools in Merseburg and Hamburg, and his *Kurtze Fragen aus der alten und neuen Geographie* ('Short Questions on Old and New Geography', 1693) and *Biblische Historien*, a children's Bible published in 1714, were among the first specialist German textbooks written for schools.

In the same way as the great French cartographic dynasties, the house of Homann survived Johann Baptist's death in 1724, though that of his son Johann Christoph, aged just 27 in 1730, might have put an end to it. Yet it not only survived in the hands of its manager Johann Georg Ebersberger as Homanische Erben ('Homann's heirs'), but even flourished, publishing in 1752 the *Atlas Silesiae* and going on to produce a series of

regional and country atlases such as the *Schweizer Atlas* (1769), *Böhmischer Atlas* (1776) for Bohemia, and the *Niederländischer Atlas* (1788) of the Netherlands. The extent of its reach is indicated by the 50 sales offices which the Homann company had within the Holy Roman Empire alone in 1750 (with a further 25 in other European countries), making it probably the leading supplier of maps in northern Europe.

Among the Homann company's rivals were publishers in Britain. That nation was steadily acquiring an overseas presence which grew from nuclei in North America (above all with the establishment of Jamestown in Massachusetts in 1627) and the Caribbean (where English forces seized Jamaica from the Spanish in 1655). Somewhat later, a first tentative foothold in the Mughal empire acquired in Surat in 1629 mushroomed after the victory of Robert Clive against Siraj-ud-Daula, the Nawab of Bengal in 1757, into a substantial territorial domain. This rapid expansion was accompanied by maps documenting the expeditions of explorers and navigators such as Captain James Cook in Australasia and the South Pacific. Hermann Moll (1654–1732), whose *Atlas Geographicus* (1711–17), which was optimistically sub-titled '*A Compleat System of Geography, Ancient*

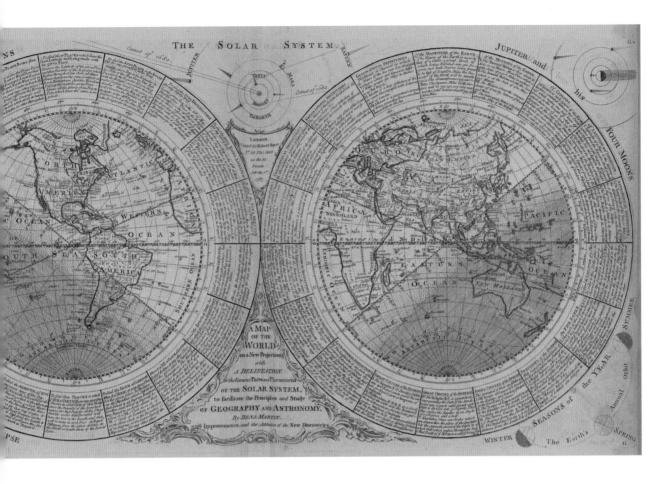

and Modern' – even though it only had two maps of India – was typical. John Senex (1678–1740) was a great rival of Moll. Senex had abandoned a career as a bookseller at the Stationers' Company (one of the old London guilds) to become a cartographer (though with an eclectic range of interests that included geology and astrology), and published his *English Atlas* in 1714, which, despite its name was a collection of two-sheet maps of the world. Its success meant it remained in print until the 1760s (boosting the not-insubstantial profit that Senex made from his other commercial mainstay in terrestrial globes and the reduced edition of Ogilby's *Britannia* which he published in 1719, p.153). By then it was being supplanted by newer rivals such as *A New Atlas of the Mundane System* (1774) by Samuel Dunn (1723–94), a Devon mathematician and astronomer, who fitted it in amidst a plethora of works on seamanship, the calculation of latitude and navigational tables.

A further impetus to the British map trade was given by the duty of 30 per cent on imported books and maps which was levied from 1712, a measure which protected the domestic map trade from outside competition, allowing a new generation of cartographers to flourish. As well as Moll and Senex (who in 1729 added local mapping to his portfolio with *A New Map of the County of Surrey,* drawing on his own surveys), the most prominent was Emanuel Bowen (1694–1767). Born in Carmarthen in Wales, he was apprenticed to John Senex's associate Charles Price – seemingly undeterred by the doubtful prospects of a career which had seen Price reduced to flogging cut-price maritime charts from Fleet Prison, where he had been incarcerated for debt. Among Bowen's most renowned works was one of his earliest, the *Britannia Depicta,* or *Ogilby Improv'd,* published in 1720, which was, as its name suggests, a version of Ogilby's road atlas (p.153), with 273 maps presented in strips like the original, though updated and with additional historical detail included. The printing of the maps on both sides of the paper also made possible a much more portable edition than had been the case with the original *Britannia.* Despite this, and his engraving of a number of other important maps and atlases, including the first based on a triangulation survey of the Orkney Islands and *The Large English Atlas* (1749) produced with his former apprentice (and son-in-law) Thomas Kitchin (1718–84), Bowen's skill and reputation never brought him a fortune, and he died in 1767 in poverty.

As well as producing the map of Scotland surveyed by the military engineer John Elphinstone in 1745 (which in the proprietorial way the English had towards their northern neighbours was entitled *A New and Correct Map of Northern Britain,* with no mention of Scotland at all), Kitchin engraved one of the key maps in North American history. Surveyed by John Mitchell (1711–68), a Virginia born physician and botanist with a penchant for cartography who had studied in Edinburgh. It was compiled as part of an effort to establish (and if possible expand) British claims as against those of the French in eastern North America. With exceptional access to archives as well as his experience of his home territory in Virginia, Mitchell (and Kitchin) did a fine job. The map was sufficiently respected by both sides in the American Revolutionary War that it formed the basis of the negotiations in 1782 that led to the Treaty of Paris which sealed the end of the conflict the following year (including the definitive British recognition of the independence of the United States). So hallowed did the Mitchell map become that it was used as a reference in US–Canadian border disputes about their maritime frontier as late as 1984. Kitchin, meanwhile, received more direct recognition back home than his father-in-law had when he was appointed royal hydrographer to George III in 1773.

Yet another of Bowen's apprentices, Thomas Jefferys (1719–71), received a similar accolade, in being appointed Geographer to Frederick, Prince of Wales, and then (after the prince's death from an abscess in his lungs) to his son George, the future George III, in 1760. He also played a key

role in the mapping of North America, beginning with his publication of *A Map of the Most Inhabited Part of Virginia* (1753) and *An Accurate Map of His Majesty's Province of New Hampshire* (1757). He also developed a curious sideline in board games and puzzles based on maps, including a 1770 map game entitled 'The Royal Geographical Pastime, a Complete Tour Thro' England and Wales' (followed up a year later with a global version in which intrepid players could navigate the north-east and as-yet-undiscovered north-west passages into the Pacific Ocean). His own apprentice John Spilsbury (1739–69) devised an entirely new form of puzzle in 1766, when he appended a map entitled *Europe Divided Into Its Kingdoms* to a wooden board and then carved it into pieces, with each of them representing an individual kingdom (though Italy, was, curiously, shown as single piece, a century ahead of its eventual reunification). This, the first jigsaw puzzle, spawned many imitators, but it shows the diverse uses to which cartography was now being adapted.

Mitchell's map was extensively drawn on for the very first map of the independent United States, compiled by the Connecticut silversmith Abel Buell (1742–1822) in 1784. His early career was chequered: when he was only 22 years old, in 1764, he was convicted of counterfeiting and sentenced to branding and mutilation by having his ear cut off. Fortunately, he had won over the judge by making him a ring, and so was branded as high on his forehead as possible – where his hair would largely cover the mark – and only the very tip of his ear was excised, and the judge allowed this to be sewn back (where, apparently, it healed). A reformed and chastened Buell set himself to more legal means of enrichment and in 1787 minted the State of Connecticut's first silver pennies, but also compiled his *New and Correct Map of the United States of North America Lay'd Down from the Latest Observations and Best Authorities Agreeable to the Peace of 1783*, which was published the year after the Treaty of Paris, and was the first American-published map to use the name of the new country. Buell made extensive use of Mitchell's 1755 map, as well as Thomas Hutchin's 1778 map of the Trans-Allegheny region. He included some novelties, including the type, which he had cast himself (making him the first in North America to do so), and he placed the prime meridian not through Greenwich, but, in a cartographical declaration of independence, through Philadelphia (where the map was published). A serial inventor, Buell later set up his own textile mill, but the business foundered, and he died in poverty in the New Haven almshouse in 1825. Very few copies of his map were printed, but it (and he) achieved immortality through its inclusion in *Geography Made Easy*, the first United States geography textbook for schools, designed by the Congregational Minister Jedidiah Morse, with the map prepared by Amos Doolittle, one of Buell's assistants.

The new nation was in sore need of mapping (and its borders, even between states, were somewhat ill-defined: those of New York so much so that Buell simply omitted them, allowing it to rest unnamed and swallowed up by a bloated Connecticut). The original charters of the colonies of Maryland and Pennsylvania had been so ambiguously drafted that their borders overlapped, and a 1681 compromise enacted by Charles II which centred on a line created by a circle of 12 miles' radius from New Castle in Maryland failed to specify where in New Castle its centre point should lie. Decades of disputes followed, partly prompted by fears that the hard-pressed residents on the border might end up paying tax twice (though the authorities were worried that they would pay none at all).

In addition to his maps of North America, Jefferys produced a number of the Caribbean, which were gathered together and published in 1775, four years after his death. As well as 16 sheets mapping the whole of the West Indies, there were 17 maps of individual islands, including this one of Cuba.

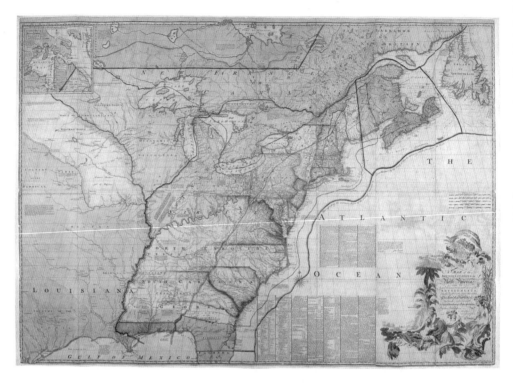

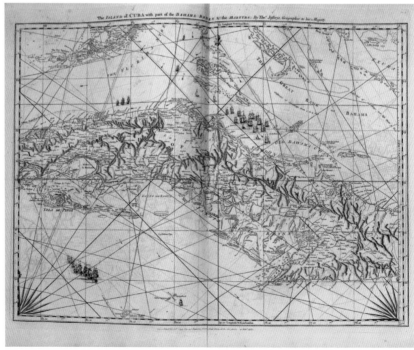

Finally, after another settlement made in 1732 broke down, a survey was set up in 1760 to demarcate the line, to be carried out by the British surveyors Charles Mason (1728–86) and Jeremiah Dixon (1733–79), who were seen as neutral parties. It took eight long years of lugging the equipment, which included heavy quadrants, transit and altitude-measuring instruments with spirit levels, a zenith sector (a telescope with a shifting mount whose eye piece was so low that the user needed to lie on his back), through rugged and sometimes hostile territory and hampered by the suspicions of local Native American groups. Finally, though, having pushed on beyond the western edge of Maryland to extend the survey to a stretch of the Virginia–Pennsylvania border, Mason and Dixon finished their work in

October 1767 and returned home, leaving the last few miles of the survey, the first measurement of a degree of latitude in North America (along the line of 39°43'), to be competed by a team of American surveyors in 1784. Although it did quell the antipathy between Maryland and Pennsylvania, the parallel, which came to be called the Mason–Dixon line, was to become best known as the symbolic cultural dividing line between the northern and southern states of the United States.

The fledgling nation had many other competing priorities. The Postal Services Act of 1792, which mandated the establishment of post offices across the country including in the remote new frontier regions, led the assistant postmaster general Abraham Bradley Jr (1767–1838) to publish his *A Map of the United States, Exhibiting the Post-Roads*, in 1796. This showed the thickening network of roads along which the increasing volume of US mail (largely carried by horse) was travelling, together with the expected times taken to traverse them (so that a letter posted in the most northerly post office, at Brewer, Maine, could expect to take 46 days before it reached the southernmost at St Marys, Georgia). A year before Bradley's map, the first US-published atlas of the country appeared, produced by the Irish-born printer and cartographer Mathew Carey (1760–1839), who had been forced to flee to Paris, and then to Philadelphia, after publishing a pamphlet criticizing the iniquities of the Irish Penal code. Among his voluminous publications, which included the country's first Roman Catholic Bible, and the *Encyclopaedia Americana*, his 1795 *American Atlas* included 17 maps of the newly independent states, as well as of South America and the West Indies. It was, though, just a first tentative step towards the great age of American atlas publishing in the next century (p.204).

The mapping of North America did not, though, become a British (or American) monopoly and cartographers from other countries continued to produce atlases; the success of the Revolutionary forces in the war against the British from 1775 even motivated the Italian map-maker Antonio Zatta (*c.* 1722–97) to compile a 12-sheet map of the rebellious colonies (entitled *Le Colonie dell'America Settentrionale di nuova projezione* – 'The Colonies of North America on a New Projection').

The British loss of territory in North America in 1783 – although the Loyalist provinces in Canada were preserved – was partially offset by gains and discoveries elsewhere. The elusive search for the southern continent, which the Dutch had won, to little fanfare and much secret mapping in the seventeenth century (p.138), was pursued further by the British in the form of Captain James Cook (1728–79). The ostensible purpose of his voyage with the *Endeavour* was to observe a Transit of Venus (a rare astronomical event which occurs twice every 120 years when the planet crosses the disc of the Sun) and to take measurements which would allow the calculation of the distance from Earth to Venus. Yet in addition to this, he carried sealed orders to proceed further south, after the Transit itself in June 1769, charting and claiming any lands he might encounter.

The result was the survey of the east coast of the Australian landmass which he conducted between April and September 1770, during which he made the first landing by a European in eastern Australia at Botany Bay on 29 April (and had the first, violent, encounter with indigenous peoples that same day). Cook was already an accomplished

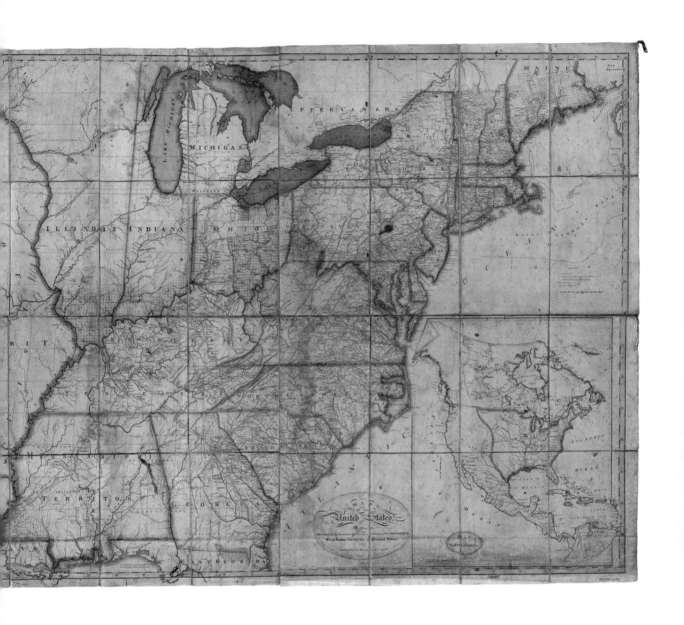

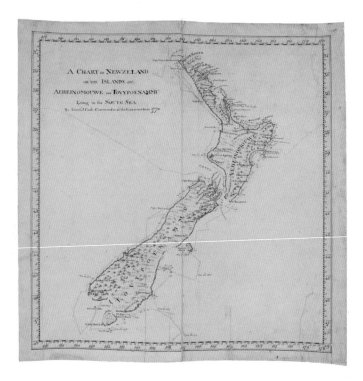

ABOVE

Chart of New Zealand,
James Cook, 1770

OPPOSITE

A Map of Hindoostan,
James Rennell, 1788

cartographer who had surveyed the St Lawrence river basin in Canada and the coast of the Carolinas in the 1760s, and during the *Endeavour* voyage he also mapped the coastline of New Zealand. Further investigation of the Australian interior, though, had to wait until the British government identified Australia as the solution to its problems of what to do with prisoners who could no longer be shipped to North America. The start of colonisation began with the arrival in January 1788 of the First Fleet in Botany Bay carrying around 750 convicts. The first atlases of Australia were only published in the nineteenth century, although the results of Cook's third voyage to the Pacific, in which he discovered the Hawaiian islands, were published in an atlas supplement to the *Voyage to the Pacific Ocean*, his account of the expedition.

The growing British territories in India were in much more obvious need of mapping. The imperative to defend them against established powers (including the weakened Mughal empire, the Marathas and the Rajputs), as well as to establish more precisely the details of the land the British East India Company could tax, led Robert Clive, victor of the Battle of Plassey and Governor-General of Bengal, to assign James Rennell (1742–1830) the task of creating an overall map of Bengal. The survey began in 1764 with the mapping the Ganges river course down to the Hooghly and Calcutta (a strategically important route and so an obvious priority), followed by the lower Ganges the following year, and then a more general triangulation survey. An appointment as Surveyor-General of Bengal in 1767 took Rennell out of the field, but he was able to continue with the work – in sometimes hostile territory (he was badly wounded in February 1766 in an ambush by local tribesmen) – until 1771.

A year after he returned home in 1778, Rennell was allowed to publish the results of his survey as *The Bengal Atlas* (no decades of secrecy as the VOC had imposed on its East Indies). Its subtitle 'Containing Maps of the Theatre of War and Commerce on that side of Hindoostan' clearly showed the preoccupation of the East India Company, whose transition from a trading operation to a land-occupying one would more and more embroil it in campaigns of conquest. Much of the print-run of the first edition of Rennell's *Atlas* was impounded by the French when they attacked the ships carrying it in April 1780, but this impelled him to produce a second, revised edition and, in 1788, a much reproduced four-sheet *A Map of Hindoostan*. Although the East India Company did continue to fund surveys, including that of Captain Mark Wood (whose 23 years of service for the Company made him something of a survivor and led eventually to the award of a baronetcy in 1808), which resulted in the exquisite maps of the *Survey of the Country on the Eastern Bank of the Hooghly* (1780–84), a more systematic and detailed map of its holdings would have to wait until its institution of the Great Trigonometrical Survey almost 30 years later (p.202).

While the English and French were establishing new maritime empires (and the Dutch stood in the twilight of their own, much of it to fall to the British in the margins of the Napoleonic Wars from 1799), other European countries were emulating the two front-runners in carrying out their own national mapping for the first time. In Denmark, the Royal Scientific Society began a triangulation survey led by Thomas Bugge (1740–1815), an astronomer, mathematician and physicist, whose busy life included service as Crown

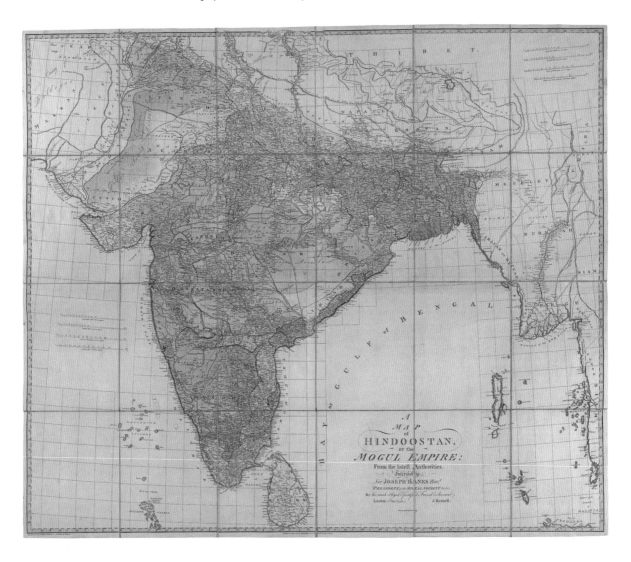

RIGHT

*Survey of the Country on the
Eastern Bank of the Hooghly,*
Mark Wood, 1780–84

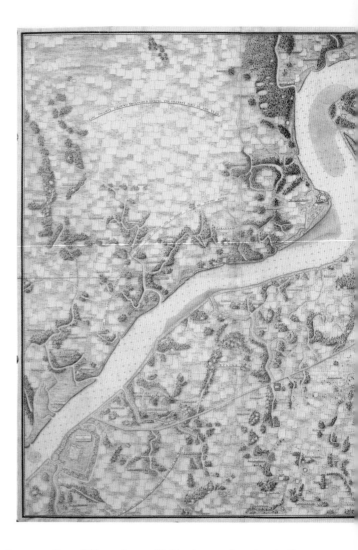

Prince Frederick's tutor, three stints as rector of Copenhagen University, a role as head of the Rundetam Observatory, and the positions of Professor of Astronomy and President of the Royal Danish Agricultural Society, as well as membership of the Commission that supervised the Copenhagen Fire Brigade. Somehow he found time from 1762 to lay out a base line to the west of the Danish capital from Ting Hill to Brondby Hill, supplemented with further triangles that eventually yielded a national topographic map of Denmark published between 1766 and 1834.

Across the Øresund in Sweden, matters proceeded even more slowly. Little new mapping was undertaken there, although the cartographer and mathematician Anders Bure (1571–1646), who was appointed the country's chief surveyor in 1628, carried out extensive surveys. As was the way with many national surveys, the final resulting

comprehensive map had only been published in 1688, and it was incorporated into the first Swedish atlas of sea charts, published by Peter Gedda (1661–97) in 1695. The land portion, however, was considered a state secret, and the atlas that Erik Dahlbergh (1625–1703) produced in 1698 had, as a result, only a single copy, which was given to Charles II, and it was not until 1735 that maps of the individual Swedish provinces were able to be published. Trigonometric surveying did not commence until 1758–61, while a modern survey was not set up until 1805. Meanwhile in Norway, then under Danish rule, a start on a topographic survey was only made in 1773 under the auspices of the Mathematical Military School.

Russia fared little better with its very first atlas (as opposed to those published abroad which included maps of its territory) being produced in 1745. It included an overall map of the country and 19 regional maps: 13 of European Russia and six of its Asian territory beyond the Urals – an area of particular interest to the court as Russia steadily expanded into Siberia and the Central Asian emirates. Russia's mapping had advanced more quickly under the guiding hand of Peter the Great (*r.* 1682–1725), who was keen to have his country modernize along western European lines (and whose drive to do so brought him to spend several months learning ship-building in Amsterdam, and then nearly four further months in Greenwich in 1697–98 to study the Royal Navy's methods – including a side trip to the nearby Royal Observatory). On his return he attracted foreign engravers, such as the French-born Peter Picard, to improve the quality of Russian maps. He also passed an imperial decree that a national survey be conducted by 30 graduates of the Imperial Naval Academy, in particular to record the new borders of the Russian Empire in Kamchatka and along the Caspian. The information these 'Geometers' compiled was then returned to the Académie des Sciences for a laborious process of correction at the Russian Cartographical Office, which the Tsar established in 1719 out of the existing Estates Department. It was led by Ivan Kirilov (1689–1737), a graduate of the Naval Academy in St Petersburg, which was one of Peter's early contributions to Russian reform. Kirilov invited Joseph Nicolas Delisle (the brother of Guillaume, p.174) to assist him. Almost immediately, the two quarrelled over Delisle's insistence that the slow grind of a triangulation survey (which would take decades in the vastnesses of the Russian steppes) should take precedence over more rapid surveying methods. As head of the Office, Kirilov naturally had his way, but their conflicting approaches meant it took 15 years to produce even a partial *Russian Atlas*, with modest coverage of 14 European governorates, and its completion at a higher level of detail and greater scope was delayed by his death in 1737. This gave Delisle the opportunity to slow things down, so that the results of the Great Northern Expedition led by Vitus Bering from 1732, which explored the Arctic Ocean as far as Sakhalin, took many years to incorporate. By that time Bering himself was long dead, having perished on an uninhabited island off Kamchatka during a second expedition in 1741 when his ship was driven aground by storms, but not before he had glimpsed the coastline of Alaska, beginning the short-lived dream of a Russian Empire in North America. Even when the new version of the *Russian Atlas* was finally published in 1745, it did not include all the findings of the Great Northern Expedition.

Elsewhere, a trigonometric survey of the Austrian Netherlands (what is now Belgium and Luxembourg) was begun in 1768 by the Austrian general Count Joseph de Ferraris (1726–1814), yielding a first map in 1777, while similar surveys for other Habsburg territories were carried out in Bohemia, Moravia, Silesia, the Tyrol and Lombardy, meaning that by 1787 all of Austria's many provinces had been mapped, though without any general topographic map or atlas resulting. Even so, they allowed the Austrians to publish 125 map sheets of their empire between 1814 and 1839.

By then, the political geography of the European continent had been thrown into turmoil by the French Revolutionary and Napoleonic Wars (which simplified the multiplicity of German states down from the befuddling mosaic of more than 300 at the time of the Peace of Westphalia to a more manageable 39 by 1815), and the secession of Belgium and Luxembourg from Austrian rule in 1830. Maps could not stand still in the face of political reality and new generations of cartographers and atlases faced the challenge of mapping them (see Chapter 7). In addition, maps began to reflect new philosophical ideas (much as they had done, in a way, in Babylonian times, and from the Christian-centred *mappae mundi* of the Middle Ages to the mapping of the new empires which arose from the Age of Exploration). The European Enlightenment in the seventeenth and eighteenth centuries, which privileged reason over faith as the guiding spirit of intellectual endeavour, yielded advances in science, philosophy and economics, as well as the study of the past. In France, its most obvious literary manifestation and the flagbearer for the whole movement was the *Encylopédie* of Denis Diderot (1713–84). A mammoth undertaking, published in 28 volumes between 1751 and 1772 (when that containing the plates was finally issued), it contained a distillation of much of Enlightenment thought and, just as its medieval predecessors, incorporated a number of

BELOW

Trigonometrical Survey of the Austrian Netherlands, Joseph de Ferraris, 1777

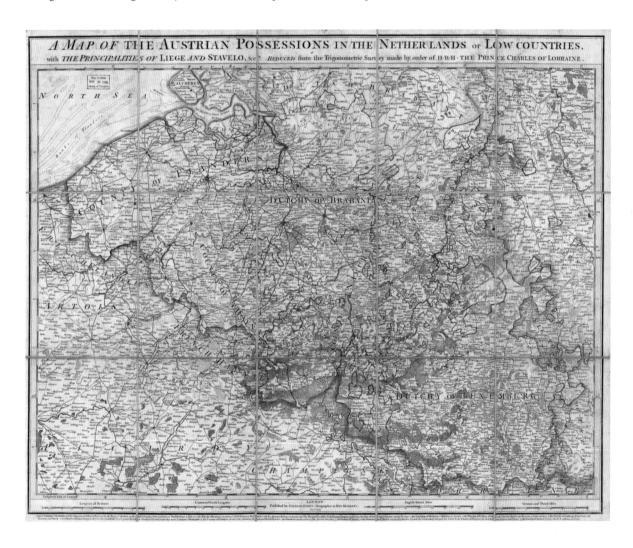

ABOVE

North America, *Encylopédie of Denis Diderot*, Didier Robert de Vaugondy, 1772

maps, notable among which is one of North America, engraved by Didier Robert de Vaugondy (p.171), that shows Fusang, a mythical Chinese-settled land, which was supposed to lurk, as yet undiscovered, somewhere in the interior.

The Enlightenment urge to reform and sweep away longstanding practices seen as a bar to progress would encourage the radical thinking of men like Rousseau and ultimately lead to the French Revolution. But it had gentler effects. In education, a new science of pedagogy replaced the rod with reason, leading Frederick the Great of Prussia to issue regulations in 1763 that made schooling compulsory between the ages of five and thirteen, and to set up a National Board of Education in 1787, and in Russia to the establishing of parochial schools across the country in 1803. The new schools needed new books to educate a wider range of pupils, and among these were the first school atlases. Already in the 1660s, the *Orbis terrarum veteribus cogniti typus in binis tabulis* ('An Arrangement of Knowledge of the Old World in Two Tables'), a posthumous publication by the German schoolmaster Johann Strube (1600–38), had been brought out. This consisted of an atlas with two maps for each country, one including the place-names and the other left blank for the pupils to fill in, a method that must still be familiar to many twenty-first-century teachers. By 1710, Johann Hübner (the publisher of the *Short Questions on Old and New Geography*, p.175) had brought out the *Kleiner Atlas*

Scholasticus ('Small School Atlas'), the first to proclaim its educational purpose in its title, and nine years later the Homann firm published its *Methodischer Atlas*, with specially simplified maps for schools. Soon, the proliferation of school atlases caused the German Academy of Science to sanction its own version in 1753, the *Atlas geographicus omnes terrarum regions: ad usum potissimum scholarum et institutionem juventutis editus* ('The Geographical Atlas of all the Regions of the World. Edited for the Best use of Pupils and the Use of Youths'). It was compiled by no less a figure than Leonhard Euler (1707–83), the great Swiss mathematician and pioneer of number theory, whose interest in maps was such that he solved an age-old cartographic puzzle, the Seven Bridges of Königsberg, in which the problem posed is to trace a route through the city, crossing each of bridges just once, without back-tracking and ending at the start point (he proved that it was not possible to do so). The atlas also included world maps showing winds, monsoons and magnetic declination, a leavening of scientific information that has continued in school atlases to this day.

The French, too, first published school atlases in the seventeenth century, beginning with *Parallela geographiae veteris et novae* ('Parallel Geography of the Old and New'), a kind of hybrid of geographical and historical atlas, which had ancient and modern maps of the same region side by side, produced by Philippe Briet (1601–68). As well as more straightforward school atlases published by mainstream map-publishers such as Didier Robert de Vaugondy's *Nouvel Atlas portatif* (1762), other French educational cartographers innovated: Jacques-Nicolas Bellin (1703–72) produced *L'enfant geographe, ou nouvelle méthode d'enseigner la géographie* ('The Child Geographer, or a New Method of Teaching Geography', 1769), which included highly simplified maps for the youngest students; and Jean Palairet (1697–1774) – whose other accomplishments included being French tutor to the children of George II of England and introducing the game of cricket to the Netherlands – used several maps for each region, each with gradually more information, as a means of progressively introducing a greater level of geographical knowledge to the students. Edme Mentelle (1730–1816), who turned from a failed career as a comic playwright to the teaching of geography, acquiring a position at the prestigious *École Militaire* in Paris, where he taught Napoleon Bonaparte geology and geography, compiled the *Atlas Nouveau*, which included maps showing the physical, and not just the political, geography of the world. Meanwhile, another professor of geography, Claude Buy de Mornas (d. 1783), included explanatory texts with each of his maps, as well as lists of former and modern place-names of important localities.

A new desire to reassess the history of the past in more rational and dispassionate terms yielded Enlightenment masterpieces such as the magisterial *The History of the Decline and Fall of the Roman Empire*, published in six volumes between 1776 and 1788 by Edward Gibbon (1737–94). Even so, the eighteenth-century was not a golden age for historical atlases, but it did see an advance with the compilation by Johann Matthias Hase (1684–1742), professor of mathematics at the University of Wittenberg, of a series of 28 maps of 'great empires' which were bound, together with a set covering the epochs of German history, into an *Atlas Historicus* in 1750. Published by Homann Heirs, it was the first real historical atlas, attempting to give an overview of history in chronological order by charting in map form the changes that unfolded over time. It was a format

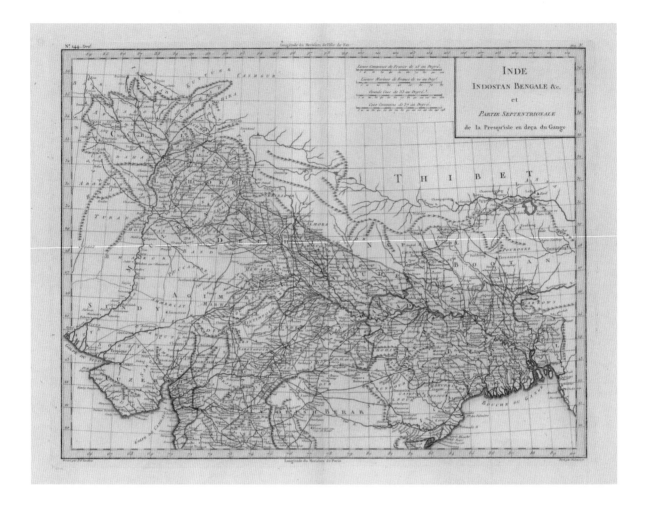

much imitated, including by the Italian cartographer Antonio Rizzi Zannoni (1736–1814) in his *Atlas historique et géographique de la France ancienne et moderne* ('Historical and Geographical Atlas of Ancient and Modern France', 1764). This principally dealt with French history as Zannoni had been commissioned by Augustus III of Poland to carry out the first triangulation survey of his kingdom and was unlucky enough to be caught up in the fighting in the Seven Year's War and was captured by the French at the Battle of Rossbach in November 1757. Taken back to Paris as a prisoner-of-war, he found it so much to his taste that he remained there for 20 years. From works such as theirs, the more voluminous output of the next century and all their successors as far as today's *Times History of the World* have taken their model.

In 1800, Europe stood on a threshold. The French Revolution had begun to export notions of mass democracy and a revolutionary fervour that threatened the established

monarchies, while the wars that it ignited were already a decade old and would engulf Europe for a further 15 years before the final defeat of Napoleon. The Industrial Revolution had started its transformation of the economic, social and demographic landscape, first of Britain, and then of other European countries, as James Watt's improved steam engine (patented in 1769) was adapted to use in textile factories, sparking heady growth in cities, which offered lucrative jobs in the burgeoning factories and squalid living conditions to new urban slum-dwellers. Those nations that emerged out of this furnace, most notably France, Britain and Germany, and outside Europe the United States and Japan, had more need than ever to map their territories with ever greater scientific precision, asserting their dominance over their empires, and turning to new forms of mapping to aid their policymaking.

ABOVE

British conquests in Normandy and Aquitaine in the 12th century, *Atlas historique et géographiqe de la France ancienne et moderne*, Antonio Rizzi Zannoni, 1764

THE HEYDAY OF IMPERIAL MAPPING

(1800–1900)

The nineteenth century saw a vast expansion in the areas of the globe controlled by European powers, in particular by France and Great Britain, as large parts of Africa came under their control (a process accelerated by the 'Scramble for Africa' in the 1880s, which drew in Germany, whose ambitious Kaiser, Wilhelm II, was keen for Germany not to miss out on what he termed its 'place in the sun'). In Asia, the remaining parts of the Indian sub-continent fell into Britain's sphere of influence, while Indo-China (modern Laos, Vietnam and Cambodia) was colonized by the French, and Malaya by the British. The need to map these territories, both for the purposes of imperial administration and to sate the appetite of those back in Europe craving information about the new empires grew in tandem with an increasing sophistication of surveying and mapping in the homelands. In Britain, the Ordnance Survey was established in 1791, and the nineteenth century also saw the publication of new national maps in France, Russia and, ultimately, of the newly united Germany and Italy. Geography was also put to new uses with collections of maps to enable government planning, and the appearance of the first truly thematic maps, such as population atlases. An entirely new front in the history of cartography also opened with the employment of maps to press for social reforms, such as Charles Booth's Poverty Maps of London's East End in the late 1880s (p.210). Maps no longer merely showed an image of the world (theological, ideological or actual), or a means to navigate within it. They now began to point to a (hoped-for) better future.

The great national survey of Britain owed its genesis to military and national rivalry (as did so much in the architecture of nineteenth- and twentieth-century Europe). National pride had already been piqued in 1783, when Joseph Banks (1743–1820), the President of the Royal Society, received a letter from Cassini de Thury, director of the Paris Observatory and the latest in the Cassini cartographic dynasty (p.166), suggesting that mutual co-operation in a triangulation survey that extended the mesh of survey lines from France over the Channel to England to establish the precise co-ordinates of the Greenwich Observatory would be useful to both countries. His proposal, with the clear implication being that the existing French estimates, which were a full 11 seconds of longitude and 15 seconds of latitude adrift from those of the English, were superior, was not exactly received favourably by the Reverend Nevil Maskelyne (1732–1811), the Astronomer Royal. It was in his tenure that the knotty problem of accurately measuring longitude at sea had finally been resolved by the marine chronometer designed in 1735 by John Harrison, who thus earned the Royal Society's long-standing offer of a prize of £20,000 to anyone who achieved the feat (though he was never paid out in full, causing much bitterness between him and Maskelyne). As a result, the Astronomer Royal may well have felt that he knew a thing or two about measuring geographical co-ordinates, and so the British scientific community instead chose a homegrown solution, with Banks asking the military engineer Major General William Roy (1726–90), to undertake a survey.

Roy was a singular character. He was an inveterate mapper, who began his career in the military in 1747 after the campaign to suppress the Jacobite Uprising of Bonnie Prince Charlie had exposed the woeful lack of modern mapping of Scotland, which had proven a hindrance to the English forces. Moving military units without getting lost and hunting down remaining Jacobite hold-outs proved vexingly difficult when the most recent surveys turned out to be those of John Adair from the 1680s, while that made more recently by John Elphinstone in 1745 was nowhere near detailed enough to be of much practical use. Lanark-born Roy joined the Board of Ordnance which, based in the Tower of London, was in charge of military supplies, but also had supervision of the army's engineers, and hence of whatever mapping it might produce or commission. Having shown his worth in completing the southern part of the survey of Scotland with the aid of six parties of surveyors, he began the mapping of southern England in 1756, but then the exigencies of the Seven Years' War took him to more direct military duties, and he was unable to return to the task.

Roy had by chance just surveyed (partly for his own amusement and partly to sting officialdom into some kind of action) a 2,362 m (7,750 ft) base line extending from the Jew's Harp (a tavern and tea garden in Marylebone, just south of Regent's Park), east to Black Lane in St Pancras, when he received the invitation from Joseph Banks to survey

BELOW

Grand Duchy of Saxe-Weimar-Eisenach, Joseph Meyer, 1849

Included in the *Zeitung Atlas* published by the German industrialist Joseph Meyer three years later, this map is one of the earliest scientifically surveyed maps of Saxony.

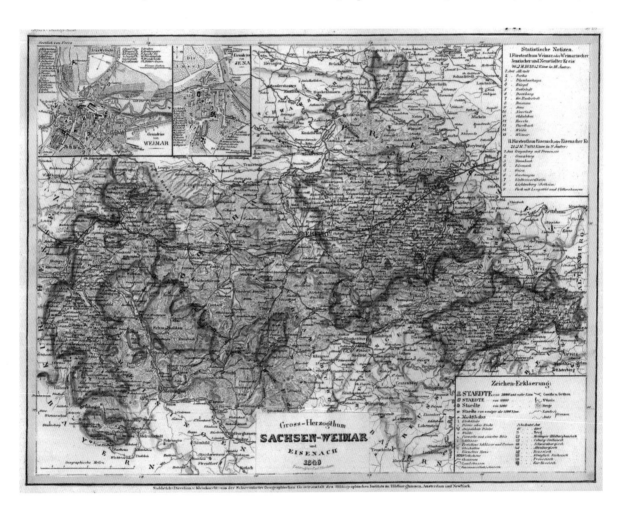

the stretch of land from London to Dover. Scarcely hesitating, for this was the opportunity for which he had waited for 30 long years, Roy assembled a team and had instruments made up (including rods of Riga pine) to use as a standard gauge against which the day-to-day metal surveying rods (which could expand or contract in heat) might be checked. By 16 June 1784, all was ready and a first base line, some 5 miles (8km) long, was begun on the flat ground of Hounslow Heath. Matters almost ground to a halt when it was found that the wooden rods were expanding and contracting too much as heat and humidity rose and fell, leaving Roy to comment that he had 'no hopes of being able, by their means, to determine the length of the base to that degree of precision we had all along aimed at'. Only the suggestion that glass rods be substituted saved the day, since while they did contract and expand, it was by a much smaller amount that was fairly easily accounted for.

Three years elapsed between the completion of the very first base line and its extension to form a triangulation between London and Dover, a delay caused by needing to construct an even more sensitive instrument than the initial transit telescope used to take measurements. This was finally delivered by the instrument-maker Jesse Ramsden

(1735–1800) in August 1787, described by Roy as 'a great theodolet, rendered extremely perfect'. The survey resumed with the revival of the proposal to link the French and English triangulations across the Channel, assisted by a French delegation including the cartographer Jean Dominique Cassini (the son of Cassini de Thury). Enormous reverberatory lamps were used to pass signals between the English base stations at Dover Castle and Fairlight Head and their French equivalents on the other side of the Channel, at Cape Blanc Nez, Montlambert near Boulogne and the church of Notre Dame in Calais. The initial triumph, and the start of triangulation back into Kent towards London, was tempered by difficulties over the translation of the two parties' incompatible measurements, from French toises into British leagues, and a disagreeable re-emergence of the argument between British and French over whether the Earth was an oblate or prolate sphere (p.168). The British authorities also proved resistant to Roy's proposal that the survey be extended to cover the whole of England.

Very shortly after he had completed his final report, Roy died on 1 July 1790. The idea of a national triangulation survey might have died with him but for the enthusiasm of Charles Lennox, the 3rd Duke of Richmond, Master-General of the Ordnance, who had become fascinated with Ramsden's precision-surveying instruments and persuaded George III to allow the survey's continuation. As a result, the Board of Ordnance was officially reconstituted in 1791 as the Ordnance Survey, under the control of the military, and headquartered in the Tower of London. Under the supervision of Lieutenant Colonel Edward Williams (d. 1798), a start was made on the triangulation of Kent and Essex (chosen for their strategic importance, given the ever-present threat of invasion from France). The survey, aimed at producing maps on the scale of one inch to a mile, continued under his successor William Mudge (1762–1820, godson of the critic, essayist and lexicographer Samuel Johnson), who extended the work into northern England and in 1813 sent out a meridian line into Scotland. By then the very first Ordnance sheet map (of Kent) had been published in 1801, priced at the handsome sum of three guineas (which was around three weeks' wages for a skilled craftsman).

The work was interrupted for 15 years between 1825 and 1840 when its surveyors were diverted to producing a map of Ireland. This one had a more clearly financial motivation, at least as far as the British government was concerned, as the land valuations that drove the taxation system there were hopelessly out-of-date. Leading the new Ordnance Survey of Ireland was Colonel Thomas Colby (1784–1852), who had been one of William Mudge's chief assistants at the British Ordnance Survey and who had succeeded him as its director in 1820. Colby had overcome the handicap of the loss of one hand in a shooting accident in 1803 to become a key member of the Survey and lieutenant governor of the Royal Military Academy in Greenwich. When called upon by the Duke of Wellington – then prime minister – to carry out the Irish Survey, Colby became dissatisfied with the quality of the instruments being used to lay out the initial almost 8-mile- (13km-) long base line and so constructed his own metal bar, made of brass and iron (whose slightly different qualities compensated for the contraction and expansion due to changes in temperature). So successful was this 'compensation bar' as a measuring tool, that, after the Houses of Parliament in London were burnt down on the night of 16 October 1834 (when stoves being used

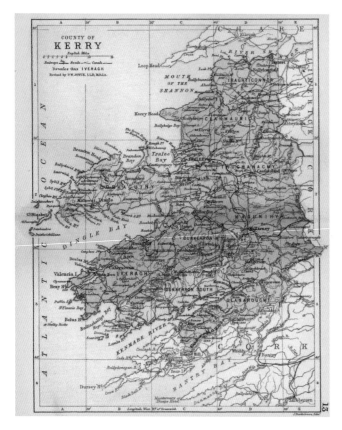

ABOVE

County Kerry, *Handy Atlas of the Counties of Ireland*, George Philip, 1883

to incinerate old wooden tally sticks used in the Exchequer for accounting reignited), destroying among the general wreckage the rod that was the official measure of the imperial yard, Colby's was used as part of the process of recreating it. This six-inch-to-one mile survey (a scale of 1:10,560) took the labours of more than 2,000 staff, civilians and soldiers of the Royal Engineers, and was only completed in 1842, with publication of the maps following three years later.

By then the matter of Land Valuation was temporarily moot, as Ireland was in the grip of the Great Famine, which destroyed its potato crop, leading to mass starvation and the emigration of a million of its people, transforming the demography of the island. Even so, the mapping did eventually resume, beginning with a resurvey of the towns and then of rural areas at a scale of 1:2500. The task extended from the 1880s to 1913, when the sheets for Westmeath and Roscommon were published just before the First World War and nine years before Ireland finally attained its independence after 550 years of occupation, struggle and rebellion.

By then, more general atlases of the country had become commonplace, such as the *Handy Atlas of Ireland*, published in 1883 by the firm of the Liverpool-based map publisher and cartographer George Philip (1800–82), who had moved there in 1819 from his native Aberdeenshire. His company, founded in 1834, became one of the most respected cartographic publishers of the nineteenth century in Britain, continuing as an independent unit for almost 150 years until its acquisition by Reed Elsevier in 1988. Philip's atlases became a mainstay of many Victorian households (and their twentieth-century counterparts), creating products ranging from its premium *Imperial Atlas*, to pocket atlases and its *School Atlas*, first published in 1852, which by 2021 had reached its 100th edition. Among Philip's main rivals in the atlas-publishing field was the Edinburgh-based John Bartholomew & Company, established by John Bartholomew Senior (1805–61) as a vehicle for his map engraving in 1826, and then for the production of atlases by others, before finally venturing into its own publishing. Its flagship would become *The Times Comprehensive Atlas of the World*, which it first issued as *The Times Survey Atlas of the World* in 1920 (having taken over from *The Times* newspaper the compilation of what had first appeared as the *Times Atlas* in 1895, but which derived ultimately from the German *Andrees Algemeiner Handatlas* of 1887).

Colby, meanwhile, had transferred back to England with many of his staff, and the survey there continued with even greater vigour. By 1851, it was complete, consisting of over 108,000 sheets, though an inconsistent approach to scale (with the Admiralty and military in general wanting larger-scale maps and those in government keen to keep the Survey's costs under control arguing for a more modestly scaled effort) meant that by 1850 a mere 23 sheets had actually been published. The decision in 1853 to resurvey the whole country (though again at a variety of scales) ensured the Ordnance Survey's continuation. Until the age of satellite mapping it owned the rights to the base mapping on which almost all other maps of the United Kingdom were drawn, creating if not a single atlas (which would, until the digital age have been impossibly wieldy), then at least the most comprehensive set of maps available for any country in the world.

The triangulation mapping of Britain (and Ireland) did not exhaust the British appetite for scientific surveying of their territory. The survey ordered by the East India Company of its domains was the largest such effort, its implementation entrusted to Lieutenant William Lambton (1756–1823), a rather unassuming infantry officer who had served with Arthur Wellesley (the future Duke of Wellington) in the Fourth Anglo-

BELOW

North Polar regions,
The Times Atlas, 1895

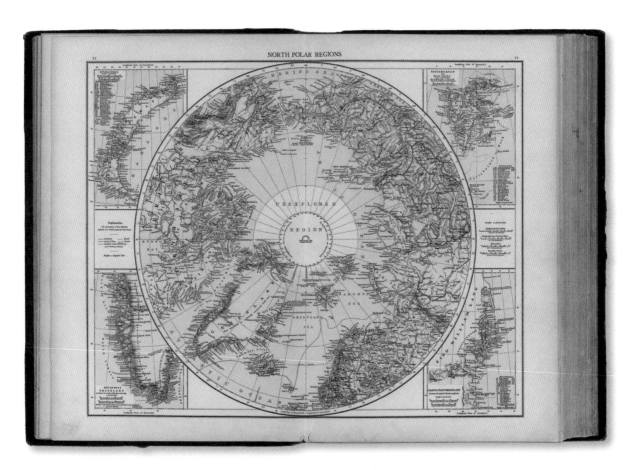

Mysore War (1798–99), during which he had demonstrated his navigational skills by using the observation of the stars to make sure a column advancing on Mysore did not get lost. His proposal of a survey, however, was initially rebuffed by James Rennell, the Surveyor-General (and compiler of the *Hindooftan* map of India, p.184), who considered that further mapping was unnecessary. Word, however, had got back to Neville Maskelyne, the Astronomer Royal, whose interest in India stemmed from his sister having married Robert Clive, the victor of Plassey and first East India Company Governor of Bengal. With this powerful backing, Lambton managed to overcome Rennell's objections, helped by the fortuitous arrival of a set of surveying instruments which had formed part of the gifts brought by Lord Macartney's mission to the Chinese Qing emperor in 1793. The Emperor had contemptuously dismissed Macartney's offerings, deeming (with some justification) that the Europeans had little to offer that China needed. In India, though, they found their worth. Included among them was a 1.5 m (5 ft) zenith sector telescope constructed by Jesse Ramsden, which was ideal for the proposed survey, and once they were discovered in Calcutta in 1800, East India Company officials snapped the instruments up for the bargain price of 2,400 rupees (£240). Even then, though, the difficulty of obtaining craftsmen able to repair the by-then rather dilapidated telescope held up its use, and so the beginning of Lambton's survey, until 1802.

But then, in mid-April, what came to be known as the Great Trigonometrical Survey began outside Madras, laying down an initial baseline along the 7 miles (11.3km) between St Thomas Mount and Pernambauk Hill using specially prepared wooden measuring rods mounted on trestles. It took a few weeks to complete this first stretch, but the next stage of the triangulation, crossing southern India from coast to coast, beginning at Cannanore (Kannur) in Kerala, took four years to lay down its network of triangles across the 350-mile (563km) expanse. Extending the survey to cover the whole of India and into the foothills of the Himalayas took even longer. Indeed, it consumed the entire career of the next Surveyor General, George Everest (1790–1866), for whom the world's highest mountain is named), who served from 1830 to 1843, and who had pushed it as far as Dehra Dun, south of Delhi, before he resigned in a fit of pique over a series of lectures criticizing his methods, which had been given by Thomas Jervis at the Royal Society in London.

Everest was succeeded by Andrew Scott Waugh (1810–1878), who carried out the tricky task of surveying the Himalayas, including parts of Nepal and Tibet which lay outside British control and were distinctly unfriendly territory for outsiders (who might easily be accused of espionage). To carry it out he employed Indian surveyors who traipsed the mountain routes in the guise of pilgrims or simple travellers. Trained to walk at a constant, steady tempo of a thousand paces to the mile, these 'pundits', as they were known, carried special sets of Buddhist rosary beads, which assisted in counting out longer distances. Inside a specially modified prayer wheel they also concealed tiny sheets of paper on which to record the number of the steps they took each day (and hence the distances between points). Among them was Nain Singh (1830–82), who made three expeditions on behalf of the company between 1865 and 1875, covering more than three million paces, and making the perilous trip to the Tibetan capital,

Lhasa, three times (on one of which he deflected attention from his surveying activities by taking employment as a teacher of accountancy).

The Company's control expanded remorselessly, absorbing Punjab following the Anglo-Sikh Wars between 1845 and 1849 and pushing against Afghanistan on the North-West Frontier. Then, the British hold on India was almost overthrown by the Indian Mutiny in 1857, followed by the cancellation of the Company's trade monopoly and the assumption of direct rule over its territories by the British Crown. But through it all the Great Trigonometric Survey continued serenely on its way (though subsumed into a more general Survey of India office in 1875), and by the time that it published the final map of the topographic survey in 1905, 103 years had passed since William Lambton had begun the effort. Over time he was forgotten and the bust of him unveiled in 2003 on St Thomas Mount (in what by then had been renamed Chennai), to mark the bicentenary of the Great Trigonometrical Survey, was largely ignored by the pilgrims who came to pray at the spot where the apostle St Thomas is said to have been martyred. Lambton's true monument is rather the hundreds of maps on a scale of 1 inch to 4 miles, covering the whole of India and parts of the neighbouring states, which his persistence and vision made possible.

Other European nations faced their own challenges in producing up-to-date atlases. Despite the prolonged gestation period of the Cassini atlas of France (pp.171–73), a decision was taken to replace it almost as soon as it was complete. The challenges posed by the mass warfare of the Napoleonic era showed that the Cassini survey had its shortcomings, and a new one was proposed as early as 1802. Work did not actually get under way until 1817, when surveys for the new *Carte de France de l'etat Major* were begun. Not quite as prolonged as its predecessor, the survey took until 1866, and the publication of the resulting maps until 1880, when the final one of the 596 sheets covering the whole country was completed. Yet it, too, was fated to be superseded almost the moment it was finished. The *Service géographique de l'armée*, which was set up in 1887 to co-ordinate the national cartographic effort, deemed that the 1817–66 survey, too, was inadequate and ordered the commencement of what was termed the 'Nouvelle Triangulation de la France'. This new iteration of the national survey of France began work in 1892 and was not finally completed until 1982. As the Cassinis had discovered, the cartographer's work is never done.

Switzerland was among the most difficult countries in Europe to map, since making scientific surveys of its mountainous terrain was a daunting task. Early attempts by officials working for the military general staff from 1809 were fitful and so General Guillaume Henri Dufour (1787–1875) was given the task of accelerating the process.

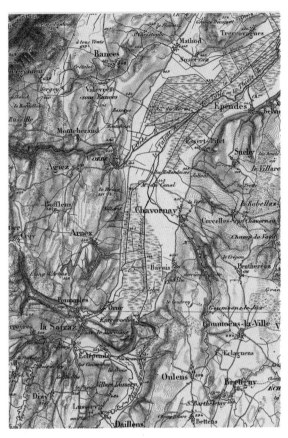

ABOVE

Canal d'Entreroches, topographic map of Switzerland, Guillaume Henri Dufour, 1849

Even under his more vigorous leadership, however (which involved the foundation of the Federal Swiss Cartographic Bureau in 1838), the construction of a nationwide network of triangulation was slow, and the first map sheet was not issued until 1845. The last of the 25 projected sheets, all on a scale of 1:100,000, was only published in 1865 and then reissued in atlas form shortly thereafter. Hardly was it complete when work on a new survey began in 1868, covering the country at an improved scale of up to 1:25,000.

Although the United States had acquired its first maps soon after Independence (and its first atlas by Mathew Carey in 1795, p.182), the country's steady expansion into new territories and the consistent growth of population through natural increase and migration which led new towns to appear almost overnight and existing ones to expand at a heady pace, meant that these were soon out of date. The passing of the Land Ordinance in 1785 at the behest of Thomas Jefferson, the longer title of which 'An Ordinance for Ascertaining the Mode of Disposal of Lands in the Western Territory' gave a clue as to the government's real intent, which was to divide up any land it acquired into geographical squares, which could be easily surveyed and then sold off to settlers.

That intent was soon to be tested. The purchase of the vast tract of land collectively known as 'Louisiana' from the French in 1803 for the bargain price of $15 million (which worked out at around $18 a square mile for the 828,000 mi^2 (2,144,510km^2) territory), pushed the territory of the United States far to the west and led Jefferson to dispatch an expedition under Meriwether Lewis (1774–1809), his former private secretary, and William Clark (1770–1838) to explore and survey the new lands, and if possible to reach the Pacific coast. The journey there consumed just over 18 months, reaching the western shoreline of the North American continent on 15 November 1805, and it took the Corps of Discovery (as the expedition members were known) until 23 September the following year to return to their start point in St Louis. Along the way they had almost starved to death, been exposed to freezing temperatures, their boat had capsized and they had been attacked several times by Native Americans and once by an irate brown bear. That they had survived at all was in no part thanks to the presence of Sacagawea, a Lemshi Shoshone woman, whose husband Toussaint Chardonneau had been hired as a guide, and who proved adept at smoothing the way among the various indigenous tribes they encountered.

Clark was the expedition's cartographer, taking along in his luggage a selection of instruments that included a hand compass, a quadrant, two sextants, a tape measure and a chronometer (the last of which on its own consumed 10 per cent of the expedition's equipment budget). With these he made daily observations, including the calculation of latitude and longitude, drawing up maps as he went along. His calculations, many of which had to be made from the unsteady platform of a moving boat, were so precise that his reckoning of the distance they had covered in reaching the Pacific turned out to be only 40 miles (about 65km) off.

Despite this early promising start, the very success of the United States in absorbing territory until it stretched from coast to coast bedevilled any real attempts to carry out a comprehensive topographic survey. With the acquisition of Alaska (purchased from Russia in 1867 for the bargain price of $7.2 million to the derision of many at the time, who mocked the US Secretary of State William Seward's negotiation of the deal as

'Seward's Folly') and the annexation of Hawai'i in 1898, the United States reached what was to be its full territorial extent. Large parts of the new territories west of the 100th meridian were surveyed by the 'Wheeler Survey', led by Captain George Montague Wheeler (1842–1905) between 1871 and 1879. A simultaneous campaign under the geologist Clarence King (1842–1901) surveyed the 40th Parallel between Wyoming and California, along the way exposing the great 'Diamond Hoax' in which a pair of unscrupulous prospectors had seeded a remote location in Colorado with diamonds and so persuaded hapless investors to part with hundreds of thousands of dollars to exploit the fictitious find. The efforts were merged in 1879 under the auspices of the US Geological Survey, fulfilling some of Wheeler's hope, but as he pointed out six years later, 'in the line of progress towards systematic and final results, the United States is in arrears of fourteen other nationalities'.[1]

If the interior of the united States was slow to be mapped, then earlier progress should have been made on its coastline and particularly the Atlantic coast, where President Thomas Jefferson's proposal for a survey was approved by Congress in 1807. But tensions flared between Ferdinand Hassler (1770–1843), the Swiss scientist appointed as the Survey's superintendent, and the Navy Department under whose supervision it was placed, and by the 1840s, only glacial progress had been made under the weight of the

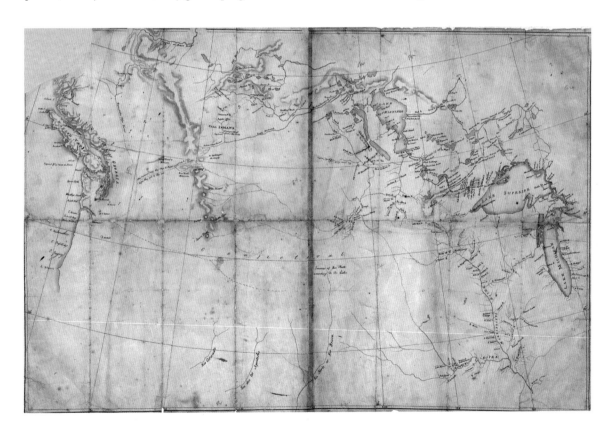

thousands of miles of coastline that fell within its domain. To add to its difficulties, the lack of any consistent approach to the mapping of the inland areas meant that these were added to the Coastal Survey's lengthening list of responsibilities. So it was in 1878 the United States Coast and Geodetic Survey was formally born, and it has been the US government's principal mapping arm ever since (though since 1970 as the United States Geodetic Survey). For a time, though, it had a military rival in the Corps of Topographical Engineers, which was born out of the Lewis and Clark Expedition and officially established in March 1813, specifically tasked with collating the results of military explorations and surveys, particularly along the expanding western frontiers, such as Major James Duncan Graham's 1841–42 survey of the sensitive border of the then-independent Republic of Texas (though it also later published a selection of maps of US Civil War battlefields before it was wound up and merged into the Army Corps of Engineers in 1863).

A small start had been made with the display of scientific information in map form in the eighteenth century, with publications such as Leonhard Euler's 1753 school atlas (p.191), which showed magnetic declinations, but it was not until further advances in printing techniques which increased the fineness of shading that could be shown on maps, that such thematic mapping really took off. A key development was the invention of lithographic printing by Alois Senefelder (1771–1834), a German actor and playwright who was searching for a cheap way to publish his own plays, who saw a profitable sideline in printing the music compositions of his contacts in Bavaria. His *A Complete Course of Lithography* (1818) described a method that was easily adaptable to maps: by tracing an image in ink on a 'stone' (at first limestone, and later zinc), which was then etched in a nitric acid solution, and then washing the uninked areas with gum arabic, a surface was created over which an inked roller could be passed to create an image.

Fine, thematic cartography also involved the conceptual leap from using colour merely to delineate political borders, as had been the case since the seventeenth century (although often these were hand-tinted rather than part of the original printing process). A start of sorts had been made by William Playfair (1759–1823), a Scottish engineer born near Dundee, whose chequered career included a scheme to destabilize the French Revolutionary government by printing large numbers of forged *assignats* (paper IOUs issued as an emergency cash supply) to provoke hyperinflation. His *Commercial and Political Atlas*, published in 1786, was the first to present statistical information in visual form (leading him much later to be called 'the father of the infographic'), including the first ever pie chart and bar charts, many of them produced in colour.

The early nineteenth century, however, saw the process taken much further and adapted to true maps. William Smith (1769–1839), an engineer for the Somerset Coal Canal Company in the late 1790s, developed an intense interest in geology from observing the strata that formed in coal-bearing rocks. He used his research over two decades to produce *A Delineation of the Strata of England and Wales*, published in 1815, with the principal type of rock formations in each region of Britain identified by different-coloured shading, all done by hand. Such thematic mapping was carried to a new level by August Heinrich Petermann (1822–78), who had studied at a specialist cartographic school established by Petermann's foster-father, the geographer Heinrich Berghaus (1797–1884), in Potsdam. Berghaus had some experience in the field, having

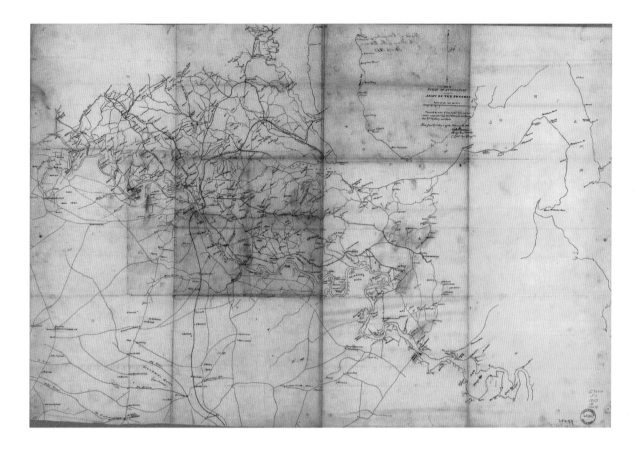

published his *Physikalischer Atlas* ('Physical Atlas') in 1848, with more than 90 maps covering a diverse range of scientific subjects, including meteorology, climatology, disease and botany, which had been intended to accompany the *Cosmos* of the explorer Alexander von Humboldt, a round-up of the current state of knowledge of science and nature, but which was in the end published as a standalone atlas.

Petermann moved to Edinburgh in 1845, as a result of negotiation with the Scottish cartographer Alexander Keith Johnston (1804–71), for the publication of an English edition of the *Physikalischer Atlas*. There, although the translation project never came to fruition, he worked on several other atlases, including *Physical Geography* (1848) which covered a similar range of subjects, and G.H. Swanston's *Royal Illustrated Atlas of Modern Geography* (1854). A move south to London followed, where Petermann founded his own publishing company, ambitiously named 'The Geographical Establishment', from which he issued a stream of innovative maps and atlases, including the *Atlas of Physical Geography* (1850) and the *Physical Statistical maps of the British Isles, showing the geographical distribution of the population and inland hydrography*, which used the data from the 1841 British Census (which enumerated the country's population as 26,707,091) and showed its density by varying levels of shading. He also made a pioneering contribution to

BELOW

Cholera map of Soho,
London, John Snow, 1854

OPPOSITE

Illiteracy of the adult
white male population,
Francis Walker, *Statistical Atlas
of the United States*, 1874

medical topography, by mapping the cholera outbreak of 1831–33 (the first to hit Britain) and showing the number of cases by the density of dots, which in the worst affected areas such as the north-east, Lancashire and the central belt of Scotland, merge into a single ominous black blob. It mapped on a national scale what the more famous map by the London doctor John Snow (1813–58) charted for the outbreak of cholera which hit London's Soho in the summer of 1854. Snow plotted the deaths onto a map of the area and found a cluster around the pump on Broad Street which supplied the neighbouring streets. When he persuaded the local Parish Board members to remove the pump handle, temporarily preventing its use, the cholera infections and deaths dropped away, proving both the link between contaminated water and cholera (previously scientific opinion had tended to consider the disease was caused by 'miasma' or bad smells), and that, in the right hands, cartography can save lives.

Petermann's growing fame, meanwhile, led to his appointment as Physical Geographer-Royal to Queen Victoria and the sponsorship of a number of exploratory expeditions to Africa and the Arctic, in large part motivated by his simple desire to fill in the last blanks on the map of those areas (including the location of the elusive North-West Passage, which was only finally navigated by the Norwegian explorer Roald Amundsen in 1903–06). His influence can be seen in the series of atlases produced by the US census department, beginning with a partial map based on the 1850 census and culminating in a national *Statistical Atlas of the United States*, published in 1874 under the guidance of the department's superintendent Francis Walker (1840–97), who used the data from the previous census to show the westward expansion of the frontier on the occasion of the country's first centennial.

Further atlases were published on the basis of the 1880 and 1890 censuses, but by the time of the latter the wave of settlers moving east from California and Oregon had merged with the one moving west across the prairie, leading the historian Frederick Jackson Turner to note that it marked a symbolic closure of the frontier that had been such a defining feature of American consciousness since the birth of the Republic.

The techniques of thematic population-mapping were further refined by the engineer Louis-Léger Vauthier (1815–1901), who in 1874 published a series of population maps of Paris that used contour lines as a means to show not the elevation of the landscape, but the density of its population. As the capital, Paris received special treatment in a country which was already renowned for its cartographic excellence. In 1742 Philippe Buache (1700–73) had already published a cross-section of the city showing the geological strata which underlay it,

MAP
SHOWING THE
ILLITERACY
OF THE
ADULT WHITE MALE POPULATION.
Compiled from the Returns of Population at the Ninth Census
OF THE UNITED STATES 1870.
BY
FRANCIS A. WALKER.

Note: In the construction of this Map the whole N? of
White Males 21 years of age and upwards is compared
with the N? of such persons who cannot write.
Explanations.
The Blue Lines indicate the boundaries of Groups of Population.
The figures in Blue 2-6-12-18-45-45: express the number of inhabitants
to the Square Mile found within each group.
The Shaded Lines in Blue indicate the outside limit of a population
of 2 or more to the Square Mile. The shading points towards the
regions which have a population of less than 2 to the Square Mile.
Note: The occasional abrupt intervals between the shaded portions
and the line of population, are doubtless due in many cases to errors
in the census returns, incident to the operation of settlement.

SCALE
Under 3 Pr cent
3-10
10-20
20-30
30-40
40 and over

while in 1769 the architect Pierre Patte (1723–1814) produced a comprehensive street-by-street cross-section of Paris in his *Memoires sur les Objets les plus Importants de l'Architecture* ('Memoirs on the Most Important Objects in Architecture), and in 1855 Eugène de Fourcy (1812–89) produced his *Atlas Souterrain de la ville de Paris*, which showed what lay under the city's streets and was presented at the Exposition Universelle in Paris that year. The appointment in 1878 of a municipal commission to centralize the gathering of statistics on the city, which included eminent statisticians such as Toussaint Loua (1824–1907) and Louis-Adolphe Bertillon (1821–83), led to a new wave of statistical atlases including Loua's *Atlas statistique de la population de Paris* ('Statistical Atlas of the Population of Paris', 1873) and Bertillon's *Atlas de statistique graphique de la ville de Paris* ('Graphical Statistical Atlas of the City of Paris') in 1888, which illustrated subjects as diverse as the population density, the tonnage of goods travelling by train and the consumption of oysters.

More conventional atlases of Paris's topography had been produced by J.S. Bellanger, whose *Atlas general des quarante-huit quartiers de la ville de Paris* ('General Atlas of the Forty-Eight Districts of the City of Paris') was published in 1827–36, mapping the city which was, like the other great European urban centres, growing apace, from around 780,000 in 1831 to over 2.2 million 50 years later.

The sheer size of London, Paris's main rival, almost defied cartographers, its medieval maze of alleys in the centre, the prolific laying out of new squares in the Georgian era, as aristocratic entrepreneurs made quick money out of previously unprofitable fields, and the engorgement of outlying villages such as Paddington and Islington into the urban mass as the nineteenth century wore on meant that barely was a map issued than it was promptly out of date. Although the Ordnance Survey mapped the city at five feet to the mile between 1848 and 1850, this produced 847 sheets, which would have made an unwieldy atlas, let alone one that was any use for practical navigation. Edward Mogg's *Ten Thousand Cab Fares Map*, published in 1859, provided a partial solution, although it dealt only in point-to-point fares for cabs along fixed routes, so was no use for free-form exploring or finding particular streets or addresses. A true portable atlas of London would have to wait until the 1930s.

Poverty, though, was far more tangible, visible every day to those who walked London's streets (or those of any large city) and who cared to notice. As well as the many other uses to which it was harnessed in the course of the nineteenth century, mapping was used as an illustration of this poverty (and in the hope of piquing politicians to take action to ameliorate the plight of the poor). Charles Booth (1840–1916), who made his fortune in the shipping trade in the 1860s and 1870s, set out to disprove the assertion by Henry Hyndman, the leader of Britain's Social Democratic Federation, that a quarter of London's population lived in complete poverty. However, his research, conducted with the aid of assistants including the sociologist and radical social reformer Beatrice Webb, which yielded the monumental *Life and Labour of the People* published between 1889 and 1891, showed that, if anything, Hyndman had underestimated the scale of the problem. It also resulted in a series of 'poverty maps' laying out in stark graphic format the human cost of London's uncontrolled expansion. Each street in the central areas (and in particular in the East End) was colour-coded in one of seven shades, which ranged from yellow for the richer, upper-class quarters, to black, which were zones inhabited by the 'lowest class

of occasional labourers, loafers and semi-criminals'. So powerful was the effect of his laying bare of the plight of London's indigent that – quite apart from its impact on the use of quantitative methods in sociology – his work promoted the case for a state old-age pension to alleviate the plight of the elderly poor and reinforced the case of those arguing for better urban sanitation.

By the end of the nineteenth century, it seemed that there was no aspect of philanthropy, demography or urban planning which did not merit its own series of maps or atlases. The age-old role of maps in acting as a record of the boundary between agricultural land-holdings (first seen in a Mesopotamian map from Yorghan Tepe from the twenty-fourth century BC, p.13) took on a new cast in the early eighteenth century due to the spread of enclosures – measures meant to consolidate the often-fragmented pattern of fields in rural areas to encourage greater food production (and as a by-product enrich larger landowners who could afford to buy up smaller plots). Enclosures, by a quirk of the law, needed an act of parliament to sanction them, and between 1790 and 1815 these reached 75 a year in number, culminating in General Enclosure Acts in 1836, 1840 and 1845. Each of them needed commissioners to inspect the land and to map out both its current lay-out and the proposed new system once the fields had been consolidated and the land enclosed. Although not published as collections until modern times, together they constitute an extraordinary document of Britain's changing landscape.

THE STREETS ARE COLOURED ACCORDING TO THE GENERAL CONDITION OF THE INHABITANTS, AS UNDER:—

Lowest class. Vicious, semi-criminal.	Very poor, casual. Chronic want.	Poor. 18s. to 21s. a week for a moderate family.	Mixed. Some comfortable, others poor.	Fairly comfortable. Good ordinary earnings.	Middle class. Well-to-do.	NIL Upper-middle and Upper classes. Wealthy.

A combination of colours—as dark blue and black, or pink and red—indicates that the street contains a fair proportion of each of the classes represented by the respective colours.

That landscape was being transformed in other ways, too. New forms of transport, canals and, from the 1820s, railways, were being added to the earlier post-roads that the seventeenth- and eighteenth-century cartographers had documented. Britain gave birth to the railway craze, as more and more lines were approved by parliament (with about two thousand miles of track operational by the end of 1843). The very first railway map showing the spreading network was published by the Birmingham engineer James Drake in 1838, showing the stretch of the London & Birmingham and Grand Junction railways which operated between London and the Midlands. Soon after, railway maps appeared in Ireland, with the publication the same year of the Second Report of the Railway Commissioners, who had been tasked by Parliament with examining how the new transport technology might be managed in Ireland and a centralized network constructed out of the chaos of lines already laid down and those proposed by various railway companies. Accompanied also by a geological map (presumably to assist engineers who were looking to avoid difficult terrain for their employers' lines), its railway map showed a network in its infancy but, unsurprisingly, already radiating out from the central hub of Dublin.

A truly national railway map followed, issued in 1851 by Zachary Macaulay of the Railway Clearing House (which was set up as a way of helping passengers navigate through the confusing proliferation of tickets offered by rival companies), supplemented by George Bradshaw (1801–1853), whose *Map of the Canals, Navigable Rivers, Rail Roads &c. in the Midland Counties of England,* had already been published in 1829, and who ten years later began issuing his monthly railway timetables, supplemented with maps of the network. With their familiar yellow covers they became a ubiquitous feature of travel on the rails until the publication of the very last edition in 1961.

Where Britain led in railway terms, the United States followed, but the vast distances involved outside the most settled areas on the east and west coast meant that progress in creating a transcontinental railroad – which would need to traverse a distance of more than two thousand miles – was slow and expensive. With the Civil War over in 1865, the Union Pacific railroad company began building west from its railhead in Omaha, and the Central Pacific started laying tracks east from California, but it cost them a prodigious $10,000 per mile of track (although the

OPPOSITE

East Central district, *Map Descriptive of London Poverty,* Charles Booth, 1898–99

BELOW

Relative quantities of traffic in Ireland, *Second Report of the Railway Commissioners,* 1838

New Railroad and Distance map of the US and Canada, Gaylord Watson, 1871

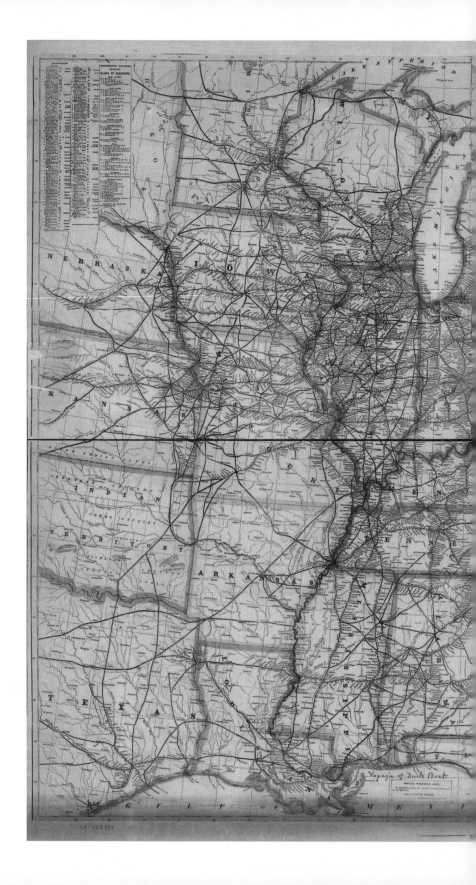

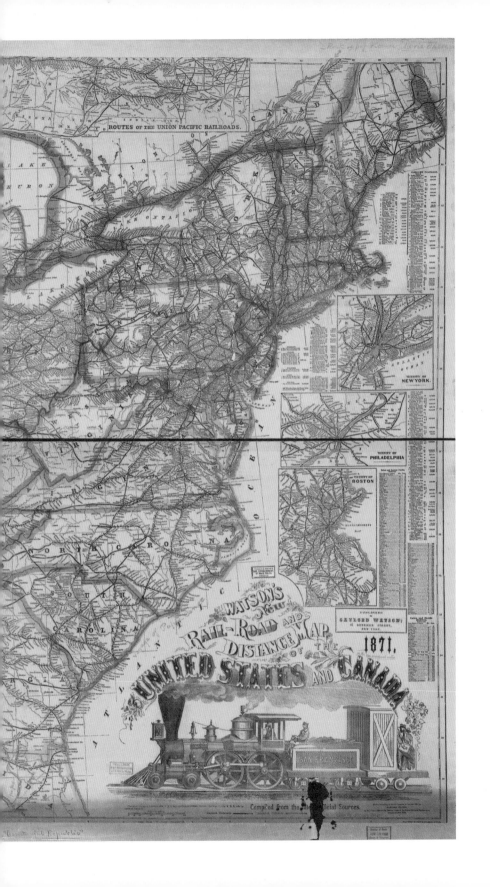

government paid them more and the opportunities for corruption in the procurement process meant the opportunities for enrichment were even greater). When on 10 May 1869 a golden spike was driven into the ground by the directors of the two companies at Promontory Point, Utah, the point their lines met, it meant that the United States's rail network, if not quite complete, was at least now joined up. Even before the completion of the transcontinental railroad, the United States's railway network had been mapped by cartographers such as James T Lloyd, who at the start of the Civil War, in 1861, published his *Lloyd's American Railroad Map*. This focused on the eastern part of the country, cutting it off at Missouri and Arkansas and including a time dial showing the time difference between 30 different locations and Washington, D.C., in a period when there was as yet no legally sanctioned system of time zones (adding a certain haphazard nature to railway travel as the hapless passenger tried to guess exactly what time was being shown on timetables). The culmination of this mapping came with Gaylord Watson's *New Rail-Road and Distance Map of the United States*, published in 1871, which showed the whole country, with distances and times (by rail) between major cities, a potent symbol of a country where previously forbidding distances could now be overcome. Watson (1833–96) followed this up in 1875 with a *Railroad Atlas of the United States* showing each state in more detail and with additional information on post offices, shipping routes, tariffs and even property prices.

The US Civil war yielded maps of a different sort, with the demands of manoeuvering large armies across now-unfriendly terrain creating huge strains for military cartographic departments that had been woefully underfunded or (for the South) non-existent at the start of the war. Map-makers such as Jedediah Hotchkiss (1828–99), who signed on as a humble teamster, but became chief cartographer to the Confederate Army of North Virginia, produced a stream of maps (which were later published in the *Confederate Military History* in 1899), while William E. Merrill (1837–91), who provided similar services to the Union Army of the Cumberland, issued official maps from his base at Chattanooga which were carried by virtually every union officer in the later stages of the war. Newspapers, too, printed their own maps for their news-hungry readers, which were often drawn by their own correspondents on the battlefields. So annoyed was General George McClellan, commander of the Army the Potomac, when he saw a front page of the New York Times in December 1861 with a detailed drawing of the defences of Washington, D.C., then under threat from a northward thrust by Confederate forces, that he tried to have the newspaper closed down.

It was in the documentation of more distant eras of history that the historical atlas really came of age during the nineteenth century, beginning with the *Genealogical, Chronological, Historical and Geographical Atlas* published by the French exile Emmanuel de las Cases (1766–1842) in London in 1801. Organized on geographical, rather than chronological lines – a dilemma which historical atlas publishers have wrestled with ever since – it was a huge success, appearing in French, English and Italian editions. A rival publication appeared not long after. Produced by Christian Kruse (1753–1827), the *Atlas und Tabellen zur Übersicht der Geschichte aller europäischen Länder und Staaten* ('Atlas and Tables with an Overview of the History of all European States and Provinces') was organized on chronological lines, presenting snapshots of European history and the

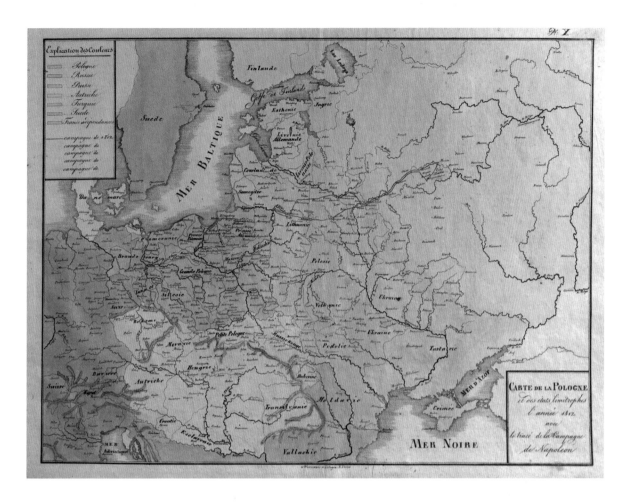

changing borders of states at 100-year intervals. It was published between 1802 and 1818 (financed through the nearly two-decade-long publication process by issuing individual instalments for separate sale).

A spate of historical atlases followed, many originating in the established German cartographic tradition of the Weimar Cartographic Institute, such as the *Historischer Schul-Atlas* by F.W. Benicken, who published it in 1820, five years after he had brought out a smaller-scale project mapping the campaigns of Napoleon. Oddly, to modern tastes (and perhaps to those of some of his contemporaries) he almost entirely eschewed placenames, telling his story with bands of colour, arrows and copious legends and timelines.

The visual display of a country's actual, historic or hoped-for borders was harnessed to the cause of nationalism, with publications such as Stanislas Plater's 1827 *Atlas Historique de la Pologne* solemnly charting the stages by which his homeland had been dismembered by its neighbours Prussia, Russia and Austria-Hungary since the First Partition of 1772. Works such as the *Atlas physique, politique et historique de l'Europe*

('Physical, Political and Historical Atlas of Europe', 1829) by the former head of the French army cartographic office, Maxime-Auguste Denaix (1777–1844), took a more all-embracing view, covering the whole continent thematically, including its flora, fauna, ethnographic details of its peoples, and the sites of battlefields and peace congresses. A more traditional focus, survived, too, in works such as that by the Cornish Bible scholar John Kitto (1804–54). Having survived a difficult childhood, in which he was beaten frequently by his stonemason father and became deaf when, aged 13 he fell from a roof, he managed to get an education at a missionary college in London, learned the printing trade and became a missionary. His *Complete Biblical Atlas,* published in 1850, was in that sense a personal triumph of faith against adversity, although its coverage, from the settlement made by the descendants of Noah, of the land occupied by each of the Tribes of Israel, down to the missionary journeys of St Paul, harked very much back to an earlier age.

Journeys of entirely different kinds had been undertaken by explorers on the edge of the new colonial acquisitions Britain had made since the end of the eighteenth century. In Australia and Africa in particular, vast expanses of land in the interiors of the continents lay unsurveyed and unmapped. In Australia, expedition after expedition went in search of a vast inland sea which ultimately proved to be a mirage, while in Africa the state

of knowledge about the source of the Nile progressed little between Ptolemy's 'Mountains of the Moon' in the first century AD (p.28) and John Hanning Speke becoming the first European to gaze on the source of the Nile at Lake Victoria in 1858.

The expeditions of Speke's great rival, the Scottish missionary-explorer David Livingstone, were charted by one of the stream of great cartographers operating in mid-Victorian London. John Arrowsmith (1790–1873) joined his family map-making business in 1810, but by the 1820s had struck out on his own, labouring long over perhaps his greatest achievement, the *London Atlas of Universal Geography,* first published in 1834 and 10 years later reaching its fifth edition, having added along the way maps of parts of the world which were becoming more familiar to a British public, including the Australian colonies, Texas and the course of the River Niger. Despite his being awarded a gold medal by the Royal Geographical Society largely on the basis of this, it is perhaps for his 1857 map of Southern Africa, including the Livingstone expeditions, for which he became best known. It was, by coincidence, also the year of the first publication of *The Church Missionary Atlas* published by the Church Missionary Society (a rival body of the London Missionary Society which sponsored Livingstone), whose missionaries ranged far and wide from South China and the Pacific Islands to Africa and the Caribbean, providing useful intelligence for the map-makers back home.

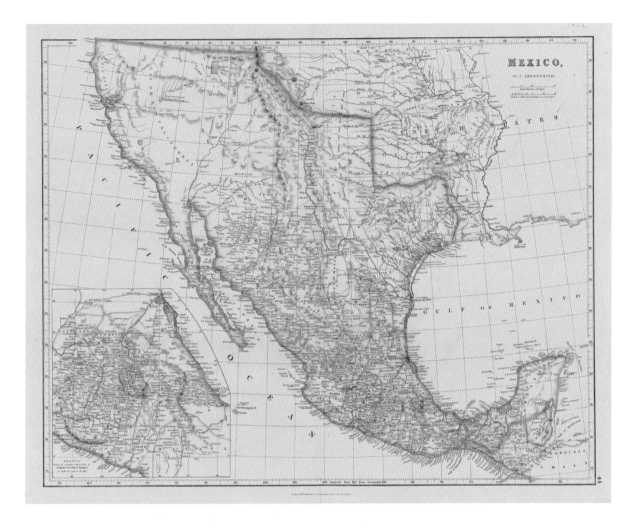

Among the best early maps of Australia was one published by a man who never been there. James Wyld (1812–87) inherited the family mapmaking business in 1836, and with a commercial acumen that ensured its success, published a stream of maps that captured the popular imagination, including one of California, aimed squarely at the spiralling interest inspired by the Gold Rush of 1849. Then, with the colonies of Victoria and New South Wales equally in the grip of gold fever after the discovery of the previous metal in Bathurst near Sydney in 1851, he came out with his *Map of South Australia, New South Wales, Van Diemens Land and Settled Parts of Australia.*

By then his mercurial attention was distracted by yet another project, the erecting of a giant 18m- (60ft-) diameter globe as a means to promote his map business. This, the globe to beat all globes was, Wyld hoped, to be one of the star exhibits in the 1851 Great Exhibition but, much to his disappointment, the organizers turned him down and he instead had to turn it into a side-show located in Leicester Square Gardens. Nonetheless, it was a striking achievement – the inside of the hollowed out 'Great Globe' had a staircase that led to a special platform from which those willing to pay the shilling (or two shillings and sixpence for peak-rate days on Thursday and Saturday) entrance fee could view scale models of the earth's topography, mountains and all, built onto its interior surface. Other exhibitions inside the Great Globe featured models of Stonehenge and the battlefield of Sevastopol and a stuffed polar bear. Over a million people came to see this fantastical pot-pourri, handsomely rewarding Wyld's investment, although after the Great Exhibition itself closed in October 1851, visitor numbers dwindled, other competing nearby attractions such as the Panopticon of Science and Art sucked further life out of the venture and expensive litigation over his promises (which he failed to fulfil) to restore

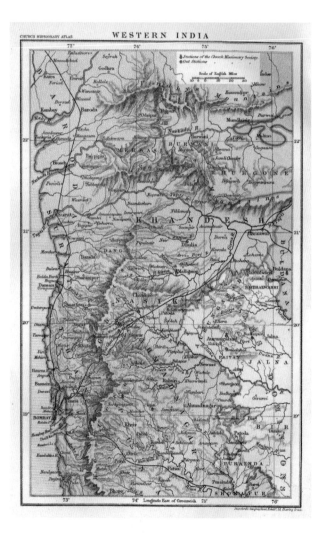

the gardens to their original state caused Wyld to lose control of the business. In 1862, the Great Globe was finally demolished, bringing a sad end to the largest (to that date) ever map of the world.

That world was becoming a smaller place, at least conceptually, as the 'blanks in the map' (if only from a European perspective) were filled in and atlases could at last become close to being truly comprehensive. The latter part of the century saw the publication of all-encompassing atlases such as Adolf Stieler's *Hand Atlas* (first published in 1872). Its American equivalent, Rand McNally's *Indexed Atlas of the World* (1881) was created by the publishing pair of Chicago-born William H. Rand (1828–1915) and Irish immigrant Andrew McNally (1836–1904), who first ran the printing press of the *Chicago Tribune*, then bought out the business and branched out into railroad guides and, finally, atlases.

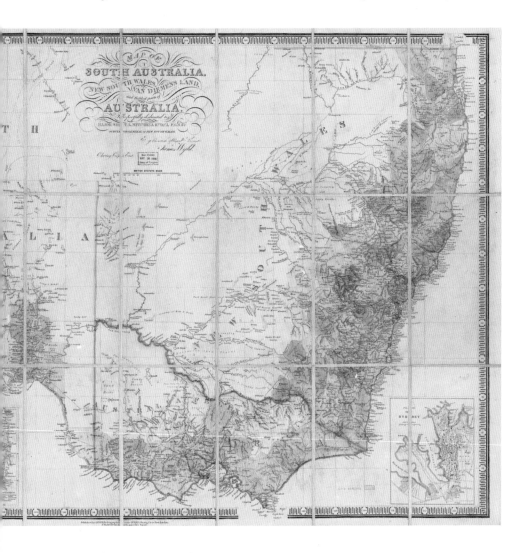

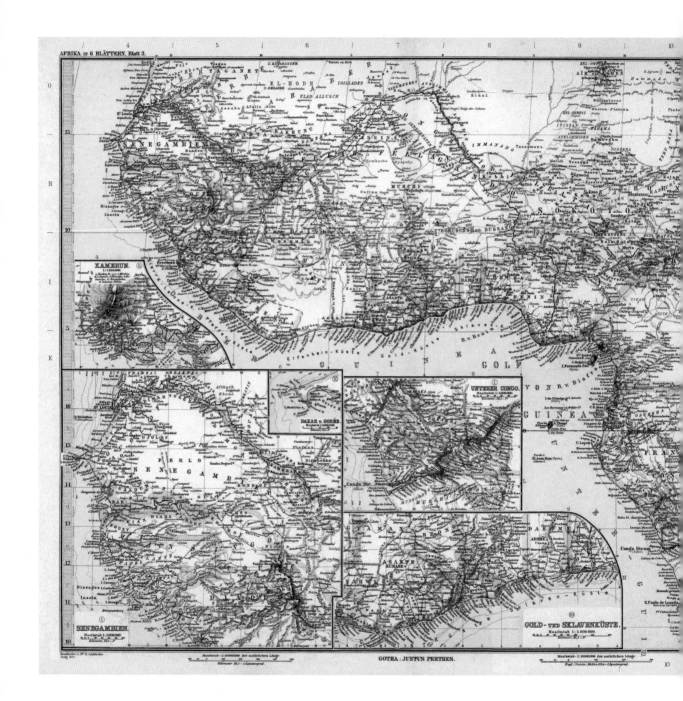

So dedicated were they to the business that when the Great Fire ripped through Chicago in 1871, they took time to bury two printing machines in the sands beside Lake Michigan to ensure the business got back up-and-running within two days, and so influential did its atlas publishing business become that when, in 1917, it pioneered a consistent system for numbering America's highways in one of their road atlases, this caught on and became the model for today's official system. In Britain, Cassell's *Universal Atlas* of 1893 was taken up by the redoubtable *Times* newspaper and republished under its own branding as *The Times Atlas*, the lineal ancestor of *The Times Comprehensive Atlas of the World*, which weighing in at over 12 pounds (5.5kg) in its fifteenth edition (2018) is probably the heaviest (and most authoritative) atlas currently published in the English-speaking world; in 2011 it caused a stir when it depicted the ice on Greenland as having shrunk by 15 per cent compared to the previous edition.

Perhaps, though, the summit of this 'imperial' mapping as least in its intent and visual impact was the map of the British Empire published in 1886 by the splendidly named John Charles Ready Colomb (1838–1909). He was an ardent supporter of Imperial Federation, a political strand popular in the last decades of the nineteenth century that argued for the creation of an imperial superstate centred (of course) on London, but in which the (predominantly white) colonies such as Canada and Australia would have political representation, binding them permanently to Britain and banishing troublesome notions of an independent destiny. His map, therefore, had several purposes. One was to display the extent of Empire, with Britain's holdings tinted in the inevitable reddish-pink (though had he waited just a little longer, even greater stretches of Africa would have turned red), and the borders of the map adorned with caricatures of various peoples from around the empire all presided over by a behelmeted personification of Britannia, carrying a trident and languishing pensively on a globe (held up by a rather pained-looking figure of Atlas). Another was to argue the economic case for Imperial Federation by highlighting the network of trade routes that bound the Empire together and from which Britain could profit on a longer-term basis if it could be established. And finally, Colomb simply wanted to commemorate the Golden Jubilee of Queen Victoria, which would take place the following year.

It seemed as though Empire and imperial mapping was for ever. Yet within 15 years the Queen would be dead and, though the Empire continued, the new century would see it face challenges, as new rivals the United States and Germany began to take it on economically. With the American acquisition of the Philippines in 1898 and the German move into Africa (where they took what are now Namibia, Rwanda and Burundi) and New Guinea and parts of the Solomon Islands and Samoa in the Pacific, Britain faced military competitors, too. For Britain, France and the other colonial powers, the coming century would mean crisis and the reshaping both of their worlds and of the world map itself.

OPPOSITE

Senegambia in Africa, *Hand Atlas*, Adolf Stieler, 1872 (1891 edition)

THE ATLAS AND WAR

(1900–1950)

The French and British Empires were at the height of their self-confidence in 1900, having partitioned much of the African continent between them while holding onto their possessions in South and Southeast Asia. Germany and Italy had entered the imperial sphere, too, albeit on a much smaller scale, and it seemed little could shake the hold of European powers over their colonial empires. The second phase of the Industrial Revolution at the end of the nineteenth century had brought advances in printing technology and the rising incomes of the middle classes in Europe and the United States created a growing market for maps of all sorts, from traditional world wall maps, to general atlases, school atlases and portable guides to the major cities, whose growing populations (that of London increased from a million in 1800 to seven million in 1900) meant that they were constantly acquiring new suburbs in need of mapping.

Yet the next half century saw this confidence shattered and the turning of mapping to other uses as two global wars devastated the European continent, large parts of the Middle East and North Africa and (in the case of the second) swathes of the Pacific, China and Southeast Asia. For a time, mapping became the purview of the military, and civilian surveys ceased, large-scale mapping being restricted as a matter of national security. Even so, maps of the colonized territories (including Palestine and India) were still produced, as were new national atlases of those countries (such as Canada) whose territory was not directly affected by the wars. Thematic mapping continued to develop in sophistication, while the constant demand for school and general atlases meant that maps were more than ever an essential part of day-to-day life.

It is a commonplace that the boundaries of many post-colonial nations, above all in Africa (and in the particularly egregious case of the Partition of India), were created at the stroke of the pen of a colonial administrator, giving little regard to traditional territories or divisions between ethnic groups on the ground. The terrible results of this rather casual approach, including civil wars, international border disputes and forced migrations, have bedevilled large parts of the world ever since. Yet, though they did indeed largely ignore considerations of local demography, they were not entirely whimsical creations, but were based on 'imperial' cartography in which the colonial powers sought to map their possessions, delimiting the borders against the holdings of other powers (though rarely going to the expense of a full-scale topographical survey such as that undertaken in India in the nineteenth century). In often difficult climatic conditions (above all for the European surveyors, whose tolerance for heat and resistance to endemic diseases was slight) and with limited instruments, map coverage concentrated on heavily settled areas such as Egypt or Java or those that were economically lucrative (such as the diamond mines of the Witswatersrand in South Africa), and rarely yielded formal atlases. The exception was those nations (generally where Europeans had settled in larger numbers) that became Dominions, reaching a semi-detached status in respect of the British Empire. In Canada, a national atlas was produced as early as 1906; by 1957, it had separate French and English editions, reflecting the complex linguistic politics of the nation, and, in 2006, its sixth edition was freely available on the internet. Elsewhere, progress was slower. Australia would have to wait until after the Second World War and the publication of the *Atlas of Australian Resources*, in 1953, which as befits a country with some of the largest deposits

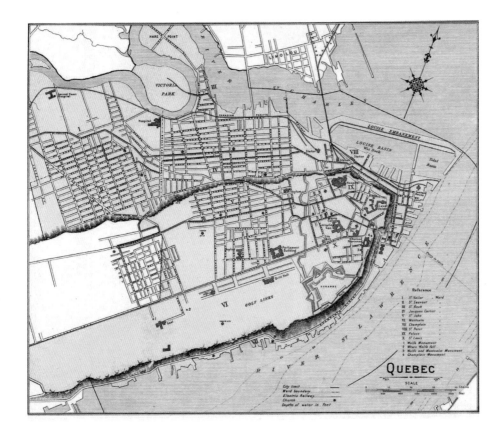

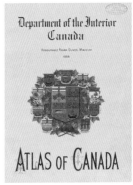

of natural resources such as coal and uranium, had a strong focus on maps of Australia's mineral wealth. New Zealand's first comprehensive national atlas, the *New Zealand Atlas*, was only published in 1976.

The increasing focus of European nations on their empires (even though their control over them was loosened by the First World War and shattered by the effects of the Second), and the continued need for imperial mapping projects of the colonies, did not detract from the demand for genuinely world atlases. And, in a surprising reversal of the general tendency to increased nationalism in the period (of which the two world wars were themselves the most catastrophic manifestation), these became for the first time something like global atlases. *The Times Survey Atlas of the World*, first published in 1920 (and which in due course would become *The Times Comprehensive Atlas of the World*, the flagship atlas of British cartographic publishing), had more than 100 maps, with just a third devoted to Europe. Although Rand McNally's *Indexed Atlas of the World* (1908) still concentrated heavily on the American sphere of influence, by the time of the company's *Cosmopolitan World Atlas* (1949), the balance had been redressed, together with the incorporation of a number of maps of physical geography and other thematic subjects to create the geographical-thematic hybrid that was becoming the norm.

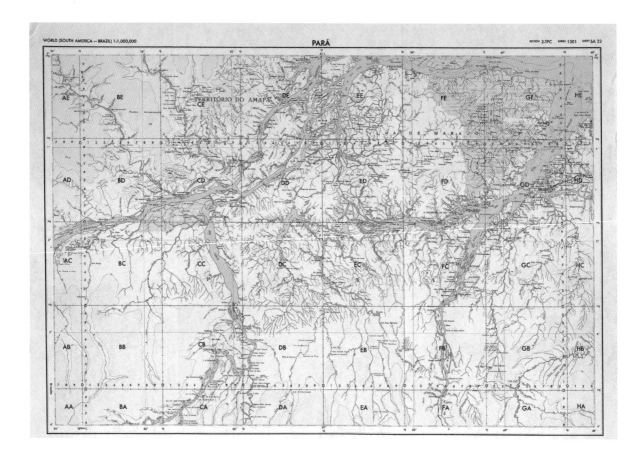

ABOVE

Marajo Island, Brazil, Sheet
SA-22 of the *International
Map of the World*, 1950

There was, though, a growing sense that the world was being reshaped and not always
in the image that the major European powers desired. Geopolitics, the discipline that
examined the interplay of global political rivalries, was the brainchild of the geographer
Halford Mackinder (1861–1947), whose busy career included being a founder director
of the London School of Economics (1895), first professor of Geography at Oxford
University (1899), being a member of the first European expedition to climb Mount
Kenya the same year, lobbying for the creation of a National Theatre, a stint as a Liberal
Unionist MP for the Glasgow Camlachie constituency and a posting as British High
Commissioner in Southern Russia during the Russian Civil War (1919–20). He also
helped found the Geographical Association in 1893 to promote the teaching of human
geography in schools. In 1904, he delivered a hugely influential paper entitled 'The
Geographical Pivot of History' to the Royal Geographical Society in London in which
he argued that powerful interconnected forces were reshaping the world in ways that
Britain needed to understand to address, and in which a proper study of geography could
play a key role. As he put it: 'Every explosion of social forces, instead of being dissipated in
a surrounding circuit of unknown space and barbarian chaos, will be sharply re-echoed

from the far side of the globe, and weak elements in the political and economic organism of the world be shattered in consequence'.[1] As the virtual founder of the discipline of geopolitics, Mackinder perceptively predicted that it would be Central Asia and not the British Empire which would be the 'pivot region of the world's politics' and pushed his point with a map of the 'natural seats of power' that showed Asia at its heart, and Britain firmly at the margins.

It was perhaps as a means to avoid the disasters of war that an international effort grew up to compile a truly global map, with the co-operation of the major powers, constructed according to an agreed set of standards. The *International Map of the World* (or *IMW*) was the brainchild of the German geologist Albrecht Penck (1858–1945), who proposed it in 1891 at an International Geographical Congress in Berne. He believed that a map on a scale of 1:1,000,000 should be possible to replace the chaos of existing world maps which had a variety of scales and whose coverage was in places patchy. He estimated it would take 2,500 maps to cover the entire earth, creating what he termed 'An Atlas of the World' of which his illustrious predecessors such as Mercator would have been proud. Each would cover four degrees of latitude and six of longitude using a common projection (a modified conic projection). He estimated that the cost could be covered by selling each sheet for two shillings a copy, but that much of this had in any case already been met by existing surveys, so that the finances should present few obstacles.

International conferences beget international bureaucracy and international squabbling and so it was that it took until 1909 even for an International Map Committee to explore the idea to be set up. It did, though, at least agree the general shape of the project and by 1913 had issued six sheets covering Europe. The outbreak of the First World War, the desire of the British to control the project and a rival initiative by the United States in South America caused even Penck to disown it in frustration, and by 1925 just 200 maps had been completed, 90 per cent of them failing to conform to the minimum standards that the Map Committee had laid down. Even the choice of the *IMW* as the approved map for the Paris peace conference at the end of the war failed to spark the project back into life. By 1953, when it was transferred to the United Nations Cartographic Office, the *IMW* had limped painfully on to reach a total of 400 maps. Despite efforts over the following decades to bring it back to life, the UN finally put it out of its misery and cancelled the little-lamented *IMW* in 1989. A true 'world atlas', when it came, would be in a far different form to that which Penck had expected (p.256).

Russia, where Mackinder had spent two instructive years as British High Commissioner as the Bolsheviks consolidated their rule and the pro-Tsarist White Russian armies collapsed, had long had political ambitions that brought it vast territories to the east (and to some extent in the west after it gobbled up much of Poland between 1772 and 1793). Yet despite the efforts of reformist rulers such as Peter the Great to reposition it, the country lay outside the European political mainstream. In the field of mapping, though, the aspirations of its later imperial rulers were the equal of those of their rival monarchs to the west. The last product of the imperial Romanovs was the *Atlas Aziatskoy Rossii* ('Atlas of Asiatic Russia'), published in 1914 on the eve of the First World War, a conflict that would finally bring down the dynasty after more than 300 years of rule. It bore the hallmarks of Piotr Stolypin, Russian Prime Minister from 1906 to 1911 during the false

BELOW AND RIGHT
Title page (below); Russian
dominions in Asiatic Russia
(right), *Atlas Aziatskoy Rossii*,
1914

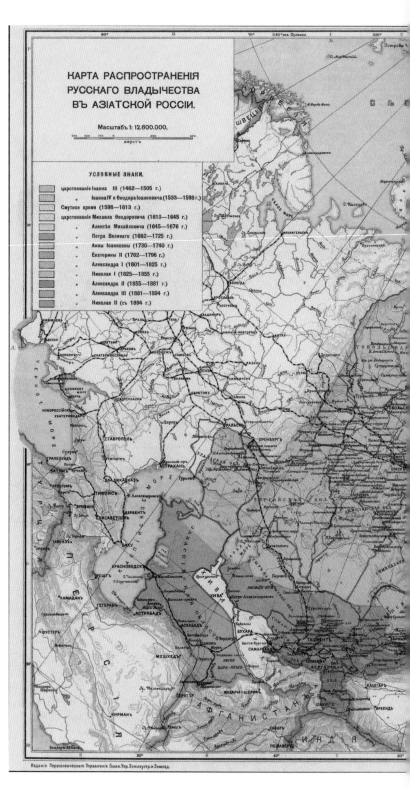

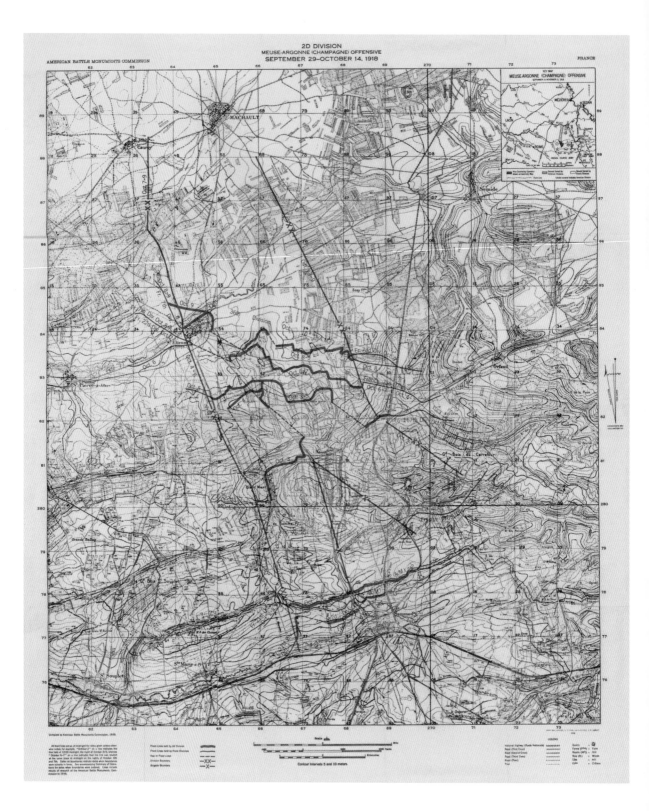

KEY MAP
MEUSE-ARGONNE (CHAMPAGNE) OFFENSIVE

Contour Intervals 5 and 10 meters

LEGEND

dawn of democratic reform that followed the Revolution of 1905, an early uprising that foreshadowed that of 1917 without resolving any of the problems that sparked the later, disastrous, conflagration. His agrarian reforms of 1906 freed peasants from being tied to communal lands (to which millions had still been bound despite the notional abolition of serfdom in 1861).

As a result of this, and more direct encouragement, more than a million of them moved to Russia's Asian territories beyond the Urals, there to prosper, until as *kulaks* (rich peasants) they were demonized as enemies of the new Soviet state in the 1920s and dispossessed or slaughtered *en masse*. This migration also transformed Russia's Siberian lands, which had been something of a backwater (albeit one which bestowed significant imperial bragging rights), into a centre of policy concern. The Resettlement Department of the Chief Directorate of Land Management and Agriculture, a bureaucratic mouthful whose head Grigory V. Glinka oversaw the project, sent surveyors out into the remotest areas on an eight-year mission that yielded a magnificent atlas with 72 maps and numerous diagrams charting the demography, mining and agricultural potential of the region. It did not, though, save the Tsar, who was shot with his family in July 1918 in Yekaterinburg, just at the western edge of the atlas's coverage.

The new Soviet authorities did, though, value the scientific precision with which it had been assembled and it formed the basis for the next great Russian mapping effort, the *Bolshoi Sovietskii atlas mira*, or 'Mira Atlas'. In a sign of the times it was produced under the 'co-operative' editorship of Alexander Gorkin (1897–1988), who was Secretary of the Executive Committee of the Soviet Union from 1938 to 1953 at the height of the Stalinist repression, the show trials which saw many of the original Bolshevik leaders executed, and during the Second World War. In deference to the political realities of the period it tactfully included vignettes of Lenin and Stalin above its title, but the turmoil of the decades in which it was being compiled meant that only two of the three projected volumes were ever published.

The hopes symbolised by the *International Map of the World* that co-operation between nations on a common project might avoid misunderstandings and war proved profoundly overoptimistic, and instead of a joining of hands, Europe experienced an arms race, particularly in the naval sphere, as Germany raced to catch up with Great Britain, the previously undisputed maritime power. The German building of warships to rival the ultra-modern dreadnought fleet which Britain began launching in 1906, the unlikely Anglo-French Entente Cordiale (1904) breaching a wall of centuries of mutual distrust, and German meddling in Morocco were all sparks on the dry tinder of European politics that finally erupted into the First World War following the assassination of the Austrian Archduke Franz Ferdinand by a Serb nationalist in Sarajevo in 1914. To fight, the rival sides needed maps. Britain already had a Topographical Section of its General Staff (formed in 1904), later renamed the Geographical Section, General Staff (or GSGS). Under the auspices of the Committee of Imperial Defence (whose name clearly indicates British priorities in any future war), it began mapping defensive positions in towns and particularly those areas along the country's long coastline which might offer tempting avenues for foreign invasion forces.

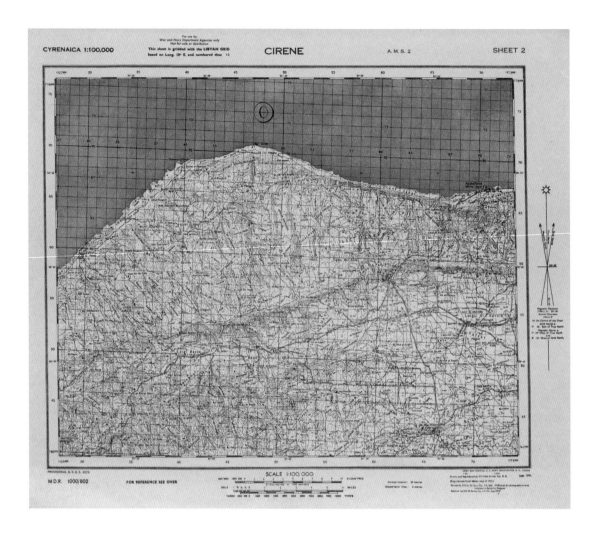

CYRENAICA 1:100,000   For use by War and Navy Department Agencies only Not for sale or distribution   This sheet is gridded with the LIBYAN GRID based on Long. 18° E. and numbered thus 43   CIRENE   A.M.S. 2   SHEET 2

SCALE 1:100,000

M.D.R. 1000/802   FOR REFERENCE SEE OVER

Cirene [Cyrenaica], Libya topographic map, US Army Map Service, August 1942

The map was based on an Italian original map of 1931, revised by the US 514 Field Survey Company and then further amended in 1942 using American military aerial photography.

The outbreak of war led to a huge demand for maps for use by the British Expeditionary Force that left for France in August 1914, but it was not initially met by new surveys (though the delays caused by having to print maps in Britain and then transport them across the Channel to the front lines led to the establishment of a military Base Stationery Unit at Abbeville in Normandy, meaning military formations received up-to-date maps in time for planned operations). The French mapping proved inadequate once the two sides settled down into the 500-mile-long snake of the Western Front trench lines, where plotting the opposition's trenches against the landscape was a vital aid for planning local and larger offensives. By the end of 1914, survey sections had been established, which grew inexorably into whole survey battalions. While these largely withered away during the inter-war period, the GSGS itself remained intact, concentrating on mapping areas of international tension within and on the borders of Britain's Empire where it was anticipated future conflicts might occur. Hong Kong was mapped in the 1920s using aerial photography taken by flying boats launched from HMS *Pegasus*, while Malta, Britain's strategic fortress-island in the central Mediterranean, was similarly mapped by the Royal Air Force.

In 1936, when it became clear that there was a real prospect of a new European War, the GSGS commissioned a new map of northern France and Belgium, where it was anticipated that the main fighting would take place. In a sign of the underfunding of the military that had been the norm since 1918, however, much of the work had to be carried out by the Ordnance Survey and was incomplete by the time the war did break out in September 1939. During the course of the Second World War, around 350 million maps were printed for the British military, with survey units directly deployed to major operations, and with the capacity to print updated maps in the field for use in front-line operations.

The most significant new mapping was carried out for the D-Day landings, the Allied invasion of north-western Europe in June 1944, which opened up a new front against the German army and was the largest amphibian landing in history, and for which a series of 'Benson' maps were produced at 1:25,000 scale covering the whole of France and Belgium, adapted from existing mapping but heavily modified using aerial reconnaissance photography. United States military mappers played a key role in this, building on their experience in the latter stages of the First World War, in which they had transferred experience gained using observation balloons in the Spanish-American War of 1898 into the new technology of airplanes (so that by 1917 a school had been set up at Cornell University to train aerial photographers). Between the wars, work continued at a lower tempo, refining the technical processes so that, for example, transparent overlays could be produced to modify maps rather than marking them up with hand-lettering, but already before the United States formally entered the Second World War, a new Map Section had been established (renamed the Map-Chart Division in January 1942), which supervised the production of aeronautical charts in particular and became responsible for producing maps for field operations throughout the war. Among its major achievements was the aerial photography of over ten million square miles of territory in areas of the world where existing mapping was either inadequate or non-existent.

Although Germany's strong cartographic tradition should have placed its military in a commanding position at the start of the First World War, the fragmentation of the German constitutional system, which still maintained separate establishments for the kingdoms that made up the German Empire, hampered its efficiency. The Prussian General Staff in Berlin was the largest, but in the production of a general map of Germany, the *Karte des Deutschen Reiches* ('Map of the German Empire'), responsibility was split between its allocation of 545 sheets; Bavaria was meant to produce 80, Saxony 30 and Wurttemberg 20. Large-scale maps of neighbouring countries were woefully inadequate. Once war did break out and the fighting congealed into the trench lines, field survey squadrons and units for the analysis of aerial photography were rapidly formed, allowing large-scale maps of the Western Front to be available to the Germans sooner than to their Allied counterparts and front-line printing units were created capable of delivering updated maps almost daily.

The rearmament of Germany carried out by Adolf Hitler's Nazi regime from 1933 also included a cartographic effort, with a Ninth Division responsible for mapping the Reich and beyond established in 1936 (that in 1939 became the Division for War Maps and Surveying). It was responsible for producing tactical and strategic mapping, making use of new surveys (including along the front lines) as well as captured foreign maps (which amounted to a collection of over 200,000 by 1943). In all, the map units of the German Army employed 1,500 officers towards the end of the war and produced over 1.3 billion printed copies.

Some of those were targeting maps for use by the Luftwaffe, the German air force (which in common with its Allied counterparts both carried out aerial surveillance, which was used to compile maps, and used those maps in delivering tactical support and, in particular, in conducting bombing raids). German targeting maps covered all the major cities, including London, Southampton, Portsmouth, Liverpool and Coventry, where strategic installations such as docks and factories were based, and were used to direct streams of attack operations during the Blitz, the eight-month-long bombing campaign against British cities which left over 40,000 civilians dead, and more than a million houses damaged or destroyed in London alone. To record the damage and to help with the clearance of the rubble and eventual reconstruction, surveyors from the London County Council's Architects Department compiled a series of bomb damage maps, recording the extent of the devastation with coloured shading (from black indicating total destruction, purple for buildings damaged beyond repair, down to orange for generalized blast damage and yellow for minor damage). As well as providing an essential tool for planning repairs of devastated infrastructure during the War, the bomb damage maps also formed the basis on which London's future shape was plotted and were used extensively in the drawing up of the Greater London Plan in 1944.

The First World War shattered the European empires of Russia, Germany and Austro-Hungary (the first two of which reconstituted themselves in another form, while the Austrian empire, which had already lost its Italian provinces by 1871, dissolved into a series of successor states). Although they little realized it, even the victors of that war, principally France and Britain, but also including Belgium and the Netherlands, were living through a last imperial twilight. Maps and atlases of their colonial possessions were still required and surveying parties still went out, often to adjudicate on boundary disputes between the European powers. In 1922 an international boundary team was sent to East Africa as the former German possessions there had been divided between Britain and Belgium as League of Nations mandates, and there was now a need for the borders between what had become British Tanganyika and the new Belgian territories of Ruanda and Urundi (modern Rwanda and Burundi) to be delineated. Its surveyors, working in treacherous mountainous jungles and swamps, completed their report by 1924. A protest when the British tried to shift the line to accommodate the path of a railway they were building from Uganda to Tanganyika was adjudicated in favour of the Belgians, so creating the lines which would appear on the *Atlas géographique et historique du Congo belge et des territoires sous mandat du Ruanda-Urundi* ('Geographical and Historical Atlas of the Belgian Congo and of the Territories under the Mandate of Ruanda-Urundi') in 1938.

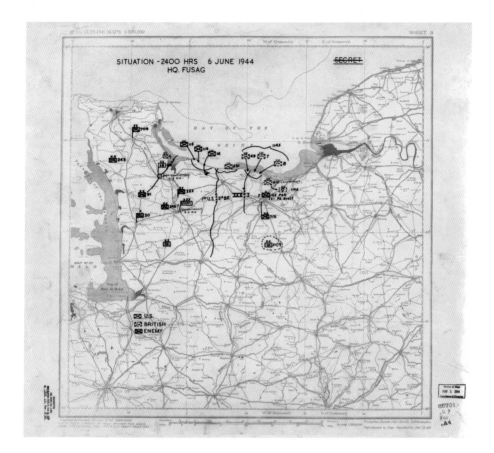

The position of the 12th Army Group, adjacent Allied Forces and German units at 2400 hours on D-Day

In-theatre mapping was vital to the Allied success in opening up a new front against Germany after the D-Day landings in Normandy on 6 June 1944. Here we can see that the Allies have secured bridgeheads along the coast, but no breakout has yet occurred.

The League of Nations mandate over Palestine, awarded to Britain in 1919 (and which became effective in September 1923), saw the British Empire reach its largest ever extent, encompassing a quarter of the globe and over 450 million people within its bounds. Those bounds, as they had been since Victorian times, were charted in countless atlases in red, with *Philip's School Atlas of Comparative Geography*, whose fifteenth edition was published the year the mandate's operation began (proclaiming that it was 'showing the territorial change effected by the peace treaties' which ended the First World War), continuing a publishing strand which would reach its one hundreth edition in 2021. While British-produced school atlases tended to have a more political approach, giving pride of place to the Empire, German-language maps intended for education continued to stress physical geography, with maps of temperature, rainfall, vegetation or population density in atlases such as the *Kartographische und Schul-geographische Zeitschrift* ('Cartographic and School Geographical Journal'), published by Freytag in 1912. In turn, as the United States transformed itself into a global power, its school atlases lost their primarily American focus, with products such as *Goode's School Atlas* (1922), which also reduced the number of place-names on each map to help a younger market understand

Triest als Kartenbild.

Bearbeitet von J. G. Rothaug.   Maßstab 1:100.000.   3 Kilometer   G. Freytag & Berndt, Wien.

Der sichtbare Teil des Bildes ist auf der Karte bezeichnet.

PLATE 9.

EUROPE
IN 1648
after the
PEACE OF WESTPHALIA

English Miles

Note.—The Boundary of the Empire is shown
by a deep red line

Oxford: Clarendon Press

W. & A. K. Johnston, Del. & Lith., Edinburgh.

geography (and, as it used the foreign-language forms of place-names in their respective countries, it also included a pronunciation guide).

Another type of atlas with an educational purpose, the historical atlas continued to explain history, particularly to a school market. With the increasingly nationalistic tinge to much publishing in the inter-war period, the preoccupation with historical boundaries often took on a more pointed hue, such as in atlases published in Germany under Nazi rule, which pushed the narrative that German-speaking countries such as Austria and countries in which there were large numbers of German speakers (such as Czechoslovakia) belonged within the bounds of the Reich. The 1933 edition of F.W. Putzger's *Historischer Schul-Atlas* ('Historical School Atlas') took things a stage further with a map showing potential air threats to Germany, reinforcing the message that the country needed its own air force, something explicitly forbidden to it by the Treaty of Versailles. Less overtly nationalistic, *William Shepherd's Historical Atlas*, published in 1911, which became a standard fixture on British bookshelves, inculcated a sense that the British Empire was the rightful successor to the Roman Empire of old (with the Angevin domains of the Plantagenets in France being another exemplary case of the wide-ranging

OPPOSITE

Railway network, Trieste, *Kartographische und Schul-geographische Zeitschrift*, 1912

ABOVE

Europe after the Peace of Westphalia in 1648, *Historical Atlas of Europe,* **R. Lane Poole, 1900**

The 90 maps in Poole's atlas reflect his interests as a medieval historian, with a significant bias towards the period before 1500. More up-do-date subjects included this one of Europe after the Peace of Westphalia, which ended the Thirty Years' War in 1648.

ABOVE

Ancient Italy (Northern part), *Historical Atlas*, **William R. Shepherd, 1911**

OPPOSITE

Lake District, *Stanford's Geological Atlas of Great Britain and Ireland*, **H.B. Woodward, 1907 (1914 edition)**

An expert on crustaceans, Woodward was also an expert in geology, serving as the Keeper of Geology at the British Museum and the editor of the *Geological Magazine* for over 50 years, from 1865 to 1918.

nature of British power), so feeding into the preconceptions of a British elite which had been brought up on a strict diet of classical history. Setting the standard in the United States was Charles Oscar Paullin's *Atlas of the Historical Geography of the United States* (1932), compiled by a team of leading historians, often dealing with very specific topics such as population distribution or the impact of treaty negotiations rather than the traditional almost rhythmic portrayal of the rise and fall of great empires.

Historical atlases were in one sense a specialized example of a wider trend in atlases during the first half of the twentieth century, in which purely regional atlases, such as the German *Saar Atlas* (1934) or the Russian *Atlas Moskovskoy oblasti* (1933) began including a high level of maps portraying natural resources, cultural sites, anthropology, religions, health and other demographic data, which edged them across the line into being thematic atlases. A tighter focus came from works such as Hans Kurath's 1939 *Linguistic Atlas of New England*, which charted dialectal differences across the northeast of the United States, and C.W. Thornthwaite's *Atlas of Climatic Types in the United States* (1941), whose geographical scope was wider, and which became the pioneer for environmental atlases later in the century. The *Atlas of Central Europe* published in Budapest in 1926, meanwhile, included demographic maps of the highly complex situation in the former Austro-Hungarian Empire, whose multi-ethnic nature had led to a mosaic of different linguistic communities which were, after the empire's dissolution in 1918, beginning to coalesce into the harder-edged national states of the inter-war period.

Those states in turn would go to war in 1939, compounded by a Pacific War as Japan's attack on the United States turned a European conflict into a global one. It would have devastating effects on the countries within which it was fought and corrosive effects on the European empires which had begun as its major combatants. After peace finally came in 1945, the next half-century would see hopes of a more truly international approach to resolving global issues raised, then dashed, then raised again, as a complex interplay of Cold War rivalry, the emergence of dozens of newly independent countries in Africa and Asia, and the growth of international bodies such as the United Nations and regional blocs such as the European Economic Community, made policy planners' strategies disappear into dust almost the moment they were formulated.

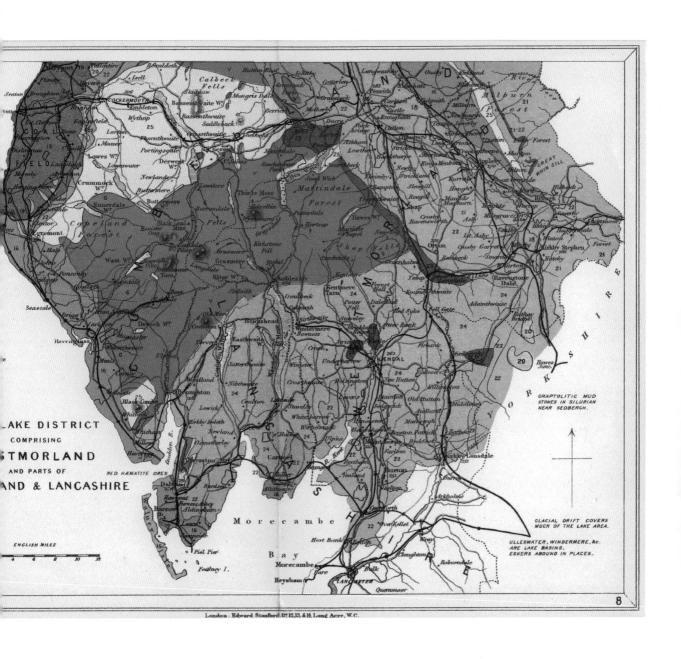

LAKE DISTRICT

COMPRISING

STMORLAND

AND PARTS OF

AND & LANCASHIRE

RED HÆMATITE ORES

ENGLISH MILES

4   6   8   10   12

GRAPTOLITIC MUD
STONES IN SILURIAN
NEAR SEDBERGH.

GLACIAL DRIFT COVERS
MUCH OF THE LAKE AREA.

ULLESWATER, WINDERMERE, &c.
ARE LAKE BASINS.
ESKERS ABOUND IN PLACES.

8

London : Edward Stanford, Ld. 12,13, & 14, Long Acre, W.C.

AN ATLAS
OF SOCIETY

(1950–2000)

The final great age of print atlases saw a wider than ever range of examples of all formats and sizes become available to consumers. As decolonisation created dozens of new independent nations, each took on the responsibility of its own mapping, creating new atlases and new visions of the country separate from the colonizing power. The Space Age provided new means of surveying as satellite photography supplemented aerial photography to allow maps to be created without ever traversing the ground. Mapping was turned to ever more uses, with the flowering of commercial thematic publishing, some of it with a campaigning intent, highlighting social iniquities or the baleful effects of Cold War superpower rivalry and the arms race, some charting the political and economic histories of countries in unparalleled detail. Towards the end of the period, digital mapping became possible for the first time, allowing the compilation, drawing and correction of maps at unprecedented speed and their publication at lower costs. Yet as the twentieth century drew to its close, the first hint of a challenge to the five-millennia-old story of maps emerged, when the advent of the internet made virtual maps, once a science-fiction dream, very much a reality.

As well as the terrible physical toll of the Second World War, which cost something like fifty million lives and left much of Europe bankrupt, its end marked a transfer of geopolitical power from the imperial powers that had dominated the world stage for the past century. The Cold War which developed in the 1940s between the new superpowers, the United States and the Soviet Union and their respective allies, soon added the threat of a catastrophic nuclear war to the already profound challenges of reconstruction. The Europeans' hold on their empires weakened, too, as the psychological will to retain them no matter the cost was broken. In the 1940s, a first wave of countries where nationalist movements had been particularly strong broke away from European control, leading to the independence of India and Pakistan (1947), Israel (1948) and Indonesia (1949).

In the cases of India and Pakistan, and Israel, all former British colonies or mandates, mapping would have a profound effect on the future of the new nations. By early 1947 it was clear to almost all that sooner rather than later Britain would have to grant some form of independence to India, severing a two-century-long period of political control. Before the Second World War it seemed likely that any independent India would encompass the whole of the South Asian subcontinent (including what are now Pakistan, India and Bangladesh). But strong lobbying by Muhammad Ali Jinnah and his All-India Muslim League from 1913, who argued that it would be impossible for India's large Muslim population to have fair political representation in a Hindu-dominated nation and that what was needed instead was to partition the land between the two religious communities, ate away at this certainty. Despite vociferous opposition from veteran proponents of a single-country solution such as Jawaharlal Nehru and Mahatma Gandhi, the British government gave way and in June 1947 it appointed Cyril Radcliffe (1899–1977), a former Ministry of Information bureaucrat, to carry out the partition of British India.

Radcliffe was given just three months to complete his work. He was hampered by the lack of time in which to conduct any meaningful new surveys on the ground or the will even to try, the shortage of staff (he had just a handful civil servants working for him), and the frosty relations between the two Muslim and two Hindu members of the

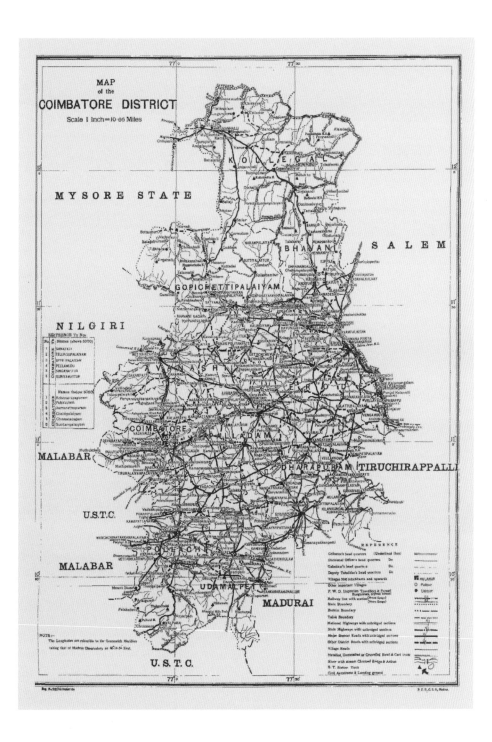

boundary commissions which were set up to adjudicate issues relating to Bengal and Punjab. The census returns on which many of the determinations were made were hopelessly out of date and Radcliffe neither attended the commissions' deliberations, nor could he use his personal knowledge to fine-tune the process: he had none, never even having visited India before.

Predictably, the process ended in disaster. Radcliffe's report was not even published until 17 August 1947, two days after independence, and hundreds of thousands of Hindus and Muslims found themselves on 'the wrong side of the line' when it was. An enormous refugee crisis was set in motion as people fled their ancestral villages by bullock-cart or automobile, on foot or by train. In the end, 15 million people were displaced and over a million died in a carnage of intercommunal violence. Subsequent disputes over the Radcliffe Line, in particular in Kashmir, have led to wars between India

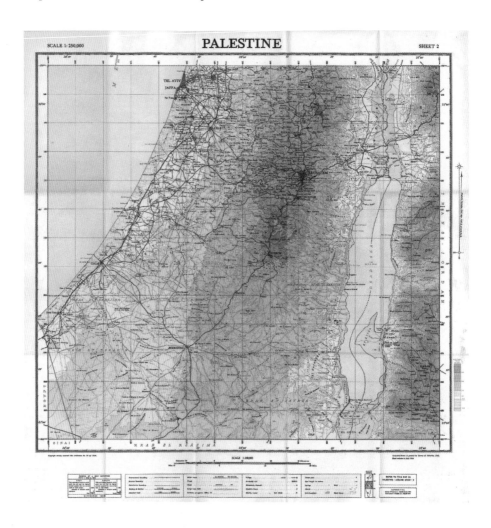

and Pakistan in 1947, 1965 and 1971 and a permanent poisoning of relations between the (now nuclear-armed) neighbours.

Although the British legacy to India was in many ways a troubled one, the new government inherited a strong bureaucratic tradition, including in the cartographic sphere. In 1956, Jawaharlal Nehru (1889–1964), who served as the country's first prime minister for nearly 17 years, established the National Atlas and Thematic Mapping Organisation, based in Calcutta, tasked with producing the independent country's first national atlas. It was the brainchild of S.P. Chatterjee (1903–89), head of geography at the University of Calcutta, who used his experience of producing a previous, smaller-scale atlas, *Bengal in Maps* (1949), to entice Nehru with the prospect of India being the first developing country to have its own national atlas (outside the western bloc only the USSR had one at that stage). The result was an eight-volume publication, with the first containing conventional political mapping and the other seven thematic mapping, including not only mineral, climate and population maps, but also covering the social geography, linguistics, culture and history of India among its total of 274 maps. A first edition was issued in 1957, but a second edition took 25 more years to complete, and the atlas remained the benchmark against which other aspirant cartographic powers could measure themselves.

If maps played a defining role in the creation of India and Pakistan, they were the key to the independence of another British territory. Israel's borders – claimed, asserted and disputed – have disrupted the politics of the Middle East since its declaration of independence on 14 May 1948 and the subsequent war with its Arab neighbours after which the new nation emerged, enlarged and in a state of permanent dispute over the legitimacy of its holding of territory initially allocated to the Palestinians. The British Mandate over Palestine, carved out of former Ottoman Turkish territory by the League of Nations after the First World War, had faced problems coping with increased Jewish Zionist migration to the region, and fears among the Muslim population about British good faith after the Foreign Secretary, Arthur Balfour (1848–1930), issued a declaration in November 1917 broadly in support of Jewish aspirations for a homeland in Palestine. By the 1930s, when it was clear some form of solution to intercommunal mistrust and violence between the Arab and Jewish populations in Palestine would be needed, the British resolved upon partition, with the 1936 Peel Commission recommending a small Jewish state centred on Tel Aviv. By 1947, with Jewish nationalist militia having fought a sapping guerrilla war against the British, and with the revulsion in Europe caused by the Holocaust raising sympathy for the idea of a Jewish state, the Arab Muslim position was weakened. A United Nations partition plan, which gave a larger crescent-shaped territory to the Jews, but left much of the West Bank of the Jordan in Palestinian hands, with Jerusalem as a rather anomalous internationally administered zone, collapsed after the British simply gave up and withdrew from the mandate in May 1948.

War promptly erupted, as newly independent Israel was attacked by its Arab neighbours and in turn sought to secure as much land as possible, and in particular to take the historic Jewish capital of Jerusalem. The conflict ended with up to five million Palestinians having fled and a huge swathe of territory east of Tel Aviv, including the western part of Jerusalem, along the Egyptian border and north abutting Lebanon, having fallen into Israeli hands. The peace settlement, ironically, was made using the

1944 British Survey Map of Palestine, which had been intended to form the basis of the failed 1947 Partition plan. From then until the present day, the region has seen a war of maps, as Israel acquired progressively more territory, in 1967 taking the Sinai, the rest of Jerusalem and the West Bank after the Six Days' War and adding parts of the Golan Heights overlooking Syria in 1973 when a coalition of Syria, Lebanon and Egypt once again attacked it. Decades of peace negotiations which followed the 1978 Camp David Accords with Egypt (after which Israel withdrew from the Sinai) yielded only disappointment. The carefully negotiated maps of the 1993 Oslo Accords which were supposed to result in a Palestinian Authority governing large parts of the West Bank and Gaza Strip proved a mirage, as Israeli security concerns, the building of a border fence cutting off Arabs within Israel from Palestinians without, the increase in Israeli settlements inside what had notionally been allocated as Palestinian territory and an increasing radicalisation of politics on both sides, corroded hopes for a lasting peace.

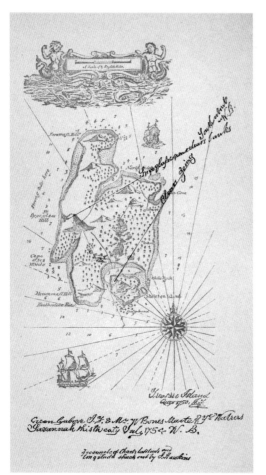

A new genre of atlas flourished in the post-war period, as printing technology improved and interest in the history of cartography increased among non-specialists. Facsimile atlases had their origins in the nineteenth century, with Edme-François Jomard's *Les monuments de la géographie, ou, Recueil d'anciennes cartes européennes et orientales* ('The Monuments of Geography, or a Collection of Ancient European and Oriental Maps'), published in 1854. Jomard was a member of the Institute established by Napoleon to study the material brought back by his expedition to Egypt in 1798, and the editor of the monumental *Description de l'Egypte* (whose map section included the first triangulated map of the country), and he included in his collection dozens of facsimiles of historic maps. A.E. Nordenskiöld's *Facsimile-Atlas to the Early History of Cartography with Reproductions of the Most Important Maps Printed in the XV and XVI Centuries* (1889) included many of the important maps from the age of exploration and remains a key work for the study of the cartography of the period. In the early twentieth century, the Egyptian prince Yusuf Kamal and Frederik Caspar Wieder, librarian of the Royal Dutch library, added the *Monumenta cartographica Africae et Aegypti* (1926–53) to the genre, making many maps of the region accessible to a wider public for the first time.

It was after 1945, however, that facsimile atlases, or other collections of previously published maps really took off, with works such as Andrew M. Modelski's *Railroad Maps of North America: The First Hundred Years* (1984). A new thematic cast on the subject as given by J.B. Post's *Atlas of Fantasy* (1973) in which readers could consult classic pieces of cartographic fantasy, such as the treasure map taken from Robert Louis Stevenson's *Treasure Island* or the map of Middle-Earth drafted for J.R.R. Tolkien's *The Lord of the Rings*.

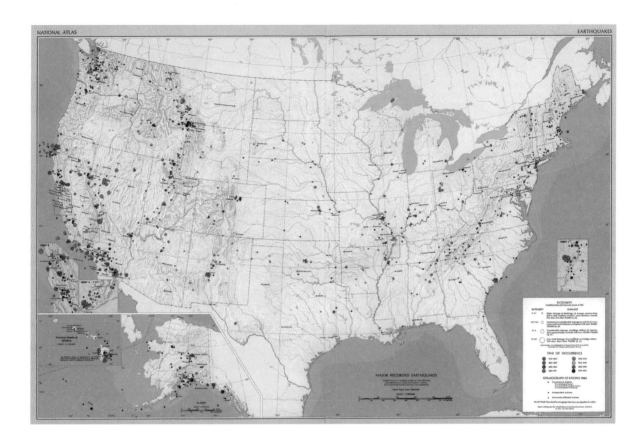

While world atlases continued to be produced, with a greater than ever wealth of data available to cartographers, the later twentieth century became a new great age of national atlases as publications such as the *Atlas der Schweiz* (1961–78) finally lived up to the aspirations of their eighteenth- and nineteenth-century predecessors to chronicle every last hamlet and stream within their territories, while publications such as *The National Atlas of the United States* (1970), which had taken 18 years to create under the auspices of the U.S. Geological Survey (USGS), began to benefit from the first adoption of computer technology into the cartographic process. An increasing interest in describing the nation not just in terms of its borders (or its roads, rivers and towns) led to a huge range of topics, from comparative regional mortality, to educational attainment, crime levels and the distribution of popular folk music styles, being visualized in national atlases such as the *Atlas van Nederland* (2011) and the *Nationalatlas Bundesrepublik Deutschland* (1999–2007).

If the later twentieth century was a golden age of any genre of atlas, however, advances in social sciences, printing technology, education and a public thirst for alternative viewpoints at a time when age-old geopolitical certainties had been upended, made it the thematic atlas. Whereas before these had been produced by isolated pioneers, or appeared in the guise of thematic maps within a larger geographical context (either world or regional),

Ravens, *The Atlas of Breeding Birds in Britain and Ireland*, BTO, 1976 (updated)

An example of a thematic atlas, this map differs very slightly from the 1976 original, in that areas of high ground are now also shown.

in the period after 1950, as many as a quarter of all atlases were thematic. Some of these were all-embracing, such as Norman Thrower's *Man's Domain*, first published in 1968, whose more than 200 maps covered a wide range of subjects – political, economic and cultural – with patterns of shading showing differentiation between areas (such as in religion), a technique which became standard in thematic atlases. Many thematic atlases have relatively few placenames and rely on devices such as chloroplethic shading (the strength of shading in a colour indicating the relative proportion of a statistical variable, such as population), or cartograms (in which the relative size of a geographical area is distorted according to the statistical variable, so that, for example, a geographically small but heavily populated area such as the Netherlands would appear correspondingly larger), and symbols and annotations to convey their message.

Many of the atlases covered a single theme, or geographical area, such as *The Atlas of the Arab World* (1991), whose more than 150 maps covered issues such as population, education and health in the 21 countries in the region, while the *Historical Atlas of the Jewish People* (1992) took a chronological approach to the subject more akin to that of a historical atlas, yet still included a broader range of cultural themes. Perhaps the most striking was Michael Kidron and Ronald Segal's *The State of the World Atlas* in 1981, which did not conceal its campaigning intent of highlighting issues such as global poverty, the arms race and the dangers of environmental degradation through dozens of thematic maps. Ideology in mapping, so often submerged, or even denied, in the race for scientific precision in cartography, had once again come to the fore. *The State of the World Atlas*'s choice of themes for presentation was as much a part of its message as the portrayal of Jerusalem as the centre of the world in medieval *mappae mundi*.

Historical atlases, too, underwent a renaissance in the second half of the twentieth century. Some, such as F.W. Putzger's *Historische Schul-atlas*, which had first been published in 1877, were simply reissues or light-touch updatings of a classic work which had stood the test of time, while others, such as Lester Jesse Cappon's *Atlas of Early American History* (1976) overlapped with facsimile atlases in their reproductions of the plans of the cities of the early United States. But the widespread adoption of offset photolithography, which enabled mass colour printing at economical costs, led to the appearance of historical atlases aimed at a more popular market, beginning in the United States with *The American Heritage Pictorial Atlas of United States History* (1966), organized on a spread-by-spread basis with short accompanying texts explaining the key points of the map and the historical development it illuminated, in an organisational scheme that would become ubiquitous for subsequent historical atlases. The culmination of this was perhaps *The Times Atlas of World History*, first published in 1978 under the editorship of the historian Geoffrey Barraclough, which has gone through eight subsequent editions, sold over a million copies, and become the benchmark against which other modern historical atlases are compared.

The twentieth century saw one final set of developments which had the capacity to revolutionize cartography. For centuries, the only way to construct a map had been to adapt those of others, or to visit the terrain in question and record it, progressively through surveys of greater scientific adequacy. The period of the First World War saw the birth of aerial reconnaissance, at first for purely tactical military purposes, but then in early 1918, the British General Edmund Allenby commissioned an aerial survey of the front with the Ottoman Turks in Palestine which was used to compile a more up-to-date map than had been previously possible. By the 1920s the British Ordnance Survey was using maps to update its own cartography and for the next 40 years, such aerial surveys became an essential part of the cartographer's arsenal. The launch of the Russian satellite Sputnik 1 in 1957 began a new era, with the first ever satellite photograph of the Earth sent back by the American orbiter Explorer 6 in 1959. Now, the Earth could be surveyed from space.

It was in such an atmosphere of new perspectives on the Earth, with finally the possibility of seeing our globe from outside as just that, a globe, that a new cartographic projection was devised by the German historian Arno Peters (1916–2002) in 1973. The Peters Projection, which set off decades of polemic, was designed, its author maintained, to correct the evident shortcomings of Mercator's projection, whose distortions, principally the disproportionate enlargement of land masses towards the Poles, gave the impression that countries – which just happened to be major political powers – in Europe and North America were larger than they really were in relation to many nations in the developing world, and in particular those in Africa. Peters did this using an 'equal areas' projection, one in which the relative size of any two areas on his map were in the same proportion as they would be on the globe. As a result, China is restored to its rightful position of being nearly five times the size of Greenland, rather than significantly smaller on most Mercator-derived maps. While much cartographic commentary focused on the similarity of the Peters Projection to that of the nineteenth-century cartographer the Reverend James Gall (1808–95), which he unveiled in 1855 (to far less fanfare and acclaim in the general press than Peters received), and on whether the equal area projection produced its own distortions at the margins, it spawned a series of maps (including many used by global Non-Governmental Organizations and charities who rather liked the notion of 'equality' it seemed to promote) and atlases (including the *Peters Atlas of the World* in 1989).

Just as Peters was announcing his projection, however, yet another development occurred which really would upend the age-old notions about how maps were made, how they were presented and, to some, how they threatened the end of the atlas altogether. Computers, digitization and the internet were coming.

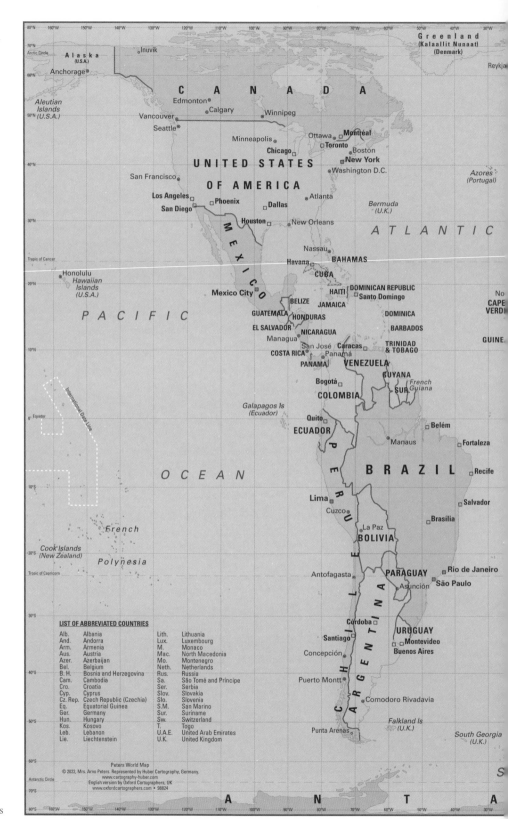

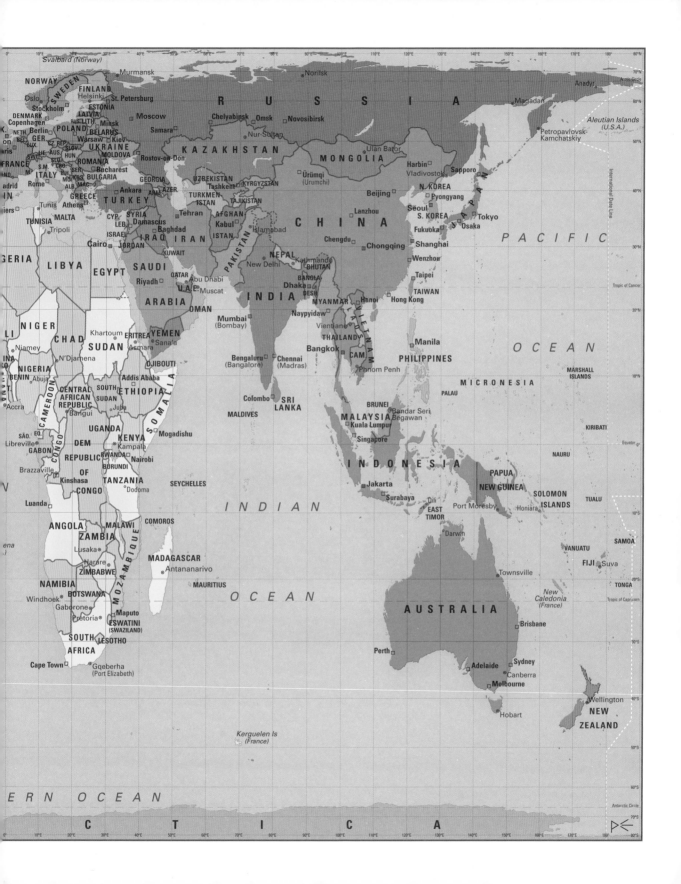

AN ATLAS
BY ANY
OTHER NAME
(2000–)

The advent of digital cartography seemed to herald a new age for atlases, as databases could now be updated rapidly and data exploited to produce a wide range of maps more quickly than ever before. Then map applications were launched on the internet, their early rather unwieldy form in simply presenting a series of static maps soon outstripped as the technology advanced. With the launch of Google Maps in 2005 and the availability of progressively more powerful smartphones, suddenly everybody had an atlas in their pocket. It became possible to access maps of virtually any part of the world with just a few clicks or touches and to create bespoke mapping with individual overlays within minutes. Updating a map once required a long and perilous sea voyage or months of surveying through jungle, desert and mountain fastnesses. Now maps could be crowd-sourced and updated with the contributions of a million people each unknown to the others, all within seconds. Does this mean that the atlas, as Mercator, Cassini or John Bartholomew knew it, is dead?

A certain amount of progress had been made in the 1950s in trying to automate the cartographic process using early computers, but it was not until the first vector graphics displays became available in the 1960s that map visualisations could be attempted, and in the same decade that the first large-scale digital databases were made, with the first geographic information system (GIS) being created in Canada in 1960. It was from Canada, too, that the first prototype of an electronic atlas came, the *Electronic Atlas of Canada* (1982), though it was only accessible on the device on which it was loaded. Before long, atlases became available commercially on CD-ROM, such as the *Electronic Atlas of Arkansas* (1986), the *PC-Atlas of Sweden* (1985) and those produced by the TIGER map service formed by the U.S. Census Bureau to create maps from the 1990 Census. Such electronic maps, however, provided only a snapshot of limited portions of the world (as did the somewhat more sophisticated *CD-Atlas of France* in 1991). Gradually, electronic maps of the world containing significant amounts of data were released, such as the *National Geographic Picture Atlas of the World* (1993). By the mid-1990s, users in effect had an analogue of a printed atlas available on a CD, which provided a much more portable format and could be interrogated to a limited extent (such as locating a place-name without having to refer to a cumbersome index).

Maps, though, and atlases were about to be transformed into something much, much more. The internet was born of the U.S. Department of Defence's ARPANET project, which was designed to create a communications network with a multiplicity of independent nodes which could survive a nuclear strike by the Soviet Union. It went live in October 1969 linking just four computers in California, and its initial development betrayed little sign of its future power. By 1971 the first email had been sent (by the programmer Ray Tomlinson), but it was not until 1991 that the first website appeared. It was the brainchild of Tim Berners-Lee (b. 1955), whose intuition that user-clickable links that led to other parts of the internet could create a 'world-wide-web' of computer servers and networks revolutionized the world of information. Computer programmers and cartographers had in the meantime been hard at work devising ways to allow users to zoom into maps and pan around them without the data stream becoming unmanageable. By 1998, Microsoft had launched Terraserver, which allowed the use of aerial photography to create virtual maps of the United States, and in 2000, the decision by the Clinton administration to make Global

Positioning System (GPS) signals (which had previously been barred to non-military users above a location of accuracy of around 100m/*c.* 330ft) open to all meant that suddenly real-time map applications based on a user's location became possible. From then, the pace of change accelerated. By June 2001, Keyhole had launched its Earthviewer 1.0 software, which allowed users to move through a digitized map of the Earth, though many parts of the world were included at a resolution which made it impractical for route-planning. Then Google acquired Keyhole and relaunched it as Google Earth in 2004, creating a similar, but more refined experience.

But the real 'atlas killer' came in February 2005 with the launch of Google Maps. Now, users could create a bespoke map of their immediate surroundings and ask the software to plan their route, by vehicle or on foot (and later by public transport) to any other accessible point. The arrival of smartphones (with the first Apple iPhone launched in 2007, and its successors and rivals 15 years later containing far more computing power in a handheld device than was available to entire governments half a century earlier). Extra functionality was included over time, with the map-maker function permitting users to add their own businesses or other local features, which are then moderated by panels of other users and the company, in effect crowd-sourcing part of Google's research

BELOW

The National Atlas of the United States, 2002

This atlas, which continued the tradition of the 1874 *Statistical Atlas of the United States,* continued as a print version until its final full edition in 1997. Thereafter, the atlas was updated online until the programme was wound down in 2014, although its archived maps remain accessible digitally.

(though its investment in satellite imagery and ground surveys, particularly in cities and towns using mobile vans to capture changes, which are then incorporated in its Google Earth imager, is considerable). As a result, Google has captured a huge percentage of the retail computer-mapping market, its databases processing in excess of 20 petabytes of data (or 20 million gigabytes) each day, while the Maps part of the business is estimated to be worth $11 billion dollars, which is more than the GDP of 22 of Africa's 54 countries.

Yet if Google provides mapping on demand to anyone with a smartphone (or even internet access), does this matter? In one sense, the answer is very much, as the data used to build the maps belongs to Google and the source code behind it is proprietary and so users cannot see the information on the basis of which the maps are created (nor do users 'own' a Google Map in the sense in which they may have owned a map in the sixteenth or seventeenth century). It is true that cartographic information was treated as sensitive during the Age of Exploration when Spanish and Portuguese sea captains would have to deliver their logs to the Casa da India in Lisbon or the Casa de Contratación in Seville (p.93) but even so this information did leak out and, despite efforts on the part of governments to suppress access to mapping – such as during the Second World War, when British map publishers were forbidden to sell high-resolution maps of the United Kingdom, including street atlases – once the cartographic genie was out of the bottle it was difficult to jam it back in. Now, technology companies have the power to do just that and to determine what users see (including the possibility that they might accede to the demands of autocratic regimes that their citizens either have no access to internet mapping, or access only to a heavily modified or censored version of it which shows only what the regime wishes them to see).

For all that, maps are more ubiquitous than ever before. Almost everybody now has in effect an atlas (or almost an infinity of atlases) in their pocket, and for those who wish for traditional printed maps, these are still available. Maps in digital form are still maps (just as they were when painted on frescoes, carved into stone or incised into clay tablets) and they are now more available and more used in an everyday setting than they have ever been.

Far from being dead, the atlas has gained another lease of life.

OPPOSITE, TOP

Extract from TIGERweb showing school districts in the states of New England, based on the 2020 United States census.

OPPOSITE, BOTTOM

Google Street View car

Where once maps were produced by surveyors hacking through jungle, trekking over mountains or laboriously recording each city block and building by hand, now Google's Street View cars simply drive through areas taking photographs from which mapping can be updated.

ENDNOTES

Chapter 1

1. Strabo, *Geographies*, trs. Howard Leonard Jones (London, 1932)
2. Ptolemy, *Almagest* 2.13, quoted in J. Lennart Bergren and Alexander Jones, *Ptolemy's Geography: An Annotated Translation of the Theoretical Chapters* (Princeton, NJ, 2000), p.19
3. Pliny *Natural History* iii, 16-17 (trs. Harris Rackham, London 1942, p.17)
4. *Ravenna Cosmography* 1.18.10-15 translation in O.A.W. Dilke, 'Cartography in the Byzantine Empire', in Harley and Woodward, *The History of Cartography*, Vol. 1 (Chicago, 1987), pp.258–75
5. Isaiah 40:22
6. Al-Idrisi *Opus Geographicum* fasc 1, p. 5 – issued in nine fascicles by the Istituto Universitario Orientale di Napoli (Leiden. E.J. Brill 1970–84)
7. Ibid., fasc 1, p.6

Chapter 2

1. Evelyn Edson, *The World Map 1300–1492* (Baltimore, 2007), p. 125, citing Gautier Dalché Guillelmi Fillastri Introduction, p.346

Chapter 3

1. Pierre d'Ailly, *Imago Mundi*, trs. Edwin F. Keever (Wilmingon, N.C, 1948)

Chapter 4

1. Gerardus Mercator, *Album Amicorum*, translated in 'The Practice of Community: Humanist Friendship during the Dutch Revolt' by Jason Harris, *Texas Studies in Literature and Language*, Vol. 47, No. 4, The Culture of Early Modern Friendship (Winter 2005), pp.299–325
2. The *Itinerary of John Leland*, Book 1: xxviii–xliii

Chapter 5

1. Lloyd A. Brown *The Story of Maps* (New York 1979), p.168
2. Willem Jansz. 'Blaeu's Wall Map of the World, on Mercator's Projection, 1606-07 and Its Influence', Imago Mundi, 1979, Vol. 31 (1979), pp.36–54
3. Johanncs Keuning, 'Blaeu's Atlas', *Imago Mundi*, 4:1 (1959), pp.74–89
4. Published in *La Verdadera Longitud por Mar y Tierra* ('The true longitude for sea and land'). See Michael Friendly, Pedro Valero-Mora & Joaquín Ibáñez Ulargui, 'The First (Known) Statistical Graph: Michael Florent van Langren and the "Secret" of Longitude', *The American Statistician*, 64:2 (2010), pp.174–184

Chapter 6

1. Jerry Brotton, *A History of the World in Twelve Maps* (London, 2013), p.301
2. Mary Sponberg Pedley, *Bel et Utile: The Work of the Robert de Vaugondy Family of Mapmakers* (Tring, 1992)

Chapter 7

1. George Montague Wheeler, *Report Upon the Third International Geographic Congress Held at Venice, Italy, 1881* (1886), p.153

Chapter 8

1. H.J. Mackinder, 'The Geographical Pivot of History', *The Geographical Journal*, Vol. XXIII, No. 4 (April 1904), pp.421–37

FURTHER RESOURCES

Bagrow, Leo *History of Cartography, Revised edition*, ed. Skelton, R.A. (London 1964)

Barber, Peter and Board, Christopher *Tales from the Map Room: Fact and Fiction about Maps and their Makers* (London 1993)

Barber, Peter and Harper, Tom *Magnificent Maps: Power, Propaganda and Art* (London 2010)

Black, Jeremy *Metropolis: Mapping the City* (London 2015)

Black, Jeremy *Maps and History: Constructing Images of the Past* (London 1997)

Brooke-Hitching, Edward *The Phantom Atlas: The Greatest Myths, Lies and Blunders on Maps* (London 2016)

Brotton, Jerry *A History of the World in Twelve Maps* (London, 2012)

Brown, Lloyd A, *The Story of Maps* (London 1951)

Delano Smith, Catherine and Kain, Roger J.P., *English Maps A History* (London 1999)

Dilke, O.A.W., *Greek and Roman Maps* (Baltimore, 1998)

Edney, Matthew, *Mapping an Empire: The Geographical Construction of British India* (London 1999)

Harper, Tom, *Maps and the 20th Century: Drawing the Line* (London 2016)

Harper, Tom and Bryars, Tim *A History of the 20th Century in 100 Maps* (London 2014)

Harwood, Jeremy *To the Ends of the Earth: 100 Maps That Changed the World* (London 2006)

Hewitt, Rachel *Map of a Nation: A Biography of the Ordnance Survey* (London 2011)

Woodward, David & Harley, J.B (Series Editors) *The History of Cartography, volumes 1 to 6* (Chicago, 1987 to 2020)

Bibliothèque Nationale, searchable map index from France's National Library
gallica.bnf.fr/html/und/cartes/cartes?mode=desktop

Cartography Unchained, essays on cartographic history before 1600
www.cartographyunchained.com

The Chart Room, links to images of antique maps
www.wildernis.eu/chart-room

The History of Cartography (Online versions of Woodward & Harley series)
press.uchicago.edu/books/HOC/index.html

Imago Mundi, The International Journal for the History of Cartography
www.maphistory.info/imago.html

Map History, cartographic gateway from former British Library map librarian
www.maphistory.info/index.html

The Map Room, large collection of historical maps and atlases
www.maproom.org/index.html

Old Maps Online, large collection of online historical maps
www.oldmapsonline.org

USGS Topoview, searchable collection of USGS mapping
ngmdb.usgs.gov/topoview

INDEX

PICTURE CREDITS

and Map Division; 217 Atlas Historique De La Pologne, courtesy Internet Archive (public domain); 218 Copyright maproom.org; 219 University of Texas at Arlington Libraries/Wikimedia Commons (public domain); 220 Copyright maproom.org; 221 Library of Congress, Geography and Map Division; 222 Kolossos (public domain); 227l The Picture Art Collection/Alamy; 227r Antiqua Print Gallery/Alamy; 228 Courtesy of the University of Texas Libraries, The University of Texas at Austin; 230l *Atlas Aziatskoi Rossii*, World Digital Library. Retrieved from the Library of Congress.; 230r–231 *Atlas Aziatskoi Rossii*, World Digital Library. Retrieved from the Library of Congress.; 232 Courtesy of the University of Texas Libraries, The University of Texas at Austin; 234 Courtesy of the University of Texas Libraries, The University of Texas at Austin; 237 Library of Congress, Geography and Map Division; 238 Earnest B (public domain); 239 Copyright maproom.org; 240 Courtesy of the University of Texas Libraries, The University of Texas at Austin; 241 Copyright maproom.org; 245 Government of India, Office of the Registrar General & Census Commissioner, India; 246 Onceinawhile (public domain); 248 Racconish (public domain); 249 Courtesy of the University of Texas Libraries, The University of Texas at Austin; 250 Reproduced with permission of BTO, from Sharrock (1976) *The Atlas of Breeding Birds in Britain and Ireland*. http://app.bto.org/mapstore; 252–53 © 2022, Mrs. Arno Peters. Represented by Huber Cartography, Germany. www.cartography-huber.com; English version by Oxford Cartographers, UK. www.oxfordcartographers.com; 257 Courtesy of the University of Texas Libraries, The University of Texas at Austin; 258t United States Census Bureau; 258b Christoph Lischetzki/Alamy

ABOUT THE AUTHOR

Philip Parker is a historian with a particular interest in the role of maps, and the ways in which we can use them to uncover history. He is the author of the *DK Eyewitness Companion Guide to World History* (2010), *History of the World in Maps* (2015), *History of Britain in Maps* (2017), *A–Z History of London* (2019) and *History of World Trade in Maps* (2020), and was the General Editor of *The Great Trade Routes: A History of Cargoes and Commerce over Land and Sea* (2012). He is also a specialist in late antique and early medieval history and wrote *The Empire Stops Here: A Journey Along the Frontiers of the Roman World* (2010) and *The Sunday Times* bestseller *The Northmen's Fury: A History of the Viking World* (2015). He studied History at Trinity Hall, Cambridge and International Relations at Johns Hopkins School of Advanced International Studies Bologna Center. He previously worked as a diplomat, the editor of a travel magazine and as a publisher running a list of historical atlases and illustrated history books, and lives in London.

ACKNOWLEDGEMENTS

In such a complex book as this, the author merely sits at the apex of the many people who helped to make its production possible. I would like to thank in particular Jennifer Barr at Quarto, who commissioned it, Frank Hopkinson, who worked on the early stages of the book, and Laura Bulbeck who worked tirelessly to keep things on track. Grateful thanks also go to Lesley Malkin for copyediting, Laurence Earle for proofreading, Helen Snaith for indexing, and Kevin Knight for the page design, without whom the author's manuscript could not have become the book you hold. I would also like to thank The London Library and its staff for presiding over one of the most congenial and well-stocked workplaces any author could hope for.